Mastering DC

*A Newcomer's
Guide to Living in the
Washington, DC Area*

by Kay Killingstad

For information regarding sales of this book, please contact:
Adventures Publishing
1-800-594-1371

Printed in the United States of America.
Editing: Sheila Donoghue
Design and Layout: Harris Design, Inc.
Printing: Kirby Lithographic Company, Inc.

Library of Congress Number: 96-084255
ISBN: 0-9631935-2-X

Although the publisher has made every effort to ensure that the
information included in this book was correct and verified at the time of
going to press, the publisher does not assume and hereby disclaims any
liability to any party for any loss or damage caused by any errors or
omissions, whether such errors or omissions result from negligence,
accident, or any other cause.

The quote on page 66 is from Howard Gillette Jr., *Between Justice and
Beauty: Race, Planning, and the Failure of Urban Policy in Washington,
DC* (Baltimore: The Johns Hopkins University Press, 1995), page 1.

ACKNOWLEDGMENTS

My thanks, especially, to Sheila Donoghue, a friend and colleague, without whose publishing experience this edition would not have been completed on time. She has guided me through the maze of writing, editing and production, and has taught me a great deal in the process. Her creativity and clarity of expression have been particularly helpful.

Dartha Dragnich and Amy Brooks have performed an invaluable service in proofreading the chapters in the final stage of the process. Their excellent editing skills are reflected in these pages. Their capable assistance and their enthusiasm for the project have been very much appreciated.

Robin Harris of Harris Design, Inc. deserves a particular note of thanks not only for her design skills but also for her patience and flexibility throughout the design and production process.

Many friends and colleagues provided review comments and substantive input, several of whom went to great lengths in their efforts to obtain material for me. I also received much assistance and guidance with equipment and software issues related to the production of this document. Individuals who contributed their time and expertise, to whom I am eternally grateful, include George Amols, Dianne Arnold, Jack Bagley, Ryan Conroy, Chet Cooper, Dartha Dragnich, David Dragnich, Dr. Saski Esteupeñan, Betty Fimiani, Bob Grevemberg, Dave Hunt, Herman Jackson, Kurt Kehl, Geoff Kieffer, Helen Moody, Melisa Moreland, Miriam Pollin, Anne Street, Blanche Theeman, Sharon Thomas, Mary Toler, Dana Toomey, Jack White and Lois Zambo.

Special thanks to Sheryl Nowitz Klein for originating the book, and for her patience, unfailing support and guidance in the transition of ownership and the publication process. Thanks also to her husband, Tony, for his advice and support.

And finally, my appreciation and thanks go to Zev and Robin Siegl, whose introduction to Sheryl led to this adventure in publishing.

This book is dedicated to my late parents, Gordon and Dorothy Killingstad, and to my brother, Jim, and his wife, Linda.

CHAPTER 3 GETTING AROUND

CHAPTER 4 DEALING WITH THE LOCAL BUREAUCRACY

CHAPTER 9 WASHINGTON WEEKENDS

Chapter 10 Young People

Chapter 11 Resources

A NOTE *TO THE* READER

When my friends Zev and Robin Siegl introduced me to Sheryl Nowitz, a young author who had just published her first book, *Mastering DC: A Newcomer's Guide to Living in Washington*, little did I realize that four years later I would succeed her as the author and publisher. I feel privileged to have acquired this well-established book with such a loyal following. The third edition carries on the theme introduced by Sheryl, and expands the book to include updated information and additional resources.

Mastering DC is a sourcebook for newcomers, and is every bit as useful for people who have been here awhile. There is a lot of information contained between the covers, some historical, some anecdotal, and some that even natives may be surprised to learn. It is my hope that you will find the book both informative and enjoyable. I welcome your comments, and look forward to incorporating many of them in a fourth edition.

Housing

When you start shopping for housing, it is important to know something about the local housing market. As with many other aspects of living in the metropolitan area, you have lots of choices available. You will probably find that you need to evaluate the choices based on information about the neighborhoods, about public transportation and other amenities, and on the cost. This chapter clues you into some general rules of thumb for real estate shopping in the DC area and lets you know what you are likely to find and how to make looking a little easier. Also included is some information on interim housing options and a list of pointers to help you out with the details of moving.

THE LOCAL REAL ESTATE MARKET

The cost of housing in the Washington area varies according to the type of neighborhood, proximity to Downtown and accessibility to the Metro system. Within that framework, the size and quality of the particular home also makes a difference. Generally, the farther away from the city you look, the less expensive you will find the housing and the more space you will get for your money.

Housing in Maryland and Northern Virginia is generally less expensive than the equivalent accommodations in the District. To get the best bargains, you have to locate close to or just outside the Beltway (Silver Spring, Takoma Park, Greenbelt, Rockville, Herndon, Alexandria south of Old Town and Falls Church). The suburbs offer more public services than the District and a wider variety of convenient shopping. Taxes are also lower.

If you choose to live in the District, having a car can be unnecessary and in many areas actually a nuisance. Having a car in the suburbs, on the other hand, can be a necessity, particularly as you go farther out. The public transportation options in and near the District are terrific, while parking is scarce and often expensive.

Housing Options

Each city has its own terminology to describe apartments and other living arrangements. Washington and its environs have the typical options, but the great number and the wide variety of life styles in the city create additional alternatives. Safety is an important consideration for many newcomers when choosing a place to live. If you are interested in finding out about a particular area, you can call the local police for the latest crime statistics. Rents vary widely throughout the metropolitan DC area depending on proximity to the city. Events such as new development can cause rent and housing price fluctuations, therefore it is recommended that you consult a real estate agent and/or current publications regarding specific neighborhood prices. For comparison purposes, typical rental rates have been included in this chapter.

Efficiencies

These are one-room apartments, usually 400 to 600 square feet, generally including a small alcove and a large closet. The bathroom is small and in many, the kitchen is along one wall of the main room. Efficiencies are normally found in high-rise buildings. You may know them as "studios" elsewhere or as "bedsits" in London. Prices range from $500 to $700 a month. Some condo buildings also include efficiencies, particularly in the more densely populated neighborhoods.

Junior One-Bedroom Apartments

A junior one-bedroom is basically an efficiency with an extra room—usually the size of a large closet—for a small bed and bureau. Everything is scaled down in size, but the separation of rooms appeals to many. Rents start at about $600 a month.

One-, Two- and Three-Bedroom Apartments

Pretty self-explanatory, these apartments or condos have the specified number of bedrooms, plus living room and dining room (usually combined) and separate kitchen. The number of bathrooms varies and is usually indicated in the ad or description. Depending on location, monthly rent usually falls in the $700 to $1,200 range for a one-bedroom, and can reach anywhere from $900 to $1,500 a month for the two-bedrooms. Three-bedrooms are more unusual, and the location and amenities determine the cost.

English Basements

This term refers to the ground-floor basements (not underground) of a row house, converted into an apartment. Usually these one- or two-bedroom apartments have separate entrances, and sometimes a terrace area. In the District, the windows often have bars for safety. Rents tend to range between $850 and $1,100, depending on size and location.

Group Houses

If you already have a large group together or you want to live with several people, you can move into one of the many "group" houses available for rent. Usually each person has a private bedroom and everyone shares the kitchen, bathroom and common rooms. Houses in the suburbs and in the more residential parts of DC also generally have a small lawn and backyard. Rent is most often under $500 a person. Group houses can be the best option for newcomers. Living with several people puts you immediately into a social circle and helps ease the anxiety of making the transition to a new city. If you are looking to live in a group house, expect to undergo an interview. Be sure you like the people as much as or more than you like the house—the emphasis on group house is on the group. Finally, find out about any "house rules" ahead of time.

Townhouses and Single-Family Homes

Townhouses are a popular choice for couples, small families and singles who want more living space without the responsibility of a large yard. These residential units share at least one exterior wall with other similar

ABBREVIATIONS IN REAL ESTATE ADS

a/c or ac	air conditioned	kit	kitchen
apt	apartment	lbr	library
avail	available	lg, lrg	large
balc	balcony	loc	location
bkyd	backyard	lr	living room
bldg	building	lux	luxury
b/k	block	lvls	levels
br, bdr, bdrm	bedroom	M	male
bsmt	basement	mo	month
CAC	central air conditioning	mod	modern
CATV	cable TV	newly ren	newly renovated
conv	convenient	nghbrs	neighbors
cpt	carpeted	nr	near
dr	dining room	pvt	private
d/w	dishwasher	pkg, prkg	parking
effic	efficiency	prof	professional
elec	electricity	rec ctr	recreation center
F	female	refs	references
flr	floor	shr	share
fr	from	TH	townhouse
frpl or fpl	fireplace	+ util	plus utilities
gar or grg	garage		(water, gas and electric)
h/w	hardwood floors	w/	with
hse	house	w/d	washer and dryer
ht	heat	w/w	wall-to-wall carpeting
incl	include/including		

units and are designed to create the feel of a block of row houses from earlier days. Many developments are like condo buildings, in that residents share in the upkeep of the common grounds, usually through a management company. Single-family homes range in size and with the wide market for new construction, two-garage, three-story townhouses, you could end up in a single-family home that is smaller than a neighbor's townhouse. The detached house does usually come with a real yard, making it a good choice for families with children. Rental rates for townhouses and single-family homes are largely dependent on size (number of bedrooms and bathrooms) and location, generally in the range of $950 to $2,000.

Getting Demographic Data

You can obtain housing, tax and demographic data on the area in which you are interested by contacting the individual **Economic Development Offices**. Call any of these offices and they will send you a packet of information.

DC

Greater Washington Board of Trade	202-727-6365

Maryland

Montgomery County	301-217-2345
Prince George's County	301-386-5600

Virginia

Arlington County	703-358-3520
Fairfax County	703-790-0600

RESOURCES

Once you have decided where you want to live and what kind of housing you are looking for, you have lots of options for resources to help you find your new home.

Advertising

Both real estate companies and individual landlords advertise available space in local newspapers. In addition to paid advertisements, you will find lots of housing notices on bulletin boards, both in local community establishments and in the offices of some larger employers.

Newspapers

Many Washingtonians find their apartment through the *Washington Post*. Fridays, Saturdays and Sundays are the best days to check its classified section for the real estate ads. *The Washington Times*, the *City Paper*, the *Northwest Current*, the *Washington Citizen*, the *InTowner*, *Hill Rag*, *Roll Call*, the *Washington Blade* and the *Journal Newspapers* also contain classified sections.

Several free guides published by area realtors list available apartments. One of the most extensive listings is the 600-page *Metropolitan Washington Apartment Shoppers Guide*. Free copies can be picked up at CVS Pharmacies, Giant and Safeway stores, and convenience stores. A bi-weekly newspaper, *Apartments for Rent*, is available at most Metro stations, Giants and Safeways.

If you are looking to buy, the Washington dailies each have special real estate sections. The *Washington Times* publishes their section on Fridays, the *Washington Post* on Saturday. The *Journal Newspapers* are worth a special mention. This chain of daily suburban papers prints a Friday "Home Report" section in each paper, geared towards the suburban city or county it serves.

Community Bulletin Boards

Hill staffers post advertisements in the **Rayburn**, **Cannon**, **Longworth**, **Dirksen**, **Hart** and **Russell** office buildings on the bulletin boards outside the cafeterias. People also post notices for available apartments on community bulletin boards at **Chesapeake Bagel Bakery's** locations in Alexandria at 601 King St., on the Hill at 215 Pennsylvania Ave. SE, in Dupont Circle at 1636 Connecticut Ave. NW, in Foggy Bottom at 818 18th St. NW, and at 4000 Wisconsin Ave. NW. You can also check the bulletin board at **Food for Thought** at 1738 Connecticut Ave. NW. The natural food restaurant's extensive bulletin board makes entertaining reading even if you are not looking for a place to live.

The **National Institutes of Health**'s bulletin board hangs outside the hospital's cafeteria in Building 10 at 9000 Rockville Pike, Bethesda, MD. At the **Brookings Institution** at 1775 Massachusetts Ave. NW (202-797-6000), you will find housing listings outside the cafeteria. The **World Bank** at 1818 H St. NW keeps a housing bulletin board so extensive that it even has its own staffer and telephone exchange. You may want to call ahead (202-473-1186) to smooth the way. The bulletin board at the **International Monetary Fund** at 700 19th St. NW (202-623-7000) is limited to staffers, but accepts advertisements from anyone.

Companies

Even when the real estate market isn't booming from an economic standpoint, the transient nature of the local population keeps a number of companies busy helping people find housing, both to rent and to own.

Real Estate Companies

If you are pressed for time during your apartment search, you may want to consider using a real estate company; their fees are frequently paid by the landlords. And if you are looking to buy, you will need to tap into the expertise of local real estate agents. On the Hill, you can stop by **John Formant Company** (202-544-3900) at 225 Pennsylvania Ave. SE, where they have listings of a variety of houses and apartments all over the Hill. If you are interested in finding a place in Dupont Circle, Adams Morgan or Georgetown, try calling **Tutt Real Estate** at 1755 S St. NW (202-234-3344). Tutt manages apartments in these neighborhoods and can also help you find condominiums or houses in the area, if you are ready to buy.

The local Bell Atlantic Yellow Pages contains a dozen pages of local and national firms under the heading Real Estate. Most of the national firms list 800 telephone numbers where you can obtain the number of a local area office.

The **National Association of Realtors (NARL)** recently unveiled an Internet service, the Realtor Information Network **(http://www.realtor.com)** that will permit anyone with an Internet connection to comb through the data contained in the Multiple Listing Services (MLS), regardless of where the browser lives. MLS is an area-wide inventory of homes for sale through member realty companies. Browsers will find a color photo, description and price of each house and a computer link with the agent handling the house.

Relocation Companies

If you are planning on buying a house, you may want to consider using a relocation service to help you find it. Most major real estate agencies have a relocation services division or a relationship with an independent relocation company. You can get regional rental information and resources through the **National Relocation Service**. Call them at 1-900-420-0040 or use **http://www.aptsforrent.com** on the Internet. At **http://www.homes.com** you can get on-line information about homes for sale.

For people involved in a job-related relocation, the **Employee Relocation Council (ERC)** can provide a range of useful information. ERC (202-857-0857) is an association of organizations concerned with domestic and international employee transfers. The membership includes corporations that relocate their employees as well as companies and individuals from the relocation industries. You can reach them at their office at 1720 N St. NW or at **http://www.erc.org/** on the Internet.

Services

In addition to the real estate and relocation companies, a number of real estate services are available to help you with more specific aspects of finding your new home.

Finding an Apartment

With six convenient locations throughout the area, **Quixsearch Apartment Finders** (1-800-486-3279) is a free apartment-finding service that covers the entire Washington-Baltimore area. You give them your preferences and their computer database offers a selection of apartments. Call them at 1-800-486-3279 for the location and hours of the office nearest you.

Apartment Search (1-800-260-3733) can also help you find an apartment in the metropolitan area free of charge. Apartment Search has offices all over the area including Dupont Circle, Bethesda, Rockville, Greenbelt, Silver Spring, Alexandria and Baileys Crossroads. Each office has access to listings for the whole metropolitan area.

Universities also provide off-campus housing resources, often open to the public. **American University**'s (202-885-3270) housing resource center is on the first floor of the Mary Graydon Center at 4400 Massachusetts Ave. NW. Apartment listings and information about the area are posted on the walls. Free telephones allow you to begin your search right there. In addition, AU has a computerized listing program that matches apartment hunters' wants and needs with available apartments.

George Washington University has a community resource center (202-994-7221) on the fourth floor of the Marvin Center. The center is open weekdays from 9:00 a.m. to 6:00 p.m. and on Saturdays from 10:00 a.m. to 2:00 p.m. For a dollar, Georgetown University's housing office

(202-687-4560) will provide you with an up-to-date listing of apartments and group houses. The housing office, on the first floor of Harbin Hall on the main campus, is open weekdays from 9:00 a.m. to 5:00 p.m.

Finding Roommates

If you already know some people here, word of mouth is of course the best way to find a roommate. If you do not, you can put an ad in the *Washington Post* or *City Paper*. The *Washington Blade*, a weekly newspaper serving the gay community, also has roommate ads in its classified pages.

If you are having trouble finding a roommate, you can contact Betsy Neal of **Roommates Preferred** at 2262 Hall Place NW(202-547-4666). Betsy will quiz you about your living preferences and habits and then suggest some possibilities. If you decide to pursue them, she will charge you $50. She is easy to work with and has an excellent track record. If you are not happy with your new roommate, Betsy will help you find another at no charge.

The **Roommate Network** at 1431 21st St. NW (202-296-5340) provides a similar service for professionals. Its computerized database matches potential roommates based on criteria such as age, sex, pets, level of neatness and smoking habits. The cost is $50 and they guarantee to work with you until you find a roommate. After you find a roommate, there is a two-month trial period to make sure everything is okay. For more information, call their 24-hour information hotline at 202-296-5326.

INTERIM ACCOMMODATIONS

For special circumstances, interim housing is a great idea. Perhaps your company is transferring you and your housing isn't ready yet. Or you are coming here on a temporary assignment and only need a place for a couple of months. Students, graduates and professors on sabbatical often find this approach suits them best.

Corporate Housing

The Washington area has several firms that specialize in short- and long-term temporary housing requirements. They own apartments, townhouses and condos in buildings throughout the area and can provide them, along with many furnishings and services, to fit your budget. **ExecuStay, Inc.** in Rockville, MD (1-800-735-7829) is one such firm. Others include **Exclusive Interim Properties, Inc.** at 1-800-776-5057 and the **National Corporate Housing Connection** at 1-800-340-6242.

University Connections

During the summer, many local universities rent dorm rooms by the week to single students or recent graduates. American University comes highly recommended. You should opt for a room with air conditioning as Washington's hot, sticky summers are not at all fun without it. Below is a list of several university housing offices. Many of these rooms are booked by April, so sign up early.

American University Summer Housing
Butler Pavilion, Room 407
4400 Massachusetts Ave. NW
Washington, DC 20016-8039
202-885-2669

Catholic University Housing
Office of Resident Life, St. Bonaventure Hall
620 Michigan Ave. NE
Washington, DC 20064
202-319-5277

George Washington University Housing
Rice Hall, Number 402
2121 Eye St. NW
Washington, DC 20052
202 994 6688

Georgetown University Summer Housing
100 Harbin Hall NW
Washington, DC 20057
202-687-3999

Howard University Office of Residence Life
2401 4th St. NW
Washington, DC 20005
202-806-6131

FOR WOMEN ONLY

Women can stay at the **Thompson-Markward Hall** (202-546-3255) just across from the Hart Building at 235 2nd St. NE. Rooms rent for approximately $134 a week, which includes breakfast and dinner. Each woman has her own room and phone; bathrooms and showers are communal. There is a two-week minimum stay.

POINTERS FOR MOVING

Planning and Packing

● Decide whether or not to use a commercial mover. Get started early, compare costs and services, and set the schedule.

● Arrange for street parking permits for all vehicles involved. For an apartment or condo, coordinate with the property manager and reserve the freight elevator.

● If you pack yourself, get instructions on how to avoid damage to your possessions. Number each box and keep a list of the contents.

● Be there to supervise packers and movers—they will be a little more careful if you are close by.

● Plan unloading and unpacking carefully. Avoid paying extra to accommodate last minute changes in where things go.

● Pack an "open-me-first" box with screwdrivers and hammer, scissors, soap and toilet paper, snacks and games, camera, phone numbers of friends back home, and other personal items for you and your family. Seal the box so it's easy to open and move it yourself.

Before You Leave

● At least a month ahead, get change of address cards from the Post Office to officially notify banks and credit card companies, magazine publishers and membership organizations, and any state or federal organizations, such as tax boards or benefit offices. Give your employer your forwarding address to mail your W-2 form.

● Schedule shut-down and start-up for utilities and services such as telephone, cable television, trash and the newspaper.

● Schedule with someone in your new location to connect appliances, light furnaces, or help out with other special details in your new home.

● Arrange for legal, medical, military, government and school records to be transferred. Have your lawyer review your will and ask doctors, dentists, and other business and medical suppliers for recommendations on who to contact after you move.

● Check with the local Chamber of Commerce for information on schools and recreation, places of worship, laws and taxes, and shopping and transportation.

● Run all your routine errands one last time—dry cleaning, recycling, library books, repairs. Get inoculation certificates for your pets.

● Call local charities (Salvation Army, Goodwill, etc.) to pick up items you won't be moving. Consider donating the food in your kitchen to local charities that feed the homeless instead of paying to have packed and moved. Ask for receipts for tax purposes.

On Moving Day

● Moving day can be hectic—make sure you have the following with you: auto registration and driver's license; cash for tips, checkbook, credit cards and travelers checks; maps for you and the movers; names and numbers for mover and realtor; local telephone directory; your "open-me-first" box; and a change of clothes for you and your family.

● Monitor unloading and unpacking. If there is damage, notify the movers and complete the appropriate paperwork before they leave.

Neighborhoods

*W*hen it comes to finding a place to live in the Washington area, there is something for everyone—urban neighborhoods of every shape and size; suburban cities and towns steeped in local history; and residential neighborhoods with single-family homes, townhouses, condos and apartment complexes. Many factors influence the decision about where to live. Cost of housing is often the most important and least negotiable issue, but factors relating to transportation time, cost and convenience can also make a difference. Local amenities and the character of the neighborhood often help people choose between otherwise comparable options.

Different life styles are better served by different parts of DC, Maryland and Virginia. Read the general descriptions in the front of the chapter to get an overview of these three areas. Or turn to the neighborhood sections for specific information to help you decide what part of the greater Washington area suits you best.

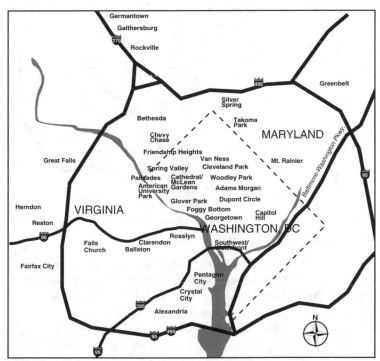

WASHINGTON, DC AREA NEIGHBORHOODS

WASHINGTON, DC

The District offers a multitude of neighborhoods, each with its own local character as well as its practical advantages and disadvantages. The Capitol Hill neighborhoods are closer to the seat of national government than any other. Not far away is Southwest, right along the Potomac River Waterfront. In the center of town, Adams Morgan and Dupont Circle offer an ambiance that reminds many of New York's Greenwich Village, with loads of coffee shops, art galleries and ethnic restaurants. Continuing out Connecticut Ave., north towards Maryland, a series of residential neighborhoods—Woodley Park, Cleveland Park and Van Ness—offers a nice compromise between the conveniences of city living and the quiet comfort of suburban space.

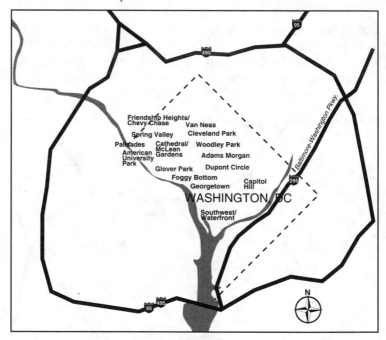

WASHINGTON, DC NEIGHBORHOODS

Not far from the White House is Foggy Bottom, a former middle-class neighborhood now best known for its proximity to George Washington University. At the foot of Wisconsin Ave., along the Potomac River, Georgetown offers a stylish, up-scale life style. The neighborhoods on upper Wisconsin Ave.—Glover Park, Cathedral and McLean Gardens— offer quiet community living and proximity to other parts of the city.

A little farther west, but still in the District, are American University Park, near the campus for which it is named, and Spring Valley, one of DC's most affluent areas. Below that is Palisades, backing up to the C&O Canal National Historical Park. Finally, along the border with Maryland you will find Friendship Heights and the DC side of Chevy Chase, areas known for their concentrations of high-rise buildings.

All five of Metro's subway lines run through Washington, and many city dwellers make regular use of Metrobus service. Running generally north-south through DC is Rock Creek Parkway—a major transportation route running through Rock Creek Park, the city's pride in public park space. Other major thoroughfares include Connecticut, Wisconsin and Massachusetts Aves. running from the center of town out to the west; Route 29 (16th St.) running north out to Silver Spring; and Routes 1 and 50 running out to the Maryland suburbs on the east side of town. The cost of housing varies widely throughout the District, depending on size, location and amenities. For many District residents, location plays a major role, as the character of a neighborhood can change within a few blocks.

SUBURBAN MARYLAND

Suburban Maryland neatly divides itself into Montgomery County on the west and Prince George's County on the east. It is one of the wealthiest counties in the country and a premier location for investing in real estate. With densely populated areas in its more urban parts closer to DC, Montgomery County still offers large expanses of open land farther out. To the west, the county boasts some of greater Washington's most expensive estates and well-to-do residents. As you make your way eastward, the county offers a more familiar, and more affordable, environment.

As in all the suburbs, residents here depend heavily on their cars to get around. Rockville Pike, the continuation of DC's Wisconsin Ave., runs through the heart of the county to the west and provides much of its shopping opportunities. The many neighborhoods in Montgomery County—Bethesda-Chevy Chase, Rockville, Gaithersburg, Germantown, Silver Spring and Takoma Park—offer a wide range of life styles with something for everyone. The northwestern end of the Metro Red Line extends out to this area, including stops at Friendship Heights; at the border with DC; and at Bethesda, White Flint and Rockville farther out. After dipping down through the center of DC, the Red Line turns back up into Montgomery County, with stops in Takoma Park, Silver Spring and Wheaton on the eastern side of the county.

SUBURBAN MARYLAND NEIGHBORHOODS

Prince George's County is considered by some to be a diamond in the rough. While it tends to suffer from a poor image concerning crime, the relatively low quality of its school system compared to Fairfax and Montgomery Counties, and a lack of upscale restaurants and shopping malls, the county does offer advantages for its residents. Living in Prince George's County, for example in Mount Rainier or Greenbelt, is less expensive than in other parts of Maryland and Virginia, for both buyers and renters. That fact alone can be enough to make a difference for many people. Another big draw is the county's particularly well-established multiracial and multicultural population and a somewhat more rural atmosphere in its smaller towns. The recent celebration of the county's 300th anniversary has called attention to other local advantages, such as a number of parks and recreational facilities and some small museums. Metro's Green Line extends out to Greenbelt, and Route 1 and the Baltimore-Washington Parkway are the major roads through the area.

NORTHERN VIRGINIA

The closer-in areas of Northern Virginia were once part of the 100-mile square plot of land allocated for the development of the new District of Columbia back in 1791. Arlington and parts of what is now Alexandria were, however, returned to the Commonwealth of Virginia in 1846. As the federal government has grown over the last 50 years, so have the business and residential areas taken up by its many offices, employees and subcontractors, with much of this growth taking place in the Virginia suburbs. Today, DC has virtually reclaimed its own. Virginians from other parts of the state barely consider Northern Virginia, and particularly places like Arlington and Alexandria, to be part of Virginia at all.

Arlington is officially designated as a county and includes no incorporated towns. Rather, it is comprised of many neighborhoods, or districts, such as Rosslyn, Court House, Clarendon, Ballston, Pentagon City and Crystal City. To meet the demands of its swelling population, Arlington's housing and shopping options have quickly multiplied. Many new residential and commercial communities have sprouted up over the last decade along Metro's Blue, Orange and Yellow Lines, all of which run through Arlington. Rental prospects run the gamut from efficiencies to group houses. Condos and houses, many small and some large, also abound.

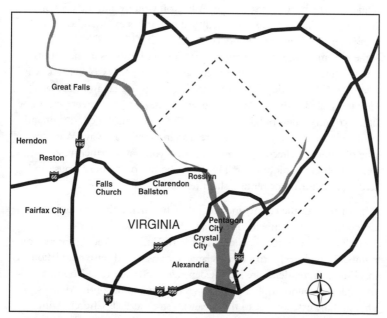

NORTHERN VIRGINIA NEIGHBORHOODS

Prices for many apartments, especially those in luxury buildings, rival those in the District and Bethesda. Farther out and away from the Metro, prices drop quickly.

Wilson Blvd. and Metro's Orange Line both connect the North Arlington neighborhoods of Rosslyn, Court House, Clarendon and Ballston. The Orange Line's quick access to Downtown makes North Arlington quite popular among commuters. The Pentagon, the world's largest office building, dominates the landscape in South Arlington. Rents here are slightly lower than in the northern part of the county and the neighborhoods are not quite as nice nor as convenient. Metrobus travels out Columbia Pike, starting at the Pentagon and continuing on to Baileys Crossroads. The City of Alexandria includes Old Town Alexandria to the east, along the Potomac River, as well as suburban areas stretching out towards the western edge of the city limits. Old Town is a nice alternative to parts of the District, offering many of the same advantages, but on a smaller scale. The many parts of the western side of the city feature more typical developments, everything from subdivisions from the '50s and '60s to high-rise condos from the '80s and early '90s. Metro's Blue Line runs through Alexandria, as do Route 1 and the southern half of the George Washington Parkway, a major road adjacent to beautiful riverfront space.

Along with Montgomery County, Fairfax County is one of the most affluent in the nation. It surrounds Arlington County and the City of Alexandria. While it is less compactly laid out, it has experienced a significant rate of growth and development over the past few decades, some of it more organized than others. In most locations in the county, you will find proudly maintained remnants of Virginia's Colonial and Civil War days, side-by-side with reminders that DC is not far away. Fairfax County is filled with a plethora of green lawns, tree-lined streets and some of the country's best public schools. It is an area long-settled, quaint and richly historic, with signs everywhere marking important Civil War sites. The overriding character is suburban, but if you travel farther west it begins to become more rural. This area is better for buying a house and settling down than for renting short term.

Popular parts of the county include Falls Church and the City of Fairfax, closer in, and the planned community of Reston and its sister city, Herndon, farther out. In general, Northern Virginia is known for its large number of high-tech firms and its large, increasingly diverse population. As in all suburbs, residents are heavily dependent on their cars. I-66 runs west through the county while I-495 crosses from north to south. Metro's Orange Line extends out to this area with stops at Falls Church, Dunn Loring and Vienna. The county-run bus service, the Fairfax Connector, runs between Springfield Plaza and Mt. Vernon. Routes 50 and 29 are also popular avenues, both for transportation and for concentrations of commercial and residential activity.

WASHINGTON, DC NEIGHBORHOODS

Capitol Hill

Capitol Hill, known simply as "the Hill," is home to thousands of congressional bureaucrats and staffers. Locals refer to the neighborhoods bordering the Capitol as being on either the "House side," in the Southeast quadrant, or the "Senate side," in the Northeast quadrant. These charming neighborhoods offer a seemingly endless array of blocks of row houses and lovely, small parks. Back in the 1960s, the Hill underwent a period of gentrification and is now considered one of the city's prime locations. Many people are lured into living here because of its proximity to "the action" as well as by the beautiful Federal and Victorian

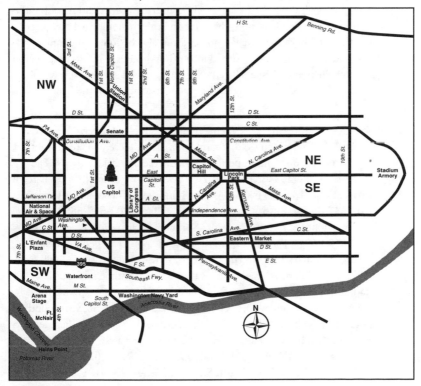

WASHINGTON, DC
Capitol Hill and Southwest/Waterfront

architecture that lends an enviable charm to the area. One of the nicest aspects of living on the Hill is that some of DC's most famous and most important landmarks are nearby. The Capitol, the Supreme Court, the Library of Congress and the Folger Shakespeare Library are within walking distance. Not much farther away are several of the Smithsonian Institution's many museums as well as the National Gallery of Art, the Botanic Garden, the Mall and Union Station.

If you decide to live on the Hill, you must keep safety in mind as you consider the choices. Safety concerns vary significantly, sometimes from block to block on the same street and conditions vary over time as well. Remember that—in general—the closer you live to the Capitol, the safer you are. The area surrounding the Capitol is protected by both DC and Capitol police. Rents vary accordingly—you can expect to pay the most for locations within a few blocks of the Capitol. The farther out you go, the lower the cost of housing.

Apartments on Capitol Hill are largely converted homes and schools rather than high-rises, lending more character to both the individual buildings and the neighborhoods. Rental housing can also be found in the many row houses that have been turned into group houses. This housing option is extremely popular, especially among younger Hill staffers. You will also discover an abundance of English basement apartments on the Hill.

This expansive neighborhood is filled with rather high-priced, mom-and-pop grocery stores. Many residents prefer to shop at **Eastern Market**, at 7th St. SE, Washington's oldest farmers' market. Here you are guaranteed to get fresh produce, meat, poultry, fish, cheese and baked goods. The blocks surrounding Eastern Market are also full of gourmet shops. Directly across 7th St. from the market, you will find Italian delicacies at **Prego** (202-547-8686), Russian food at **Misha's Place** (202-547-5858), and deli food and gourmet coffee along with an array of kitchen gadgets at **Provisions** (202-543-0694). Farther down 7th St. at the corner of Pennsylvania Ave., the aromatic **Roasters On the Hill** (202-543-8355) roasts and sells fresh coffee. A rival farmers' market turns the Redskins' home turf (RFK Stadium, parking lot 6) into a fruit- and vegetable-lovers' paradise on Thursdays and Saturdays between 7:00 a.m. and 5:00 p.m., year-round, and from July through September on Tuesdays as well. Prices here tend to be lower than those at Eastern Market. If you have a car, you can go either to the **Safeway** at 4th St. and Rhode Island Ave. NE (202-636-8640), or to the one at Kentucky and 14th St. SE (202-547-4333).

On the House side, in Southeast, just above the Library of Congress and the House office buildings, Pennsylvania Ave. has several blocks crowded with commercial activity. Local favorites include **Chesapeake Bagel**

Bakery (202-546-0994) and **Roland's** (202-546-9592), a small neighborhood grocery store. Right around the corner from the Madison Building, **Le Bon Café** at 210 2nd St. SE (202-547-7200), serves pastries, cappuccino, salads and sandwiches. If you have a big appetite and are in the mood for Mexican, there's **Burrito Brothers** (202-543-6835) at 205 Pennsylvania Ave. SE. Other local favorites include **Taverna the Greek Islands** (202-547-8360), **La Lomita Dos** (202-544-0616), the **Tune Inn** (202-543-2725) and **Hawk and Dove** (202-543-3300), a mainstay of many Hill staffers. Farther up Pennsylvania Ave., towards the Eastern Market Metro station, you will find another cluster of restaurants and a **CVS**, at 661 Pennsylvania Ave. SE (202-543-3305).

Massachusetts Ave., the main thoroughfare on the Senate side, contains a number of restaurants including **American Café** (202-547-8500), **Armands** (202-547-6600), **Cafe Berlin** (202-543-7656) and **Two Quail** (202-543-8030). **Capitol Hill Supermarket** at 3rd St. and Massachusetts Ave. NE (202-543-7428) provides the most convenient grocery shopping. Nearby Union Station has a nine-screen movie theater, a huge food court and several restaurants and bars as well as a number of shops including Brookstone, Ann Taylor, several bookstores and a train theme store.

Commute to Downtown 15 minutes by Metro Blue and Orange Lines at Capitol South in SE and Red Line at Union Station in NE

Post Office National Capitol at 2 Massachusetts Ave. NE (202-523-2628) and Southeast at 327 7th St. SE (202-547-6191)

Libraries Library of Congress at 1st St. and Independence Ave. SE (202-707-5000), Southeast at 7th and D Sts. SE (202-727-1377) and Northeast at 7th St. and Maryland Ave. NE (202-727-1365)

Police Station 415 4th St. SW (202-727-4655) and 1805 Bladensburg Rd. NE (202-727-4490)

Recreational Activities The neighborhood's parks turn into playing fields on warm weekends. The Mall has an exercise circuit at the corner of Independence Ave. and 4th St. SW, as well as huge open spaces for running, walking or biking. There is an indoor public swimming pool at 7th St. and North Carolina Ave. SE.

Southwest and Waterfront

While Capitol Hill residents tend to live in row houses, those living in the Southwest and Waterfront area are more likely to be found in a high-rise apartment building or on a boat. Across the Washington Channel is **East Potomac Park** which provides a public golf course, tennis courts, swimming pool and picnic tables. **Hains Point**, at the southern end of East Potomac Park, offers a beautiful view of the waterfront. And at the tip of Hains Point you will find a sculpture titled the Awakening, an aluminum giant rising dramatically out of the earth.

Southwest includes **Fort McNair**, one of the oldest active military posts in the United States, and the progressive **Arena Stage** (202-488-3300). Located at the corner of 6th St. and Maine Ave., Arena Stage has three theaters and hosts a variety of performances ranging from the classics to cutting-edge drama. In this area you will also find some opportunities for seafood—a row of restaurants lines the waterfront, capped by the **Maine Ave. Wharf** at 1100 Maine Ave., a market where you can choose from an enormous selection of fresh seafood. In addition to walking along the river, residents can stroll the short distance to the Waterfront, L'Enfant Plaza and the Smithsonian museums along Independence Ave. Southwest is home to many government offices, including the Food and Drug Administration, the Department of Health and Human Services, NASA Headquarters, the Department of Energy, the Department of Transportation, and the Environmental Protection Agency. Convenience alone makes this an attractive neighborhood for federal workers.

As most of the apartment complexes have garages and lots, parking is not a problem for residents. However, you should be prepared to pay an extra $30 to $50 a month for parking privileges. The **Southwest Mall**, at 4th and M Sts. SW, provides residents with the usual shopping options. At 401 M St. SW there is both a **Safeway** (202-554-9155) and a **CVS** (202-863-9227).

Unlike the more glamorous areas of the District, Southwest has blocks of high-rises adjacent to public housing areas and property crime is a concern here. Many neighborhood residents have raved about living in the area, but the common perception for people who don't live there is that Southwest is unsafe. Unlike Georgetown, Adams Morgan and Dupont Circle, Southwest shuts down in the evening. Its night life is mostly restricted to the Waterfront restaurants and the area near Arena Stage.

Commute to Downtown 10 minutes by Metro Green Line at Waterfront and Green, Yellow, Blue and Orange Lines at L'Enfant Plaza

Post Office Fort McNair at 4th and P Sts. SW (202-484-0969), L'Enfant Plaza at 458 L'Enfant Plaza SW (202-523-2013) and Southwest at 45 L St. SW (202-523-2408)

Library Southwest Branch at Wesley Place and K St. SW (202-727-1381)

Police Station 415 4th St. SW (202-727-4655)

Recreational Activities There are several small parks in this neighborhood and the Mall is just a brief walk away. There is a major DC-run recreation field and facility at the corner of South Capitol and Eye Sts. SW.

Adams Morgan

Quiet by day, crowded at night, Adams Morgan is one of the city's most culturally diverse and vibrant areas. The intersection of Columbia Rd. and 18th St. NW forms the heart of Adams Morgan. Specialty shops, bars and some of Washington's best ethnic restaurants crowd a several block stretch along each of the streets.

Adams Morgan is an area in perpetual transition. Over the past decade or so, real estate investors have begun a campaign to renovate and modernize the neighborhood. Riots in the early 1990s called media and public attention to the disadvantages—and advantages—of living in this area. As in any transitional area, safety conditions can change quickly from one block to the next, and it pays to be a bit "street smart" if you live here.

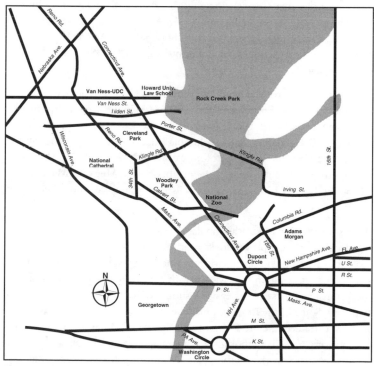

WASHINGTON, DC
Adams Morgan, Dupont Circle, Woodley Park, Cleveland Park and Van Ness

The area between 18th St. and Connecticut Ave., on the west edge of Adams Morgan, is generally considered to be the safest.

Throughout the neighborhood, you will find many beautiful townhouses and brownstones, some of which have been converted to group houses or apartment or condo buildings. There also are a number of elegant, older apartment buildings, some rental and others condo. The variety of housing choices in Adams Morgan is consistent with the neighborhood's varied and eclectic character.

As in many of Washington's more popular neighborhoods, parking is a constant challenge here. Finding a parking spot can be especially tough on weekends, when thousands of Washingtonians and suburbanites invade Adams Morgan for the restaurants and bars. There is a pay parking lot on 18th St. The closest Metro stations—Dupont Circle and Woodley Park-Zoo—are each a 15-minute walk from the heart of Adams Morgan. Metrobuses run up and down 16th and 18th Sts., providing access to all parts of the city.

The largest supermarket in the neighborhood is the **Safeway** on Columbia Rd., just east of 18th St. (202-667-0774). A better selection of fruits and vegetables can be found at the neighborhood farmers' market on Saturdays, at the intersection of Columbia Rd. and 18th St., right in front of the Crestar Bank.

Corner grocery stores and small ethnic markets fill in the gaps. At 1831 Columbia Rd. NW, **So's Your Mom** (202-462-3666), with its trademark big kissing lips, sells deli goods from New York. Latin American groceries are sold at **El Gavilan** at 1646 Columbia Rd. NW (202-234-9260) and **Americana Grocery** at 1813 Columbia Rd. NW (202-265-7455). Perhaps the most exotic store in the neighborhood, **Merkato Market** at 2116 18th St. NW (202-483-9499) sells Ethiopian spices and other specialty foods.

Adams Morgan is particularly popular for its many restaurants. You can wander along the couple of blocks near the intersection of 18th St. and Columbia Rd. and end up enjoying cuisine from just about any part of the world. The prices vary just as widely, with a delicious and often unusual meal at many of these places easily costing less than $15 a person or more than $50. Some of the more popular restaurants are **Cities**, **I Matti**, **Perry's**, **Meskerem**, **Café Lautrec** and **Straits of Malaysia**. Several of the more expensive neighborhood restaurants have individual valet parking services, and they work together, parking cars for patrons of each other's restaurants. For dessert, Adams Morgan has its own **Ben & Jerry's** (202-667-6677) at the corner of Euclid and Champlain Sts. and a number of after-dinner coffee spots such as **Jolt 'n Bolt** and **Belmont Pantry** in the Belmont Kitchen restaurant.

Adams Morgan Day is one of the city's best annual events. Usually held the second Sunday in September, this huge street fair celebrates the cultural diversity of the neighborhood with an abundance of food and music.

Just off the southeastern corner of Adams Morgan, the area along U St. from 16th St. out to the U St.-Cardozo Metro station is widely considered an up-and-coming part of town. This section, the U St. corridor, has become home to an urban eclectic crowd, with restaurants, shops and other businesses to match. Many of these establishments draw on the resident artists to design and decorate their interiors, with varying degrees of style—and success. While this part of town is not as safe as neighborhoods due west, it is developing into a safer and more desirable place. Popular restaurants include **State of the Union**, **Polly's**, **Julio's** and **Stetson's**.

Commute to Downtown 10 minutes by Metro Red Line at Woodley Park-Zoo

Post Office Kalorama at 2300 18th St. NW (202-483-5042) and Temple Heights at 1921 Florida Ave. NW (202-232-7613)

Library Mount Pleasant at 16th and Lamont Sts. NW (202-727-1361)

Police Station 1624 V St. NW (202-673-6930)

Recreational Activities Public tennis courts can be found on 18th St. between California and Kalorama Sts. The Marie Reed Center (202-673-7771) has an indoor swimming pool at 2200 Champlain Ave. NW. There is also a small park at Columbia Rd. and Kalorama St.

Dupont Circle

Dupont Circle epitomizes city living—busy streets, crowded sidewalks, the rare open parking space, an abundance of high-rise buildings, movie theaters, distinctive shops, art galleries, bookstores and a multitude of bars and restaurants. It is a vibrant, sometimes hectic neighborhood, characterized by a wide diversity of life styles and cultural interests. It is a magnet for the gay community, for professionals and for many students, especially graduates. Dupont Circle is one part of town where you can walk to just about everything, and walking is much easier than driving (and parking) in the evening and on weekends, when people from all over come to the neighborhood's many bars and restaurants.

Dupont Circle sits just above Downtown and below Adams Morgan. Technically, this neighborhood spans the area west of 16th St. and east of 24th St., between N St. and Florida Ave., but its high real estate values have led realtors to extend its boundaries and include many other nearby areas, such as Logan Circle and Shaw. These peripheral areas offer slightly lower housing costs, but are not as safe or as distinctive as Dupont Circle.

The area on the western side of Connecticut Ave. houses several hotels, many embassies and a number of art galleries as well as apartments, condos and private townhouses. The embassies lining Massachusetts Ave., as it travels northwest from Dupont Circle up to Observatory Circle, have helped this part of the avenue earn the name Embassy Row. It can be an excellent route for jogging or taking a long, romantic walk.

Housing costs here are among the highest in the city, although not quite as high as in Georgetown. The variety of Victorian townhouses and apartment buildings offers a virtually complete selection of housing solutions. Most of the more affordable housing appears on the east side of Connecticut Ave., known as East Dupont. As a result of the relatively high real estate values on both sides of the avenue, you will not find many group houses in Dupont Circle. You should look for them instead on the fringes of the area, to the east of 16th St.

If you plan on living here, you really do not need a car and in fact, may be better off without one. Most addresses are a few blocks from one of the two entrances to the Dupont Circle Metro station. Garage parking can be outrageously expensive—between $150 and $200 a month at many buildings—that is, if you ever get to the top of the waiting list.

Grocery shopping can be done at the **Safeway** at the corner of 17th and Corcoran Sts. NW (202-667-6825). There is another grocery store, **Townhouse**, discreetly tucked away at the corner of 20th and S Sts. NW (202-483-3908), and several corner markets and gourmet stores that cater to busy city dwellers. Following Connecticut Ave. north, you will find **Lawson's** (202-775-0400) right "on the circle," **Sutton Place Gourmet** (202-588-9876) at the corner of R St. and a new local establishment, **Market Day** (202-387-3858), between R and S Sts. **Chesapeake Bagel Bakery**, above the circle at 1636 Connecticut Ave. NW (202-328-7985), **Whatsa Bagel**, below the circle at 3513 Connecticut Ave. (202-966-8990), and **Bagels Etc.**, at 2122 P St. NW (202-466-7171), all specialize in good local bagels—although connoisseurs from New York may be disappointed. The neighborhood is richly populated by coffee shops, including **Starbucks**, **Hannibals**, **Soho Tea and Coffee**, **Java House** and **Cup'A Cup'A**.

The West End section, just off the southwest corner of the heart of Dupont Circle, borders Georgetown to the west and Foggy Bottom to the south. Apartment, condos and townhouses in the West End are mostly luxury residences. Residents shop at the **Townhouse** at 2060 L St. NW (202-659-8784), **Metro Market** at 2130 P St. NW (202-833-3720) or **Federal Market** at 1215 23rd St. NW (202-293-0014), which has a thriving noontime business for its terrific sandwiches. Characteristic of grocery stores in urban settings, these stores promise cramped aisles and high prices.

Commute to Downtown Five minutes by Metro Red Line at Dupont

Post Office Temple Heights at 1921 Florida Ave. NW (202-232-7613) and Farragut at 1145 19th St. NW (202-523-2506)

Library West End at 1101 24th St. NW (202-727-1397)

Police Station 1624 V St. NW (202-673-6930)

Recreational Activities Right in the center of the neighborhood is the actual Dupont Circle, with a large fountain, grassy areas, park benches and lots of people, many with their dogs in tow. This is a popular spot for picnics, reading, skating, meeting up with friends and people-watching. Rock Creek Park has numerous trails for running and biking and a mile-and-a-half long exercise trail with 18 workout stations, beginning near the Taft Bridge. Be careful running or walking through the park when others are not around or after dark.

Woodley Park

When you spot the large mural of Marilyn Monroe painted on the side of a Connecticut Ave. townhouse, you know that you have reached Woodley Park, at the north end of the Taft Bridge. This Connecticut Ave. neighborhood is home to a varied population including young and not so young professionals, students and an interesting "hotel population," for the area is home to a couple of large convention hotels. Nearby, hundreds of animal species make their home at the National Zoo, a popular spot for tourists and locals alike.

Older high-rise buildings dominate this neighborhood. Many of the apartments are boxy and small, but have a wonderful old-fashioned charm that you won't find in the suburbs. The area's popularity stems from its proximity to Adams Morgan and Downtown and to its relative safety. Many residents attribute this safety to the presence of several embassies in the area, each with its own security force. If you are looking for a group house, you should continue up Connecticut Ave. to Cleveland Park as there aren't as many of them in Woodley Park. Street parking can be difficult even with a residential parking sticker, required in all DC neighborhoods with parking restrictions.

Woodley Park's commercial strip spans a three-block area around the Metro station on Connecticut Ave. The area includes some of Washington's best ethnic restaurants including **Cafe Paradiso** (202-265-8955), **Saigon Gourmet** (202-265-1360), **Woodley Café** (202-332-5773) and the **Lebanese Taverna** (202-265-8681). Around the corner, you will find **New Heights** (202-234-4110) and an Irish bar called **Murphy's** (202-462-7171). You can also find a **CVS** at 2616 Connecticut Ave. NW (202-265-6818) and the **Washington Park Gourmet** at 2331 Calvert St. NW (202-462-5566). There is, however, no major supermarket. Serious grocery shopping requires a trip to one of the bordering neighborhoods— Adams Morgan's **Safeway** (202-667-0774) or Cleveland Park's **Brookville Supermarket** (202-244-9114).

Commute to Downtown 10 minutes by Metro Red Line at Woodley Park-Zoo

Post Office A mini post office is located in the basement of the Sheraton Hotel, 2660 Woodley Rd.; the entrance is around back, on Calvert St. (202-328-2000).

Library Connecticut Ave. and Macomb St. NW (202-727-1345)

Police Station 3320 Idaho Ave. NW (202-282-0070)

Recreational Activities The running and biking paths in Rock Creek Park are nearby, as is the Park's mile-and-half-long exercise trail, with a series of 18 workout stations that begins just below the Taft Bridge.

Cleveland Park

Historically, Cleveland Park was the first neighborhood developed outside of Capitol Hill and Georgetown. In the late 19th century, wealthy merchants began building mansions on what was then known as Piedmont Plateau. At the time, the only access to the neighborhood was through Georgetown. President Grover Cleveland sought refuge from the city heat in the 1880s by purchasing a "country house" in this neighborhood, where the temperature was approximately 15 degrees cooler than at the White House. Only when the Taft Bridge opened at the beginning of the century did the neighborhood really begin to develop as part of the city. Today, Cleveland Park offers a growing number of amenities as well as easy access to Downtown and the Hill. A good part of the neighborhood is an official Historic District.

As in Woodley Park, most of Cleveland Park's commercial activity occurs within a three-block radius of its Red Line Metro station (Cleveland Park). The **Uptown Theatre** at 3426 Connecticut Ave. NW (202-966-5400), one of Washington's best movie houses complete with old-style seating and a balcony, sits in the middle of this activity. In addition to **Brookville Supermarket** at 3427 Connecticut Ave. NW (202-244-9114), the neighborhood has more than its share of small gourmet stores, including **Vace** (202-363-1999), offering primarily Italian goods, many of which are homemade. Nearby you will find **Uptown Bakers** (202-362-6262), **Quartermaine Coffee Roasters** (202-244-2676), **Starbucks** (202-966-8118) and **Yes! Natural Gourmet** (202-363-1559). You can shop at the **Giant** at Connecticut Ave. and Van Ness St., or at Wisconsin Ave. and Newark St. or the **Safeway** at 4310 Connecticut Ave.

On the east side of the 3500 block of Connecticut Ave. sits a small strip mall called **Park 'n Shop**. This remnant of a 1920s shopping mall, reputed to be the first strip mall, was renovated in 1992. Although some traditionalists may blanch at the glitzy new site, the new mall has brought even more amenities to the neighborhood, including **Whatsa Bagel** (202-966-8990) and **Pizzeria Uno** (202-966-3225) along with a **Herman's** sporting goods store and a **Blockbusters** video store.

Several popular local restaurants can be found along Connecticut Ave., including **Spices Asian Restaurant & Sushi Bar** (202-686-3833), **Ireland's Four Provinces** (202-244-0860) and **Yanni's Greek Taverna** (202-362-8871).

Cleveland Park is known for its beautiful, posh houses, but house hunters can also choose from a wide range of apartment buildings lining Connecticut Ave. and many more apartment buildings tucked away on the quieter side streets. Most of the apartment buildings cater to professionals or students and offer efficiencies and one- and two-bedroom apartments. Those searching for a group house will find lots of relatively inexpensive options in the large, older, bungalow-style homes. Street parking is available, if difficult to find during busy times, on side streets on the western side of Connecticut Ave.

The Cleveland Park Metro station is the closest one to the main entrance of the National Zoo, and using it lets you avoid the long uphill climb from the Woodley Park-Zoo station.

Commute to Downtown 12 to 15 minutes by Metro Red Line at Cleveland Park

Post Office 3430 Connecticut Ave. NW (202-523-2395)

Library Connecticut Ave. and Macomb St. NW (202-727-1345)

Police Station 3320 Idaho Ave. NW (202-282-0070)

Recreational Activities The Cleveland Park Club at 3433 33rd Pl. NW (202-363-0756) has a small swimming pool and offers aerobics classes. There are tennis courts at 45th and Van Ness Sts. NW and next to Hearst School, off Wisconsin Ave. below Sidwell Friends School.

Van Ness

Van Ness is the last Connecticut Ave. neighborhood with access to the Metro. Above Van Ness, the Red Line turns west to Wisconsin Ave. before heading north to Bethesda and other spots in Maryland. In the high-rise apartment landscape of Connecticut Ave., Van Ness forms an island of commercial activity between Cleveland Park and the rest of upper Connecticut Ave. The presence of Howard University Law School and the University of the District of Columbia (UDC) defines much of the neighborhood's character. Modern apartment buildings provide the bulk of available housing on Connecticut Ave. itself in the form of efficiencies and one- and two-bedroom apartments. But once off Connecticut Ave., Van Ness is transformed into a suburban neighborhood of pricy, single-family homes.

Many neighborhood conveniences surround the Van Ness-UDC Metro station. Two supermarkets, **Giant** (202-364-8250) and **Safeway** (202-244-4390), and a wide variety of other stores can be found within a three-block radius. Van Ness also boasts more than its fair share of fast-food outlets, including **Taco Bell**, **Burger King**, **Pizza Hut** and **Roy Rogers**. Through an entrance on Veazey Terrace, Giant offers free underground parking—a rare treat in the District. On-street parking in Van Ness is limited, especially when the two universities are in session, but there are several underground parking garages. Most apartment buildings offer parking at about $75 per month.

Above Van Ness, blocks of apartment buildings alternate along Connecticut Ave. with pockets of commercial activity. There is a small shopping area with several restaurants, gas stations and a **CVS** (202-966-1815) near the intersection of Connecticut and Nebraska Aves. The original **Marvelous Market** (202-686-4040), one of Washington's most notable bakeries, resides here. Farther up Connecticut Ave. close to Chevy Chase Circle, you will find several more restaurants, another **Safeway** (202-244-6097), **Magruder's Supermarket** (202-244-7800) and the gourmet bakery,

Bread and Chocolate (202-966-7413). It is about a 15-minute walk from here to the Van Ness-UDC Metro station.

Commute to Downtown 15 minutes by Metro Red Line at Van Ness-UDC

Post Office Friendship at 4005 Wisconsin Ave. NW (202-523-2401)

Library Connecticut Ave. and Macomb St. NW (202-727-1345)

Police Station 3320 Idaho Ave. NW (202-282-0070)

Recreational Activities UDC has three public tennis courts just behind the Safeway; UDC students and faculty have first priority.

Foggy Bottom

There are several theories as to the origin of the rather unusual name for this neighborhood. Some say that the neighborhood was built on top of a reclaimed swamp. Others claim that the State Department's murky politics gave rise to the name. Regardless, its proximity to the State Department, the World Bank, the International Monetary Fund (IMF), the Kennedy Center and George Washington University (GWU) makes it an attractive neighborhood for those in the foreign service and for students.

In the last century, Foggy Bottom has switched from being the home of thousands of middle-class workers to a neighborhood of students and bureaucrats. A mix of moderate and luxury apartments can be found on Foggy Bottom's residential streets—the most expensive being the Watergate (an establishment known for its class and elegance long before it became a synonym for Washington corruption). Apartments at the Watergate rent for thousands of dollars a month and sell for millions, but do not despair—more economical housing can be found to the north of Virginia Ave. Buildings closest to the George Washington University campus tend to offer the most reasonable costs. You should be able to find a wide range of apartment types and get the right deal for you, with a little bit of legwork.

Residents buy groceries at the **Townhouse** (202-659-8784) at 2060 L St. NW or another **Safeway** (202-338-3628) in the basement of the Watergate Complex, in a small, rather exclusive underground shopping mall, complete with post office, **CVS** (202-333-5031) and the fabulous **Watergate Pastry Shop** (202-342-1777). In addition, several small mom-and-pop grocery stores catering to students' late-night eating habits dot the area.

Music and movie fans can get their fix at the 2000 Pennsylvania Shopping Mall with **Tower Records** (202-331-2400) at one end and **Tower Video** (202-223-3900) at the other. In the middle, you will find **One Stop News**

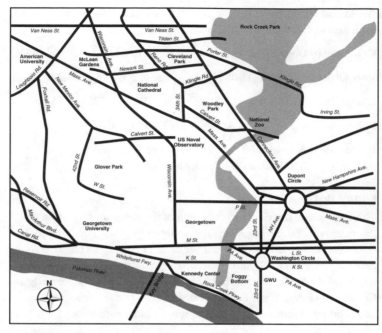

WASHINGTON, DC
Foggy Bottom, Georgetown, Glover Park and
Cathedral/McLean Gardens

(202-872-1577) and the **Cone E. Island** ice cream shop (202-822-8460) as well as a few restaurants, including **Kinkead's** (202-296-7700) and **Bertucci's Brick Oven Pizzeria** (202-296-2600). Morning coffee, bagels and muffins can be picked up at **Ciao** (202-296-6796), a favorite among GWU students.

Commute to Downtown Five minutes by Metro Blue and Orange Lines at Foggy Bottom

Post Office 2600 Virginia Ave. NW in the Watergate Complex (202-965-2730)

Library West End at 1101 24th St. NW (202-727-1397)

Police Station 3320 Idaho Ave. NW (202-282-0070)

Recreational Activities The Mall, with its vast playing fields, is just a few blocks south of the Foggy Bottom Metro station. The Federal Reserve has several tennis courts open to the public. To reserve one, call 202-452-3357.

Georgetown

Georgetown, right on the banks of the Potomac River, started out as a commercial port and remained so until the latter half of the 19th century. This helps explain the layout of this historic quarter. To the west of Wisconsin Ave., you will find some of the neighborhood's nicest homes where the wealthy merchants used to live. Less successful merchants and workers resided to the east of Wisconsin Ave. in a mix of two-story Victorian and clapboard houses. You would hardly be able to guess at the humble origins of much of Georgetown as today it attracts a predominantly well-to-do crowd. The neighborhood is filled with historic sites, as noted by plaques placed on the side of many houses.

In addition to being Washington's oldest neighborhood, Georgetown offers its residents urban elegance mixed with an active night life. The intersection of Wisconsin Ave. and M St. forms the business and entertainment hub of the neighborhood known best for its upscale restaurants, fashionable clothing stores, and many popular bars and night spots. Moving away from the hub, you find a beautiful residential neighborhood, full of tree-lined streets and cozy Federal, Georgian and Victorian townhouses. Many young professionals and a large portion of Washington's jet-set have found their niche in this neighborhood. For $6,500 a month you can rent a three-bedroom apartment at Georgetown's exclusive **Washington Harbour** (yes, they actually spell Harbour with a "u"), right along the banks of the Potomac. While Georgetown does offer a mix of apartments, English basements are probably the most popular choice in this area for rich students and young professionals.

Over the years, Georgetown's popularity has brought some problems to the neighborhood. Street parking in the area around Wisconsin Ave. and M St. is virtually impossible and it is not much easier to find spaces in the residential areas. Of course, apartment residents have the option to pay for private parking, but, as with most things in Georgetown, this amounts to a serious expense.

Georgetown's lack of easy access to the subway prevents many from choosing this neighborhood. The closest Metro station to the eastern half of Georgetown is Foggy Bottom on the Blue and Orange Lines, a 10- to 15-minute walk away. For those nearer to the Georgetown University campus, the Rosslyn Metro station, also on the Blue and Orange Lines, is actually nearer, even though you have to cross Key Bridge to get to it. Fortunately, both Wisconsin Ave. and M St. are on major bus routes.

Georgetown has a wealth of shopping opportunities, including the **Georgetown Park Mall**, with its nearly 100 shops, boutiques, galleries and cafés. An important feature of this mall is a parking garage for which validation is available. **Washington Harbour**, at 3000 K St. NW, combines commercial and residential space right on the water, with a number of popular bars and restaurants including **Sequoia** (202-944-4200).

The **"Social" Safeway** at 1855 Wisconsin Ave. NW (202-333-3223) is the largest supermarket in the area. As its nickname suggests, this Safeway is a popular spot for singles to check each other out while waiting in the checkout lines. In addition, Georgetown has several smaller gourmet markets including **Neam's Grocery** at 3217 P St. NW (202-338-4694) and **Dean & DeLuca** in the Old Market House at 3276 M St. NW (202-342-2500). Bagel lovers can choose among **Georgetown Bagelry** at 3245 M St. NW (202-965-1011), the **Booeymonger** at 3265 Prospect St. NW (202-333-4810) and **Chesapeake Bagels** at 4000 Wisconsin Ave. (202-966-8866).

Commute to Downtown   25 minutes by foot, 15 minutes by bus

Post Office   1215 31st St. NW (202-523-2405)

Library   Georgetown Regional at Wisconsin Ave. and R St. NW (202-727-1353)

Police Station   3320 Idaho Ave. NW (202-282-0070)

Recreational Activities   Before it was recently damaged by severe flooding, the C&O Canal Towpath was a great place for walking, running and biking, and ice-skating, under appropriate conditions. Until the three- to four-year reconstruction project is completed, you will have to turn elsewhere. You will find tennis courts at 30th and R Sts. NW, and at 33rd St. and Volta Place NW. Glover Park, nearby, offers hiking trails through its woods.

Glover Park

Glover Park rests just above Georgetown, bounded by Wisconsin Ave. and Glover and Whitehaven Parks. It contains many large, older homes, making it a popular spot for group houses, especially for Georgetown and American University students. You will find group houses available on the streets off Wisconsin Ave. For those who prefer apartment or condo living, there are many older apartment buildings, both high-rise and garden-style, including a number overlooking the park from which the neighborhood gets its name.

For an area so close to the bustle of Georgetown, there is a pleasant small-town feel to much of Glover Park. Apart from the main retail area on Wisconsin Ave., there are only a few businesses. A cozy Little League baseball and soccer park at the intersection of Calvert St. and Wisconsin

Ave. is surrounded by trees. You can meet your neighbors at Glover Park Day, a neighborhood block party in June. The area has its own monthly paper, the "Glover Park Gazette," and the baby sitting co-op has become a neighborhood institution. The **Glover Park Citizen's Association** (202-965-8800) can provide further information.

Glover Park's border with Georgetown stirs with commercial activity. In the 2400 block of Wisconsin Ave., you will find **G&G Market** (202-333-5300) and **Plain Old Pearson's Liquor** (202-333-6666). The local **Glover Park Market** is at 2411 37th St. NW (202-333-4030). **Bread & Circus**, at 2323 Wisconsin Ave. NW (202-333-5393), is a newly opened whole foods market carrying high-quality gourmet, specialty, natural and organic foods. Georgetown's **"Social" Safeway** at 1855 Wisconsin Ave. NW (202-333-3223) is also nearby. On Saturday mornings, a farmer sells organic and market produce at the corner of Calvert and 39th Sts. NW. An Amoco station with some of the highest prices in town sits at the corner of Calvert St. and Wisconsin Ave. Despite the high neighborhood gas prices, having a car in this neighborhood is less of a challenge than in other areas. Street parking is relatively available and access to a car makes living here much easier.

Commute to Downtown 15 minutes by bus

Post Office Calvert St. at 2336 Wisconsin Ave. NW (202-965-8966)

Library Georgetown Regional at Wisconsin Ave. and R St. NW (202-727-1353)

Police 3320 Idaho Ave. NW (202-282-0070)

Recreational Activities A recreation center located at 3600 Calvert St. NW sponsors art and aerobics classes as well as programs for senior citizens. Several small parks are in the neighborhood and tennis courts are nearby at 33rd St. and Volta Place NW. Several trails through the Glover Park woods take you south to Reservoir Rd.

Cathedral and McLean Gardens

Traveling farther up Wisconsin Ave., you reach Cathedral and McLean Gardens, two relatively small and quiet neighborhoods just above Georgetown. Cathedral earns its name from the defining landmark in the area, Washington National Cathedral, visible from points throughout the city and even across the river. Its grounds are a wonderful place to stroll and enjoy a peaceful moment right in the heart of a busy city. When open, the Cathedral's massive towers provide a splendid panoramic view of Washington.

The blocks surrounding the Cathedral host a number of older apartment buildings and single-family homes. Generally, apartment buildings line Wisconsin Ave. and the side streets to the west. Single-family homes appear on the side streets east of Wisconsin Ave. in the shadow of the Cathedral and bordering on the Cleveland Park neighborhood. Many of these homes are actually in the Cleveland Park Historical District.

Farther up Wisconsin, the former McLean family estate now houses McLean Gardens. The McLean family, one of DC's wealthier families, suffered many misfortunes often blamed on the legendary curse of the Hope Diamond (a famous 45.5-carat blue diamond now on display at the Smithsonian, which so far does not seem to have inherited the curse). In 1941, the federal government bought the estate and built apartment buildings and dormitories to shelter the many people coming to the District to work for the growing War Department. After World War II, private interests took control of the land and turned the buildings into private apartments. Today, McLean Gardens is a large garden apartment and condominium complex and includes a luxury high-rise, the Village Tower.

Most of the commercial activity along Wisconsin Ave. occurs between the two residential neighborhoods. A 24-hour **Giant** (202-244-5922) and a **CVS** (202-966-9268) face each other at the corner of Wisconsin Ave. and Newark St. The first in-town **Fresh Fields**, a specialty and natural foods supermarket, is located at 4530 40th St. NW (202-237-5800), in neighboring Tenleytown. The first **Starbucks Coffee** to open in Washington is at 3430 Wisconsin Ave. NW (202-537-6879). **Cactus Cantina** at 3300 Wisconsin Ave. (202-686-7222) offers authentic Mexican food; along with great food, their claim to fame is that there is no can opener in the kitchen.

Commute to Downtown 15 minutes by bus

Post Office Friendship at 4005 Wisconsin Ave. NW (202-523-2401)

Library Tenleytown at 4450 Wisconsin Ave. NW (202-727-1389)

Police Station 3320 Idaho Ave. NW (202-282-0070)

Recreational Activities McLean Gardens maintains its own pools, open to residents. Three public tennis courts sit near the corner of Newark and 39th Sts. You can grow your own vegetables and flowers in the public gardens also located at Newark and 39th Sts. To reserve a garden plot, call 202-576-6257.

American University Park, Spring Valley and Palisades

American University Park and Spring Valley are two of the several neighborhoods touching the fringes of American University. Massachusetts Ave., a main DC thoroughfare, runs through these neighborhoods and up in to suburban Maryland. Frequent Metrobuses provide residents with access to Downtown. American University Park is a modest neighborhood, containing reasonable housing options. The suburban feel of this area, combined with affordable starter homes, makes it popular for young families. Apartment housing, though not plentiful, is available; rents tend to reflect the scarcity. Students favor the mammoth apartment buildings just below campus along Massachusetts and New Mexico Aves.

Spring Valley, one of the most affluent sections in Washington, is known for its quiet, tree-lined streets full of large, single-family homes. For those just beginning to move into houses, leasing a house may be a more practical option. Rental prices here compare to other Northwest neighborhoods. Available rental housing options include attached houses, cluster homes and detached, single-family residences. There are few apartment buildings or complexes in this area.

Palisades includes the area west of American University down to MacArthur Blvd. Like American University Park, the neighborhoods here are family-oriented, with brick colonial homes and private yards on tree-lined streets.

Proximity to American University offers residents many entertainment options with university athletic events, performances, movies and museums open to the public. For information about upcoming events, contact the AU Student Confederation at 202-885-6400. Two popular student hang-outs in the area are **Maggie's** at 4237 Wisconsin Ave. NW (202-363-1447) and **Quigley's** at 3201 New Mexico Ave. NW (202-966-0500).

Cafe Deluxe (202-686-2233) at 3228 Wisconsin Ave. NW offers a varied menu and a nice neighborhood atmosphere. **Listrani's** (202-363-0619) at 5100 MacArthur Blvd. NW is a very popular Italian restaurant (offering pizza delivery as well) as is **DeCarlo's** (202-363-4220) at 4822 Yuma St. NW. **Crate & Barrel** (202-364-6100) and **Starbucks** (202-686-3680) are conveniently located in the 4800 block of Massachusetts Ave. NW.

Grocery shopping can be done at one of two neighborhood Safeway stores—the **Safeway** at 4865 MacArthur Blvd. NW (202-337-5649) or the **"Secret Safeway"** at 4203 Davenport St. NW, just off Wisconsin Ave. (202-364-0290). In nearby Bethesda, just over the Maryland line, there is a **Giant** at 5400 Westbard Ave. (301-652-1484). **Sutton Place Gourmet** at 3201 New Mexico Ave. NW (202-363-5800) satisfies the neighborhood's

WASHINGTON, DC
American University Park/Spring Valley/Palisades and Friendship Heights/Chevy Chase

need for gourmet food and provisions. A second, smaller **Sutton Place Gourmet** (202-966-1740) sits at 4872 Massachusetts Ave. NW.

Commute to Downtown 30 minutes by bus

Post Office Friendship at 4005 Wisconsin Ave. NW (202-523-2401) and Palisades at 5136 MacArthur Blvd. NW (202-363-2921)

Libraries Palisades at 49th and V Sts. NW (202-727-1369) and Tenleytown at Wisconsin Ave. and Albemarle St. NW (202-727-1389)

Police 3320 Idaho Ave. NW (202-282-0070)

Recreational Activities The Wilson Senior High School track and indoor pool at Nebraska Ave. and Chesapeake St. NW (202-282-2216) are open to the public. Turtle Park at Van Ness and 45th Sts. NW hosts organized baseball and soccer teams.

Friendship Heights and Chevy Chase

This tiny, high-rise neighborhood straddles the line between DC and Maryland. Its 32 acres host a variety of upscale stores and mammoth apartment buildings. The neighborhood is famous for its fashionable shopping district that includes Gucci, Gianfranco Ferre, Valentino and Saks Fifth Avenue, to name a few. Two attractive retail malls face each other at the intersection of Wisconsin and Western Aves.—**Mazza Gallerie**, with Neiman Marcus and Filene's Basement as anchors, and **Chevy Chase Pavilion**, with several specialty stores but no department stores.

As for housing, if you prefer older or cozier neighborhoods, you should look elsewhere. But if you like high-rise living and want to be near upscale amenities and the Metro, this might be just the place for you. Many choose to live here because it has an "urban feel" without the urban taxes—at least on the Maryland side of the line. Most apartment complexes have swimming pools and relatively inexpensive underground parking. The area's proximity to American University and Downtown, via the Metro Red Line, makes it a convenient location. The **Chevy Chase Shopping Center**, on the east side of Wisconsin Ave., has a **Giant** (301-718-6559) and a **CVS** (301-652-4959). A free shuttle bus service connects all of the major apartment complexes with this shopping center.

You can contact the **Friendship Heights Village Council** at 4433 South Park Ave. (301-656-2797) for information on the area. The **Village Center**, in the same building, provides residents with recreational, educational, cultural and health services.

Commute to Downtown 25 minutes by Metro Red Line at Friendship Heights

Post Office Main Post Office at 7400 Wisconsin Ave. in Bethesda (301-652-7401) and Chevy Chase at 5910 Connecticut Ave. (301-652-8508)

Libraries Tenley-Friendship at Albemarle St. and Wisconsin Ave., NW (202-727-1389) and Bethesda Regional at 7400 Arlington Rd. (301-986-4300)

Police Station 7359 Wisconsin Ave. (301-652-9200)

Recreational Activities The Wilson Senior High School track and indoor pool at Nebraska Ave. and Chesapeake St. NW (202-282-2216) are open to the public. Hubert Humphrey Friendship Park is within walking distance.

MARYLAND NEIGHBORHOODS, MONTGOMERY COUNTY

Bethesda and Chevy Chase

Chevy Chase, right on the border between city and county, is often linked up with either Friendship Heights in DC or Bethesda in Maryland, depending on who you talk to. In Maryland, Bethesda and Chevy Case have been sister neighborhoods for years and many local establishments use the two names together. Bethesda occupies the southern tip of Montgomery County and is one of the more affluent suburbs in the metropolitan region. Neighborhoods with pricy single-family homes predominate, punctuated by several important research facilities, including the National Institutes of Health, the Naval Medical Center and the Uniformed Services University of the Health Sciences. Chevy Chase is just east of Bethesda and maintains a good deal of its original village-like qualities.

While Chevy Chase has its own specific jurisdictional boundaries, as can be seen on any good map, Bethesda is a more sprawling area, with a core of commercial activity surrounding the Metro station that bears its name. There are actually five Metro Red Line stations serving the Bethesda-Chevy Chase neighborhoods—Friendship Heights, Bethesda, Medical Center, Grosvenor and White Flint. This string of stations offers an appealing alternative to driving along the traffic-congested Wisconsin Ave.-Rockville Pike corridor.

Downtown Bethesda demonstrates the recent and rapid expansion this suburb has undergone. Just 20 years ago, Bethesda was a sleepy farm town. Development accelerated in the 1970s, spurred on further by the coming of the Metro in 1982. You will find remnants of the old farm town near the Bethesda station, including a weathered old post office and a statue honoring the "Madonna of the Trail," a tribute to Maryland's pioneer women. Next to these, the Rainbow Forest, an aluminum-disc sculpture, and the recently built Hyatt Luxury Hotel stand as icons of modern-day Bethesda. During the summer, the courtyard by the Metro station rocks to the beat of outdoor concerts; in the winter, it turns into an ice-skating rink. A couple of blocks north is the **Bethesda Theatre Café** (301-656-3337), a popular spot for discount movies and light meals.

Beyond the high-rise buildings characteristic of downtown Bethesda, off to the west of Wisconsin Ave., you will find Woodmont Triangle. Many small shops and some of the area's best ethnic restaurants reside here. Your dining options include **Bacchus** (301-985-0734), **Matuba Japanese Restaurant** (301-652-7449), **La Madeleine** (301-215-9139) and the **Cottonwood Cafe** (301-656-4844), just to name a few. **Travel Books & Language Center** at 4931 Cordell Ave. (301-951-8533) offers a huge collection of travel guides and maps from around the world and proudly counts the US State Department among its regular clients. The city has built numerous parking garages, free on weekends, so parking should not be a problem.

Bethesda does not lack for appealing housing, but it does not come cheaply. The newer luxury apartment buildings near the Metro offer all conceivable amenities at top-notch prices. A multitude of older, renovated buildings along Battery Lane, a few blocks away, can be had for slightly less.

The Medical Center Metro stop farther up Rockville Pike was built on the campus of the National Institutes of Health and if you exit the Metro at just the right time, you will hear reveille blown from the Naval Medical Center across the street. These institutions border residential neighborhoods where several homeowners rent out rooms in their homes or in detached apartments, and group houses are also available. Around the Grosvenor Metro station you will find more high-rise condominiums and apartments. Some buildings offer discounts to NIH employees; if you qualify, be sure to ask at the rental office.

In this affluent suburb, grocery stores and supermarkets promise no shortage of fully stocked shelves. Residents can shop at the **Safeway** at 5000 Bradley Blvd. (301-656-8641) or opt for the gourmet **Safeway Marketplace** (301-907-0700) at 7625 Old Georgetown Rd. **Giant**, on its home turf in the suburbs, has a store at Arlington Blvd. and Elm St. (301-718-2470). A **Giant Pharmacy** (301-652-9130) is across the street. **CVS** has one store at 4601 East-West Highway (301-986-9144) and a 24-hour store (301-656-2522) at the corner of Bradley Blvd. and Arlington Rd. In addition to large grocery stores, there are several supermarket-sized gourmet stores. **Sutton Place Gourmet** (301-564-3100) has a store in the **Wildwood Shopping Center** off Old Georgetown Rd. Farther out, **Fresh Fields** at 5225 River Rd. (301-984-4860) offers its natural and specialty foods. There is also the **French Market** (301-986-9661) in the Elizabeth Arcade at 4601 N. Park Ave. On Wednesdays and Saturdays, the **Montgomery Farm Women's Cooperative** hosts a farmers' market selling fruit, flowers and Amish baked goods at 7155 Wisconsin Ave. An outdoor flea market, replete with oriental rugs, furniture and jewelry, takes over this location on Sundays.

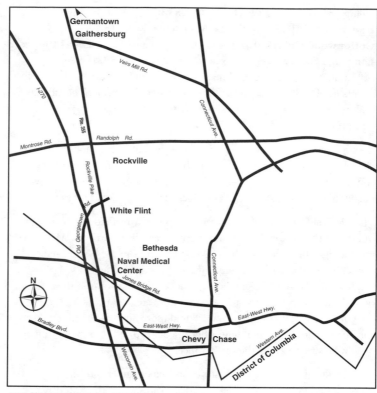

MONTGOMERY COUNTY, MD
Bethesda/Chevy Chase and Rockville/Gaithersburg/Germantown

Free information about the area is available from the Bethesda-Chevy Chase Center (301-986-4325) at 7815 Woodmont Ave.

Commute to Downtown 30 to 35 minutes by Metro Red Line at Friendship Heights, Bethesda, Medical Center, Grovesnor and White Flint

Post Office 7400 Wisconsin Ave. (301-652-7401)

Library Bethesda Regional at 7400 Arlington Rd. (301-986-4300)

Police 7359 Wisconsin Ave. (301-652-9200)

Recreational Activities Cabin John Regional Park (301-299-4555) at 7400 Tuckerman La. has tennis and handball courts, hiking trails and an ice-skating rink. **Glen Echo Park** at 7500 MacArthur Blvd. in Glen Echo (301-492-6282) is the area's gem, a national park sponsoring hundreds of classes in the arts. Its historic Spanish Ballroom offers a variety of dance classes and four dances per week from April through November. The park also operates a beautiful antique carousel from May through September.

Rockville, Gaithersburg and Germantown

Rockville has served as the seat of Montgomery County since 1776. It is an area particularly rich in colonial history and it has been neatly transformed over the years into a modern, well-planned city. Many homes are older, detached residences, yet the area offers a great deal of newer construction as well. You will find many parks and playgrounds to be an integral part of most Rockville neighborhoods. The city sponsors a popular cultural arts program. Extensive shopping, including **White Flint Mall**, can be found along Rockville Pike. Only 12 miles from DC, Rockville is connected to the District and its closer-in suburbs by excellent commuter access via I-270 as well as Rockville Pike (Route 355) and by the Metro Red Line for those who prefer public transportation.

Going a little farther out either I-270 or Rockville Pike, you come to Gaithersburg, about 20 miles from DC. Much of this community's development is due to its proximity to the I-270 corridor, a commercial and business area known for the many corporations that have relocated there in recent years. The local population of government workers, scientists and professionals enjoys a diverse mix of life styles. The City of Gaithersburg was incorporated in 1878 and both retains its historic character in the Olde Town district and welcomes the necessary expansion of more recent times.

An ethnically diverse city of approximately 50,000 people, it provides the full range of housing—apartments, townhouses, and both historic and newer single-family homes—as well as many parks and family-oriented recreation centers. Geographically in the heart of Gaithersburg is the **Lakeforest Mall** shopping center with over 200 department stores, shops, restaurants and movie theaters. Many other small shopping malls, restaurants and theaters are scattered throughout the city and there is a development plan underway to enhance the city's historic core. Community spirit is evident in such annual events as Olde Town Day and the Labor Day Parade.

About five miles beyond Gaithersburg is Germantown, home to several of the county's major employers including DOE and many high-tech firms along the I-270 corridor. The residential neighborhoods in Germantown offer many older homes as well as a wide variety of new, single-family homes, townhouses, condos and rental apartments. The combination provides for a diverse range of architectural styles. The community is bounded by two streams—Great Seneca to the south and Little Seneca to the north—and by two large parks—Seneca Creek State Park and Black Hill Regional Park. Local bus service to nearby Metrorail stations makes commuting via public transportation available to residents.

Silver Spring

Silver Spring is a sprawling area comprising the easternmost part of Montgomery County. As the local real estate market has not yet exploded like it has in Bethesda, you can find some of the most reasonably priced housing in the Washington suburbs around this area's three Red Line Metro stations—Silver Spring, Forest Glen and Wheaton.

Downtown Silver Spring is located near the junction of Georgia Ave. and Colesville Rd. (Route 29) and surrounds the busy Silver Spring Metro station. While there are a number of new high-rise office buildings there, the downtown area's last renaissance was back in the 1930s; since then most of the larger stores have left for Rockville Pike. This loss of economic vitality offers Silver Spring's residents many unanticipated advantages. The Metro station is accessible by car, even at rush hour, and there is plenty of nearby parking. A number of small, ethnic restaurants and shops have filled the vacant storefronts. You will find Italian, Ethiopian, Thai, Indian and Latin-American establishments here.

A controversial development project called the American Dream is being proposed to revitalize downtown Silver Spring. If endorsed, the massive complex will house retail, entertainment, educational and cultural facilities. Already in the plans are a waterpark, an ice-hockey rink, theme restaurants, an IMAX theater and more than 20 movie screens. The existing Silver Triangle complex would be incorporated into the new mall project.

Single-family homes and clusters of apartment buildings, both high-rise and garden-style, surround each of the three Metro stations serving Silver Spring. Group houses are available around the Forest Glen and Wheaton Metro stations. For those willing to brave the morning commute down Route 29, there are even cheaper options out Colesville Rd., at White Oak and beyond.

The area is served by several large grocery stores. **Snider's** at 1936 Seminary Rd. (301-589-3240) is a local favorite and has a steady following who rave about its meat and wine selections. Larger chains also can be found in downtown Silver Spring, including **Giant** at 1280 East-West Hwy. (301-585-1670) and **Safeway** at 909 Thayer Ave. (301-565-0686). Another **Giant** (301-949-1458) is located in Wheaton Plaza and there is a **Safeway** (301-949-7690) nearby at 11201 Georgia Ave.

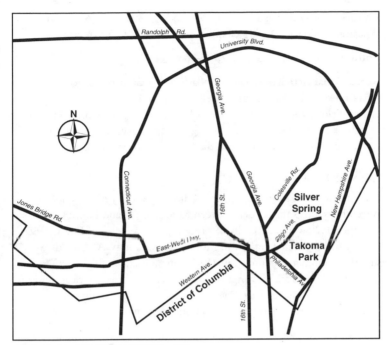

MONTGOMERY COUNTY, MD
Silver Spring and Takoma Park

To match its varied population, Silver Spring offers a huge variety of ethnic markets and restaurants. Prices are generally better than in other, more up-scale neighborhoods. For ethnic groceries, downtown Silver Spring offers **Italia** at 8662 Colesville Rd. (301-588-6999), **Muskan Fine Indian Grocery** at 956 Thayer Ave. (301 588 0331), the **Thai Market** at 902 Thayer Ave. (301-495-2779) and **Las Americas Mercado Latino** at 8651 16th St. (301-588-0882). The **Parkway Deli** at 8317 Grubb Rd. (301-587-1427) has almost everything you could want from a deli.

The area's largest shopping center, **Wheaton Plaza** (301-946-3200), lies between Veirs Mill Rd. and University Blvd. One of the major Washington department stores, **Hecht's**, anchors this mall. A new **JC Penney Co.** store is scheduled to open in the summer of 1996.

Commute to Downtown 20 to 30 minutes by Metro Red Line at Silver Spring

Post Office Main Branch at 8616 2nd Ave. (301-588-2926) and Silver Spring at 8455 Colesville Rd. (301-588-5086)

Libraries Silver Spring at 8901 Colesville Rd. (301-565-7689) and
Wheaton Regional at 11701 Georgia Ave. (301-929-5520)

Police Station 801 Sligo Ave. (301-565-7740)

Recreational Activities The area boasts two great parks. Sligo Creek
offers a hiking and biking trail as well as numerous playgrounds and
playing fields. Wheaton Regional Park has everything imaginable including
horseback riding, hiking trails, a fishing pond, a playground with both
carousel and miniature trains, and the beautiful Brookside Gardens.

Takoma Park

Takoma Park rests along the upper northeast boundary of DC and
currently straddles the border between Montgomery and Prince George's
Counties. Following the results of a recent public vote, as of July 1, 1997,
the city will be located entirely in Montgomery County. A planned
suburban community founded in 1883 along a branch of the B&O
railroad, Takoma Park was originally conceived as a healthful clean-water
alternative to Washington's malarial swamps. Despite changing times,
Takoma Park is still conceived of as an offering outside the mainstream.

A mixture of religion and politics has given shape to the community. From
1904 to 1989, Takoma Park was world headquarters of the Seventh-Day
Adventist Church. Two of the church's institutions, Washington Adventist
Hospital and Columbia Union College, remain, along with long-standing
traditions of family, vegetarianism and temperance. In recent years, signs of
the Church's waning influence have begun to appear, including a small bar
near the center of town. Takoma Park's population is politically active and
has put in place a number of progressive measures such as the declaration
of a nuclear-free zone, legal recognition of non-marital partnerships and a
so-far-unsuccessful movement to ban gas-powered lawn mowers.

Religion and politics aside, Takoma Park is a family-oriented place where
neighbors are still neighborly and residents work together to create a safe
and nurturing environment for children and adults alike. The local
population is an enviably diverse racial mix without the strained racial
tensions that tend to characterize some inner-city neighborhoods.

If you are looking to buy a house, Takoma Park may be a good place to
start. The grand Victorians near Old Town, around the intersection of
Carroll and Laurel Aves., will cost much more than those farther out, as
will anything that can be described with a straight face as within walking
distance of the local Red Line Metro station. About 60% of the housing
stock in Takoma Park is rental. Most of the high-rise apartment buildings
are on Maple Ave., but rental housing may be found throughout the city.

Takoma Old Town offers a quixotic mix of small, locally owned specialty shops. There is **Everyday Gourmet** at 6923 Laurel Ave. (301-270-2270), featuring take-out or eat-in pastries, sandwiches and other prepared items. **Mark's Kitchen** at 7006 Carroll Ave. (301-270-1884) is a Korean luncheonette offering a semi-vegetarian menu and cappuccino, and **Savory Cafe** at 7071 Carroll Ave. (301-270-2233) serves café-style food. The **Middle East Market** at 7006 Carroll Ave. (301-270-5154) is a great spot for exotic breads, coffee and spices. And from the end of April until mid-December, there is a farmers' market every Sunday in the center of town. While not as big as other area markets, the Takoma Park farmers' market has a loyal following among residents, many of whom consider it a major cultural event.

Commute to Downtown 15 minutes by Metro Red Line at Takoma

Post Offices 6909 Laurel Ave. (301-270-4392) and 1325 Holton La. (301-422-3980)

Libraries Takoma Park, MD Library at 101 Philadelphia Ave. (301-270-1717) and Takoma Park Tool Lending Library at 7500 Maple Ave. behind City Hall, where residents can borrow garden tools, drills and hand tools.

Police Station 7500 Maple Ave. (301-589-8274)

Recreational Activities Takoma Park's best park land includes hiking trails and playing fields on both sides of Sligo Creek, which runs through the eastern part of town. On Sunday, to accommodate bikers, skateboarders and the like, vehicles are banned from parts of the Takoma Park section of Sligo Creek Parkway.

MARYLAND NEIGHBORHOODS, PRINCE GEORGE'S COUNTY

Mount Rainier

Mount Rainier is a small, early 20th century "streetcar suburb," situated along Washington's northeast border, at the gateway to Prince George's County. Barely more than a mile square, it has been described by its city manager as a "working-class bedroom suburb" and by the *Washington Post* real estate section as a "place waiting to happen." Located along the Route 1 corridor (Rhode Island Ave.), Mount Rainier is barely five miles from the center of DC and the recent opening of Metro's Green Line at West Hyattsville has made it an even more convenient spot. It is one of the last places inside the Beltway where you can still find single-family detached homes selling for under six figures and is reputed to have one of the area's most compatible racial and ethnic mixtures.

As Mount Rainier is primarily residential, most of the housing stock consists of small, owner-occupied, pre-war bungalows and other modest house styles, including numerous Thirties-era Sears mail-order homes with spacious rooms and hardwood floors. A few larger Victorians can be found in the blocks just north of Rhode Island Ave. A low-rise apartment complex, Kaywood Gardens, is located along Eastern Ave. at the DC-Maryland border. A number of low- and high-rise rental apartment buildings line Queens Chapel Rd. on the city's northern edge, close to the West Hyattsville Metro station.

Downtown Mount Rainier shopping can be characterized as serviceable at best. The main draw is the **Glut Food Co-op** at 4005 34th St. (301-779-1978), the Washington area's oldest surviving food co-op and a great place to stock up on inexpensive grains, spices, whole wheat bread, fresh fruit and vegetables. One other notable downtown store is discount-minded **Party Times Liquors** at 3307 Rhode Island Ave. (301-927-3037). The nearest major grocery store is the **Giant** (301-699-0501) in **Queens Chillum Shopping Center**.

Commute to Downtown 20 to 30 minutes by Metro Green Line at West Hyattsville or by Metrobus to the Red Line at Rhode Island Ave.

Post Office 3709 Rhode Island Ave. (301-699-8855)

Library 3409 Rhode Island Ave. (301-864-8937)

Police Station 3409 Rhode Island Ave. (301-985-6565)

Recreational Activities Mount Rainier has a number of neighborhood parks scattered throughout the town, including a Nature Center (301-927-2163) on 30th St. near Arundel Rd.

Greenbelt

This suburban Maryland planned community was created in the mid-1930s by the federal government as part of the New Deal. Greenbelt provided needed jobs for people in the area during the Depression, and its row houses and apartment buildings gave them an inexpensive place to live. The government sold all of the property in 1953. The tenants of the more than 1,600 row houses formed a co-op and purchased the property; the co-op functions to this day. Much of the original landscaping is still intact, with many paths connecting little parks to the shopping center, ballfields, a 1938 movie theater and a lake.

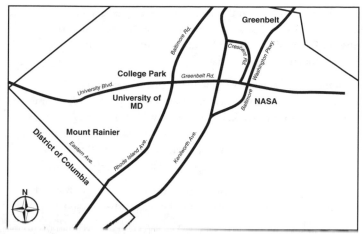

PRINCE GEORGE'S COUNTY, MD
Mount Rainier and Greenbelt

Today, the city has a high concentration of academics, scientists and engineers, many of whom work at the NASA/Goddard Space Flight Center or the University of Maryland in nearby College Park. Greenbelt is the home of many community activists, clubs and co-operatives, including the grocery store, nursery school, weekly newspaper and weekend café hosting local talent.

The town of Greenbelt sits at the intersection of five major roads, making it ideal for people commuting in all directions. The Baltimore-Washington Parkway, the Capital Beltway, I-95, Kenilworth Ave. and Route 1 all go through or around Greenbelt. Downtown DC is only about 15 miles away and Baltimore only 25. This community's place on the commuter's map was forever secured in late 1993, when the Green Line's Greenbelt Metro station opened.

Greenbelt is actually two communities in one. The original section, known as "Old Greenbelt," follows the original city plan and is essentially the same as it was when it first opened in 1937. The long apartment buildings are obvious products of the 1930s, with utilitarian lines and art-deco accents. Over the years, some single-family homes have managed to work their way into the community plan and today they line several quiet streets in the west side of town. The newer parts of Greenbelt sprawl in either direction along Route 193 (Greenbelt Rd.) and are not as neatly laid out. This section of Greenbelt is typical of the hodgepodge, suburban development seen in the metropolitan area, with modern townhouse communities taking up most of the real estate to the east. There is the public Schrom Hills Park on that side of town. For renters, Greenbelt is home to one of the largest apartment complexes on the East Coast, **Springhill Lake** (301-474-1600), with close to 3,000 units and its own public recreation center.

Many of the town's amenities, including the new Community Center, library, municipal building, pools and fitness center, post office, community stage and **Co-op Supermarket & Pharmacy** (301-474-0522) at 121 Centerway, are located within a hundred yards of each other in the middle of Old Greenbelt. Farther out, you will find **Giant** at 6000 Greenbelt Rd. (301-982-2359) and **Safeway** at 7595 Greenbelt Rd. (301-345-0150).

The main event of the year in Greenbelt is the Labor Day Festival and Parade, three days of pageants, carnivals, music, an art show and a variety of other activities.

Commute to Downtown 30 minutes by Metro Green Line at Greenbelt

Post Office 119 Centerway (301-345-1721)

Police Station 550 Crescent Rd. (301-474-7200)

Library 11 Crescent Rd. (301-345-5800). Greenbelt's wonderful library also serves as a popular community center.

Recreational Activities Community Center at 15 Crescent Rd. (301-397-2208), housed in the renovated 1937 elementary school, offers classrooms, a senior center, gym, art studios and other community services. Greenbelt Park at 6565 Greenbelt Rd. (301-344-3948) has walking trails and areas for camping and picnicking. The entire northern edge of Old Greenbelt is bordered by the Federal Department of Agriculture's Beltsville Research Center, a huge tract of government farmland criss-crossed by rarely traveled two-lane country roads great for biking and running.

VIRGINIA NEIGHBORHOODS, ARLINGTON COUNTY

Rosslyn

When you look across the Potomac River from DC to Virginia, Rosslyn seems an aberration. High-rise office buildings, forbidden by height restrictions in the District, dominate the skyline of this close-in suburb. What Rosslyn lacks in aesthetic appeal, though, it makes up in convenience, sitting directly across Key Bridge from Georgetown and across Roosevelt Bridge from the Mall. Metro's Orange and Blue Lines stop here first on their way out to other Virginia suburbs.

The main thoroughfare, five-laned Wilson Blvd., climbs up from Key Bridge and heads out to the west beyond Rosslyn. Several sky-walks were built as part of the original planning concept for Rosslyn, to separate automobile and pedestrian traffic. In reality, though, these ramps are confusing and many seem to lead nowhere. Fortunately, Arlington County has a long-range plan for enhancing the central business area with a main plaza, a river esplanade with views of Washington, tree-lined and store-lined streets filled with automobiles and people, and residential buildings that would help keep the area vital after working hours. Renovation of some of the 30-year-old buildings has already begun.

During the day, more than 36,000 workers toil away in Rosslyn's many office towers but at night the local streets are typically deserted. This lack of night-time activity should not dissuade new residents. According to the Arlington police department, Rosslyn is quite safe. One night of the year, however, the area is particularly busy as some of the best views of the Fourth of July fireworks on the Mall can be had from the rooftops of Rosslyn's towering buildings.

Despite Rosslyn's less than charming appearance, many young professionals and students, especially from George Washington University, find the neighborhood a fine place to live. Rosslyn offers a surprising array of garden and high-rise apartments, some right on the Potomac. Housing costs are generally slightly below those of the Northwest's most popular neighborhoods. Those looking for group houses should explore the streets north of Wilson Blvd. toward I-66.

Both Rosslyn and Court House, the next neighborhood out Wilson Blvd., have wonderful Southeast Asian restaurants, including Vietnamese, Cambodian, Thai and Korean.

Rosslyn has most of the usual neighborhood conveniences at or around the intersection of Wilson Blvd. and North Lynn St. You will find several dry cleaners, **CVS** (703-243-4993) and **Tivoli Gourmet** (703-524-8904). Residents do their grocery shopping at **Safeway** (703-276-9315) at 1525 Wilson Blvd. A 30-foot-tall sculpture called "Anna and David" marks the spot for this underground Safeway, making it easy to find.

Commute to Downtown Seven minutes by Metro Blue and Orange Lines at Rosslyn

Post Office 1101 Wilson Blvd. (703-525-4336)

Library Central Library at 1015 North Quincy St. (703-358-5990)

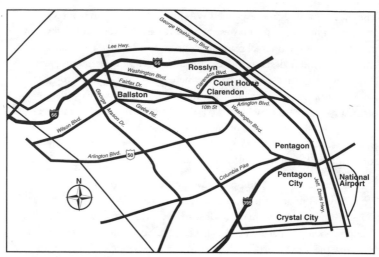

ARLINGTON COUNTY, VA
Rosslyn, Court House, Clarendon, Ballston, Pentagon City and Crystal City

Police Station 2100 North 15th St. (703-558-2222)

Recreational Activities Two tennis courts are at Lyon Village Park at the intersection of 20th Rd. and North Highland St.

Court House

It will come as no surprise that the Arlington County Courthouse is the focal point of this neighborhood. While you may not initially think that living near a courthouse is a plus, it does make handling official business a lot easier.

Relatively new luxury apartment buildings and a shopping complex can be found around the Courthouse and out along Clarendon Blvd. These buildings offer a selection of one- and two-bedroom apartments. There are several older, smaller and less expensive apartment buildings on the side streets, supplying an even wider range of apartment options. A number of large-scale developments have also been built south of Clarendon Blvd. toward Route 50.

The plaza adjoining the Courthouse contains a convenience store called the **Metro Market** (703-841-3530), several restaurants, gourmet food shops and an eight-screen **AMC movie theater** (703-998-4AMC). There are several supermarkets nearby—the **Safeway** in Rosslyn (703-276-9315) and another about a mile away at 3713 Lee Highway (703-841-1155) as well as two **Giants**, one at 3115 Lee Highway (703-527-9453) and another near the Virginia Square Metro, at 3450 North Washington Blvd. (703-358-9343).

A weekly farmers' market takes place near the Courthouse on Saturday mornings from April to October. Farmers sell their fresh produce on 14th St. between North Courthouse Rd. and North Veitch Sts., just past the police station.

Commute to Downtown 10 minutes by Metro Orange Line at Court House

Post Office 2043 Wilson Blvd. (703-525-4441)

Library Central Library at 1015 North Quincy St. (703-358-5990)

Police Station 2100 North 15th St. (703-558-2222)

Recreational Activities There are two tennis courts at Lyon Village Park at 20th Rd. and North Highland St.

Clarendon

Clarendon, just up Wilson Blvd. from Court House, has not yet been subjected to the high-rise building boom enjoyed (or suffered) by its neighbors. It remains a mostly quiet, low-key neighborhood, full of ethnic restaurants and older single-family homes. The abundance of older houses makes Clarendon a great area for group houses.

The square at the Clarendon Metro station is the hub of the neighborhood and reflects the changes taking place there. In the middle of the square, a World War I monument stands in stark contrast to the sleek, modern high-rise building that dominates the spot from its location on Clarendon Blvd. But across Wilson Blvd., you're back to older, worn-down storefronts that today are full of small shops and restaurants. The changing cultural nature of the area is evidenced by the large number of oriental establishments nearby, including some of Washington's best Vietnamese restaurants.

If you are planning to live here, you will need a car as most conveniences are not easily reached on foot. If you have a car, there are several large supermarkets to choose from, including the Safeways and Giants mentioned in the section on the Court House area. **Bread & Circus** has a new store (703-527-6596) at 2700 Wilson Blvd., two blocks east of the Clarendon Metro station.

Commute to Downtown 15 minutes by Metro Orange Line at Clarendon

Post Office 3118 North Washington Blvd. (703-525-4838)

Library Central Library at 1015 North Quincy St. (703-358-5990)

Police Station 2100 North 15th St. (703-558-2222)

Recreational Activities Washington-Lee High School at 1300 North Quincy St. (703-358-6262) has a swimming pool and a track. Six public tennis courts are across the street at Quincy Park.

Ballston

Ballston gives every indication that it will become the next Rosslyn, with many high-rise buildings crammed together within a few blocks of the Metro station that bears its name. Even the recession seems barely to have curbed the area's rapid growth.

Housing can be found in any one of the many apartment buildings or townhouses on the side streets off Fairfax Dr., Washington Blvd. and Glebe Rd. High-rise apartment buildings generally offer one-, two- and three-bedroom apartments, but not many efficiencies.

The blue-roofed **International House of Pancakes** (703-522-3118), known as IHOP, stands as an old-time landmark on Fairfax Dr., having weathered the many years of changes to the neighborhood. It stays open round the clock and is a great spot for midnight meals and Sunday morning breakfasts. In addition, the area has a large shopping mall, **Ballston Common**, and a few restaurants, including one of Washington's most popular Tex-Mex restaurants, **Rio Grande Cafe** (703-528-3131). **Giant** (703-351-9220) is at the corner of Washington Blvd. and Lincoln St., a short walk from the Virginia Square Metro and **George Mason Law School**. If you have a car, you can shop at the **Safeway** (703-524-1528) at 5101 Wilson Blvd. past Glebe Rd., the **Super Fresh** (703-237-0331) at the corner of North Harrison St. and Lee Highway, or the **Safeway** across the street at 2500 North Harrison St. (703-538-6700). **Tivoli Gourmet** (703-528-5201), right at the Metro station, is the neighborhood's only gourmet shop.

Commute to Downtown 20 minutes by Metro Orange Line at Ballston

Post Office Buckingham at 235 North Glebe Rd. (703-525-4170)

Library Central Library at 1015 North Quincy St. (703-358-5990)

Police Station 2100 North 15th St. (703-558-2222)

Recreational Activities Washington-Lee High School at 1300 North Quincy St. (703-358-6262) has a swimming pool and a track. Six public tennis courts are across the street at Quincy Park.

Pentagon City

This quiet community off Army-Navy Dr. is just south of the Pentagon. Many single-family homes and several massive apartment buildings crowd the area. This working class neighborhood lacks many of the amenities and conveniences typical in the suburbs. As a result, housing in Pentagon City is available at lower prices than in nearby, amenity-rich Crystal City or North Arlington. A wide selection of group houses occupies the streets behind the Virginia Highlands Park off South Ives St. Whether you live in an apartment building or a house, parking never seems to be a problem.

This neighborhood is home to a major mall, the **Fashion Centre at Pentagon City**, which includes one of the area's several **Nordstrom** stores. Residents particularly enjoy the mall's six-screen movie theater and huge food-court. The Pentagon City Metro, on the Blue and Yellow Lines, has an exit leading directly into the mall, which also has its own large parking garage.

While the neighborhood does not have a large grocery store, there is a convenience store in the basement of River House I at 1111 Army Navy Dr. Also, a huge **Price Club** (703-413-2324) is available in Pentagon City. The nearest **Safeway** is in Crystal City at 2129 Crystal Plaza Dr. (703-415-0422), just a Metro stop away. If you have a car, you can go to the **Safeway** at 2303 Columbia Pike (703-920-2909) or the **Giant** at either 2515 Columbia Pike (703-685-7050) or 1303 South Glebe Rd. (703-836-0245).

Commute to Downtown 20 to 30 minutes by Metro Blue and Yellow Lines at Pentagon City

Post Office Eads at 1720 Eads St. (703-979-2108)

Library Aurora Hills at 735 South 18th St. (703-358-5715)

Police Station 2100 North 15th St. (703-558-2222)

Recreational Activities Six public tennis courts are at Virginia Highlands Park, at the corner of 17th and South Ives Sts. The Carver Center at 1415 South Queen St. has three tennis courts.

Crystal City

If you have ever flown into National Airport, you have probably noticed a crowd of skyscrapers towering near the Pentagon. These complexes make up Crystal City, lining both sides of Jefferson Davis Highway (Route 1) with a mix of offices, hotels and apartments. The Navy is the predominant tenant in the Crystal City area and many private firms have located here for that reason and to be near National Airport. The core of Crystal City was planned and built as a unit and originally owned by one developer. Over the years, additional construction has only intensified the density of the area which, while lacking charm, abounds in conveniences.

This area's gigantic apartment and condominium buildings offer a variety of choices. You will easily find everything there from efficiencies to three-bedrooms at prices lower than those in North Arlington. Some older single-family homes, perfect for group houses, can be found on the west side of Jefferson Davis Hwy.

If you live in Crystal City, especially in one of the central high-rises, you could go for months on end without ever venturing out of doors as most of Crystal City is connected by miles of underground passages. Here, all "roads" lead to the **Crystal City Underground Shopping Center**, with every imaginable amenity, including a post office, several small gourmet shops, restaurants and a **Safeway** (703-415-0422). Even the Crystal City Metro station feeds into this underground mall, giving you access to all parts of the metropolitan area through connections from the Blue and Yellow Lines.

A word of caution—because of Crystal City's proximity to National Airport, airplane traffic can be heard throughout the day. The noise gets particularly loud during the early evening hours and can be a serious problem in residences facing east towards the airport. Flight departures from National are restricted after 10:00 p.m.; however, planes under a certain noise level are allowed to land after that hour. If you are looking for an apartment or house here, be sure to ask about the noise and then drop by at night or early in the morning to gauge it for yourself.

Commute to Downtown 25 minutes by Metro Blue and Yellow Lines at Crystal City

Post Office 1632 Crystal Dr. (703-413-9267)

Library Aurora Hills at 735 South 18th St. (703-358-5715)

Police Station 2100 North 15th St. (703-558-2222)

Recreational Activities Six public tennis courts are available at Virginia Highlands Park at the corner of 17th and South Ives Sts.

VIRGINIA NEIGHBORHOODS,
CITY OF ALEXANDRIA

Originally Virginia's center for commerce and culture, the 16-square-mile City of Alexandria, bordering the Potomac River, today includes one of the country's most historic communities. At the far east end of Alexandria is Old Town, the city's best known neighborhood, looking almost too good to be true. Strict zoning regulations protect its freshly painted Georgian houses, cobblestone streets and clean sidewalks. The historic quarter begins right along the waterfront and continues west along King St. and the many other quaint streets in the orderly, colonial part of town—a great place for walking tours. As you might expect, housing costs are highest here.

While greater Alexandria has as many as five Metro stops—Braddock Road, King St., Eisenhower Ave. and Huntington on the Yellow Line and Van Dorn St. on the Blue Line—none of them serves Old Town directly. It is quite a walk from the center of Old Town to the nearest station, Braddock Rd. Fortunately, there are a number of Metrobus routes as well as DASH, the local bus system, linking the many parts of Alexandria to each other and to the District. DASH runs six bus routes through Alexandria for just $0.75. Frequent air travelers may want to consider living in Alexandria, as it is less than a 10-minute commute to National Airport.

As you leave Old Town and travel south down Washington St. towards Mt. Vernon, you will find several apartment complexes that try to capitalize on their proximity to Old Town. If reasonably priced, these apartments can be a good choice as they are quite convenient. You will find more of the same type of housing out along Route 1 South. Farther to the west and southwest, there are even more high-rise and garden-style buildings along Beauregard and Duke Sts. and in the part of town known as Alexandria's West End. The West End is not far from the Van Dorn Metro station and the densely populated area offers housing in just about every price range. The northwest end of the city, near the Braddock St. Metro and National Airport, contains a mix of up-scale condos and low-rent housing. There is a lovely, quaint area along Russell Rd., in the shadow of the Masonic Temple, a visual and historic landmark not far from Old Town.

Since colonial days, space has been set aside in Old Town Alexandria's town square for a farmers' market. Today, the tradition of selling fresh produce, meats and baked goods continues at the weekly Saturday morning market on the south plaza of the City Hall at 301 King St. More typical shopping can be done at **Giant** at 530 1st St. (703-739-0751) at the north end of Old Town, about seven blocks from the Braddock Rd. Metro station, and at **Safeway** (703-836-0380) at 500 South Royal St., at the south end. In addition, Old Town boasts several gourmet stores, including **Sutton Place Gourmet** at 600 Franklin St. (703-549-6611) and the **King St. Gourmet Cellar** at 210 King St. (703-683-5439). The number of grocery stores and shopping centers in greater Alexandria is too high to count; wherever you are in the area, one is bound to be nearby, especially along the more important through streets such as King St., Seminary Rd. and Duke St. (Route 236), which turns into Little River Tpk. farther west.

Landmark Center (703-941-2582) in Alexandria includes **Sears** and **Hecht's** under its roof. While Landmark is not near a Metro line, you can get there using public transportation (Metro Blue Line to Van Dorn then DASH bus to the mall). Driving is much quicker, take I-395 to Duke St. East.

Commute to Downtown 30 to 45 minutes by Metro Yellow Line at Braddock Road, King Street, Eisenhower Ave. and Huntington or Blue Line at Van Dorn

Post Office Main Branch at 1100 Wythe St. (703-549-4201), George Mason at 126 South Washington St. (703-549-0813), Parkfairfax at 3682 King St. (703-379-6017), Trade Center at 340 South Pickett St. (703-823-0968) and Jefferson Manor at 5834 North King's Hwy. (703-960-4440)

Libraries Lloyd House at 220 N. Washington St.(703-838-4557), Ellen Coolidge Burke at 4701 Seminary Rd. (703-370-6050) and James Duncan at 2501 Commonwealth Ave. (703-838-4566)

Police Station 2003 Mill Rd. (703-838-4444)

Recreational Activities Chinquapin Park (703-931-1127) at 3210 King St. has an indoor pool, fitness room, racquetball courts, tennis courts, picnic areas and a nature trail. Cameron Run Regional Park at 4001 Eisenhower Ave. (703-960-0767) has a wave pool, miniature golf course (a tough one—no windmills and dog houses here) and batting cages.

VIRGINIA NEIGHBORHOODS, FAIRFAX COUNTY

Falls Church

While the actual City of Falls Church spans only two square miles, the area Washingtonians refer to as Falls Church is much larger. Much of the area between northern Arlington and the posh community of McLean has a Falls Church mailing address.

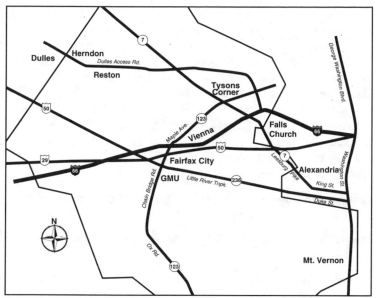

ALEXANDRIA AND FAIRFAX COUNTY, VA
Alexandria, Falls Church, Fairfax City, Reston and Herndon

East Falls Church encompasses the area between Arlington Blvd. at the Seven Corners Shopping Center and the East Falls Church Metro station. Rents here are low for the Washington metropolitan area. The high-rise and garden apartment complexes located along commercial Leesburg Pike (Route 7) supply an abundance of efficiencies and one-bedroom apartments. In general, locations closer to the East Falls Church Metro are more convenient, although slightly more expensive. Group houses can be found in and around the Washington Blvd. area.

West Falls Church, by contrast, has fewer choices for apartment seekers and more for those looking to buy. The exceptions here are the few high-rise apartment complexes between the West Falls Church Metro station and Tysons Corner.

Falls Church is a shopper's paradise. In East Falls Church, there is **Seven Corners Shopping Center**, which houses one of the area's new super-sized **Barnes & Noble** bookstores (703-536-0774) and **Starbucks** (703-534-3111). West Falls Church sits in the backyard of up-scale shopping at **Tysons Corner Center** and **Tysons Galleria**, featuring **Bloomingdale's** (703-556-4600), **Macy's** (703-556-0000), **Neiman Marcus** (703-761-1600), **Nordstrom** (703-761-1121) and **Saks Fifth Avenue** (703-761-0700).

The only way to reach one of the best supermarkets in the area, the **Giant** (703-845-0446) at Baileys Crossroads, is by car. This Giant has everything. If you choose to shop here, go during the week; the supermarket and surrounding mall are extremely popular on the weekends and the parking lot is occasionally full and often chaotic. Another **Giant** (703-237-9609) is at the corner of West Broad St. and Haycock Rd., within walking distance of the West Falls Church Metro station. You will find **Safeways** at 6118 Arlington Blvd. (703-241-4131) and 7397 Lee Hwy. (703-573-2057) and **Magruder's** (703-280-0440) on Graham Rd. **Fresh Fields**, at 7511 Leesburg Pike (703-448-1600), between I-66 and Tysons Corner, offers a large selection of organically grown produce.

Commute to Downtown 30 to 45 minutes by Metro Yellow Line at East Falls Church and West Falls Church

Post Office 301 West Broad St. (703-532-8822) and 6019 Leesburg Pike (703-671-0221)

Libraries Thomas Jefferson at 7415 Arlington Blvd. (703-573-1060), Mary Riley Styles at 120 North Virginia Ave. (703-241-5030)

Police Station 300 Park Ave. (703-241-5054)

Recreational Activities The Falls Church Community Center at 223 Little Falls St. (703-241-5077) sponsors a variety of sports activities and offers classes in cooking and dancing. The Washington & Old Dominion bike trail whisks bikers and joggers all the way east to the border between Arlington and Alexandria and as far west as Purcellville.

Fairfax City

Fairfax City dates back to the pre-Revolutionary War era and retains some of the charm of its colonial roots. However, the 12 miles separating it from downtown Washington, DC have not shielded it from the rapid growth of the metropolitan area in recent decades. Downtown Fairfax City remains village-like, with small houses and restaurants. Beyond that, however, you will find many strip malls and housing developments. The area known as Fairfax now sprawls well beyond its official boundaries; large sections of the outlying county are considered part of the city, complete with Fairfax addresses.

Just across the city line is the Vienna Metro station, actually more convenient to Fairfax than to the neighboring city that gives it its name. In addition to a number of Metrobus routes serving Fairfax, the city operates its own mini-bus system, called CUE, with four routes running about every 10 minutes connecting most of the city proper to the Metro. Most residents, however, find a car necessary.

Fairfax is home to George Mason University (GMU), one of the largest schools in the Virginia state system. While GMU students commute from all over the region, Fairfax is by no means overrun by students. In fact, residents of all types and ages benefit from proximity to the university. The Fairfax Symphony Orchestra and the Virginia Opera perform at **GMU's Center for the Arts** (703-993-8888). For the economy-minded, the **University Mall Theater** (703-273-7111) shows almost-current films for only $3 a ticket. Several bars offer live music. **T.T. Reynold's** at 10414 Main St. (703-591-9292) has live entertainment every day of the week. **Fat Tuesday's** (703-385-8660) has more of the same, with blues and rock bands playing nearly every day.

All types of housing are available for purchase and rental. Apartments and townhouses in the Fairfax Circle area are most convenient to the Metro, some within walking distance of the Vienna station. From other areas, rail commuters must use the CUE bus or drive to the Vienna station. Several apartment and townhouse communities are located along Blake La. going northwest to Fairfax Circle. There are others along Main St. (Route 236) between downtown and Pickett Rd. Rents in Fairfax follow the Washington area rule—the more accessible the area is to DC, the more you pay to live there.

There are numerous smaller shops in downtown Fairfax and several convenient shopping centers. But for serious shopping, area residents head for nearby malls, including **Fair Oaks** (703-359-8300) at the intersection of Route 50 and I-66, anchored by **Hecht's**, **Sears** and **JC Penney Co**.

Victoria's Cakery at 3995 Chain Bridge Rd. (703-273-0800) is tucked away in one of the funky Victorian houses in downtown Fairfax and is guaranteed to satisfy any sweet tooth. **Safeway** has locations at the **Courthouse Plaza Shopping Center** (703-591-8473) and at 3043 Nutley St. in the **Pan Am Shopping Center** near Fairfax Circle (703-560-6696). **Giant** is at 11054 Lee Highway (703-273-0147), 9570 Main St. (703-323-9108) and 12997 Lee Jackson Memorial Highway (703-803-7732). Fairfax also has its own **Price Club** at 4725 West Ox Rd. (703-802-1223) for buying in bulk.

Commute to Downtown 45 to 60 minutes by Metro at Vienna

Post Office Main at 3951 Chain Bridge Rd. (703-273-5571), Turnpike at 3601 Pickett Rd. (703-239-2900), Fairfax at 5616 Ox Rd. (703-250-9188) and Chantilly at 4410 Brookfield Corporate Dr. (703-968-7272)

Library Fairfax Regional at 3915 Chain Bridge Rd. (703-246-2741)

Police Station 10600 Page Ave. (703-691-2131)

Recreational Activities Burke Lake Park at 7315 Ox Rd. in Fairfax Station (703-323-6600) has an 18-hole golf course, fishing, hiking, camping and boating. Children enjoy its carousel and miniature train.

Reston

To some, Reston is the ultimate suburb, combining the best of being near DC with the best of living out in the rolling Virginia countryside. To others, this completely planned community has the look and feel of a residential theme park. The community takes its name from its visionary founder, Robert E. Simon, who willed it into being on farmland near Dulles Airport back in the 1960s. Almost half of Reston is park land or other open space, including a series of four man-made lakes around which the neighborhoods are organized. Each part of town—Hunters Woods, South Lakes, Lake Anne and Tall Oaks—has its own village center, complete with food, banking and other facilities, as well as a community center and a fellowship house for senior citizens. The neighborhoods in Reston are mainly self-contained, screened from major streets and the busy Dulles Toll Rd. by dense groves of trees.

In the past few years, Reston and other communities have been home to a blitz of development. Office buildings lining the Dulles Toll Rd. house high-tech businesses in this part of the state. Another relative newcomer to the community is **Reston Town Center** at 11911 Freedom Dr. (703-742-6500). This mall and gathering place looms up out of the landscape and is a focal point for the area's nightlife.

In the middle of Town Center is an outdoor pavilion with seating for some of the restaurants. Concerts are held here during the summer, and in the winter the pavilion is converted into an ice-skating rink. Aside from dozens of shops such as **Ann Taylor**, **Banana Republic**, the **Gap**, **Brentano's Books** and **Sam Goody**, Town Center houses a number of restaurants and a **National Amusements Multiplex Cinema** (703-318-1800). Some of Georgetown's dining landmarks have made their way out to Reston's Town Center which now includes **Clyde's** (703-787-6601) and **Paolo's** (703-318-8920). **Rio Grande Cafe** (703-904-0703) serves delicious fajitas and the **Market Street Bar & Grill** (703-709-6262) offers a good brunch and a bit of culture with live jazz Friday, Saturday and Sunday nights. Expansion plans include bringing in gourmet food and coffee stores such as **Sutton Place** and **Starbucks**.

The **Reston Visitor's Center** at 11450 Baron Cameron Ave. (703-471-7030) provides detailed information and directions to all areas. Rental rates and housing prices vary depending on the size of the unit and proximity to the neighborhood lake.

For groceries there is one Safeway at 1120 South Lakes Dr. (703-620-2444) and another at 2369 Hunters Wood Plaza (703-620-6691) and two **Giants**, at 12040 North Shore Dr. (703-478-6718) and 1450 Reston Pkwy. (703-435-4100). Reston also has a CVS at 11160 South Lakes Dr. (703-620-6691).

Commute to Downtown No Metro. The Fairfax connector provides access to the West Falls Church Metro station during rush hours. Non-rush-hour service is provided by the Reston Internal Bus System (RIBS).

Post Office 11110 Sunset Hills Rd. (703-437-6677)

Library Reston Regional at 11925 Bowman Towne Dr. (703-689-2700)

Police Station 12000 Bowman Towne Dr. (703-478-0904)

Recreational Activities Reston has lots of public swimming pools and tennis courts for its residents. In addition, there are footpaths and bike trails all over town, linking together the area's many neighborhoods.

Herndon

Herndon, Reston's next door neighbor, is quite different. Comparing the two, someone said, quite simply, that Herndon has more pick-up trucks than BMWs. While Reston was planned from start to finish, Herndon developed over time and along very different lines. Once a small village railroad stop, Herndon got caught up in the regional growth that accompanied the construction of the Dulles Toll Rd. High-tech, defense-oriented and service businesses, attracted by the convenience of the airport, have created a new commercial nexus known as the Dulles Corridor. Herndon has absorbed much of the influx of businesses, residents and related activity.

You can still sense something of Herndon's history as you travel along Elden St. through the somewhat-scruffy, old-fashioned downtown. The town still has the look and feel of the small village it was not long ago. The tiny, old railroad station, once the focal point of Herndon, still sits proudly in the center of town. Renovating late Victorian houses has become trendy here, but recent townhouse and apartment construction has begun to change the area's old-fashioned look. Renovated older homes and townhouses tend to be located close to the village center with newer accommodations on the outskirts, although in a town of just over four square miles, that does not require going very far. On average, for roughly similar housing, Herndon's prices are well below those in Reston.

Downtown Herndon is home to the **Ice House Cafe** at 760 Elden St. (703-471-4256). The small, dark jazz club has been a local institution for years. Also on Elden St. are the ubiquitous **Champion's Sports Bar** at #208 (703-306-8600), **Hard Times Cafe** at #394 (703-318-8941), **Anita's Mexican Food** at #701 (703-481-1441) and **Outback Steakhouse** (703-318-0999) at #150, as well as a discount movie theater showing almost-current flicks. A **Loew's Theater** (703-318-9290) can be found near the Dulles Toll Rd. Exit 2, in the **Worldgate Plaza**, also home to several shops and the **Worldgate Athletic Center** (703-709-9100), a popular health club with great facilities.

Residents do their grocery shopping at a gourmet **Giant Marketplace** at 1228 Elden St. (703-437-3162) or out at the Worldgate Plaza's **Shoppers Food Warehouse** at 2425 Centerville Rd. (703-793-3892). For breads and other baked goods, try **Great Harvest Bakery** at 785 Station St. (703-471-4031). In the center of town you will find a **CVS** at 1062 Elden St. (703-471-9478) and **Rite Aid** at 696 Elden St. (703-787-9830).

Commute to Downtown 45 to 60 minutes via the Fairfax Connector to the West Falls Church Metro station. An express bus runs during rush hour. Local bus routes are available at other times.

Post Office 590 Grove St. (703-437-3740)

Library Herndon Fortnightly Library at 768 Center St. (703-437-8855). The original Herndon library was formed by the Ladies Fortnightly Club, and today the library—open on a more regular schedule—retains the name as part of the area's local history. The library has meeting rooms available for community group activities and sponsors children's story times.

Police Station 1481 Sterling Rd. (703-435-6846)

Recreational Activities The Washington & Old Dominion Railroad Regional Park (703-729-0596) has trails for running, bicycling, horseback riding and hiking.

Getting Around

*T*he best approach to mastering transportation in the Washington area is to take the time to learn the layout of the city and its major suburbs. With a good map and a few insider tips, getting around the area is relatively easy. Many Washingtonians will assure you that this is because the city's grid-like layout is simple to learn. While this is certainly true in theory, the picture becomes more complex once you take into account the many special features of DC's layout and the constantly evolving nature of the Maryland and Virginia suburbs.

This chapter provides a brief overview of the area and introduces the major streets, roads and circles in DC, as well as the major arteries in adjoining western Maryland and northern Virginia. Modes of transportation for getting into, around and out of the area are also covered.

The metropolitan Washington area is comprised of the small, compact city of Washington, DC—only about 10 miles across—and the bordering counties in Maryland and Virginia. The boundaries with Maryland are designated by Western, Eastern and Southern Aves. The Potomac River serves as the boundary between DC and Virginia, with five bridges connecting the two. Each bridge is named in honor of a person or place important to local or national history, and most are best known by a somewhat unofficial name. Following the flow of the Potomac from the northwest to the southeast, the bridges are Chain Bridge, (Francis Scott) Key Bridge, (Theodore) Roosevelt (Memorial) Bridge, (Arlington) Memorial Bridge, and a complex of spans collectively known as the 14th St. Bridge.

The original boundaries for Washington, DC formed a 100-square-mile area shaped like a diamond. The diamond encompassed all of what is now DC as well as what is now Arlington County and a small piece of the City of Alexandria in Virginia. The federal government returned the Virginia property in 1846, leaving the Potomac River as the boundary line between Virginia and DC. To this day, many maps continue to show an outline of the original diamond shape.

DRIVING

Thousands of motorists drive into the city each week day. Most of these people work in the city; some are visitors, others are tourists. Most know where they are going, or at least think they do; many do not. This results

in congestion, confusion and chaos just about every day. The more you know about the area, the more successful you will be in handling the challenges.

Streets, Roads and Circles

Many of the streets and roads within DC continue out into the surrounding suburbs. Some change names along the way and are so designated in this section, where appropriate. Traffic circles are unique to DC in the metropolitan area; however, city planners are considering their potential use for handling increasing growth in certain suburbs.

DC

To understand Washington's streets, you have to understand their history. In 1791, Major Pierre Charles L'Enfant, a French engineer-architect and former American Revolutionary soldier, was commissioned to draw up plans to build the nation's capital. L'Enfant patterned elements of his design after his native city, Paris, France. Much still survives of his original concept which, once learned, can help orient you as you travel in and around DC.

The basic grid is the relatively orderly and logical part of the layout. The city is divided into four quadrants—Northwest (NW), Northeast (NE), Southeast (SE) and Southwest (SW), with the Capitol at the point where the quadrants meet. The boundaries for these quadrants are the streets radiating out from the Capitol—North Capitol, South Capitol and East Capitol Sts.— and the Mall, which is what would have been West Capitol St. The streets running parallel to North and South Capitol Sts. are numbered, with numbers going up as you go further away from the Capitol, either to the east or to the west. This means that there are two 14th Sts.—one 14 blocks east of the Capitol building and one 14 blocks west of it.

The streets running parallel to East Capitol St. and the Mall are arranged alphabetically, starting at the Capitol and moving out to the north and south. Close in, the alphabet is used for street names such as C St. and K St. As with numbered streets, there can be two streets with the same name, such as one C St. three blocks north of the Capitol and another C St. three blocks south. No matter how hard you look, though, you will not find J Street. The official explanation is that "J" was eliminated from the plans to avoid confusion with I St., as the Roman letter "I" was once written in the same way. Another, more colorful, explanation—popular in DC for its political undertones—is that L'Enfant disliked Chief Justice John Jay and deliberately left out J St. to slight him. You will find I St., commonly spelled "Eye" to avoid confusion with 1st St. (There goes the official J St. explanation!) Unfortunately, no official explanation exists for the absence of streets named X, Y and Z. One possibility is that W St. was the border of the original settled area and there was no need to continue on. As you travel farther from the Capitol, particularly going north, the streets are labeled with two- and three-syllable names in alphabetical order, and then with names of trees and flowers as you get closer to the Maryland border.

WASHINGTON, DC—A CITY OUT OF WILDERNESS

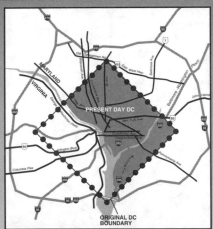

In 1790, Congress decided to build a new capital city in the midst of wilderness at the confluence of the Potomac and Anacostia Rivers, on land ceded to the federal government by Maryland and Virginia. With the exception of the port cities of Georgetown and Alexandria, the territory was largely rural and was referred to by many as "Wilderness City."

To design the city, President George Washington hired French engineer-architect Pierre Charles L'Enfant who had served under him in the American Revolution. No stranger to the ideals of the new nation, he envisioned the city as symbolic of the entire country. In a 1792 letter to Thomas Jefferson, Secretary of State and Washington's advisor to the project, L'Enfant wrote, "To change a wilderness into a city . . . to receive the seat of government of so extensive an empire . . . is an undertaking vast as it is novel."

L'Enfant incorporated prominent features of the local landscape as sites for public spaces. He strategically placed broad, elegant avenues to allow for easy access and create appealing vistas, overlaying them on a grid of streets and creating the powerful underlying geometry of the city plan. While much of the city today exemplifies the qualities of his design, his original plan included only the area south of today's Florida Ave. and east of Georgetown.

The project was not spared the influences of controversy and local politics, and quickly became tumultuous and even explosive. Within a year, L'Enfant was fired for his unwillingness to submit to the authority of the project's commissioners. He was only the first of many talented and capable architects to meet this fate in the first decade of the city's history.

Washington also hired Andrew Ellicott, the city's first surveyor, who brought with him Benjamin Banneker, a respected black mathematician. In 1791-92, they used handmade astronomical devices to survey the land and place large stones as mile markers along the boundaries of the original 100 square miles of the city. A recent five-year project using today's technology has proved they did more work in less time, with simpler tools and greater accuracy than most surveyors can imagine.

While many people built on the work of L'Enfant, he is still considered to be the primary force in the design of the new nation's capital. One of the most impressive views of Washington can be seen from his tomb in Arlington National Cemetery, a fitting final tribute.

All addresses in DC include the designation of the quadrant where they are located. This helps you keep straight about which 14th St. or which C St. you need. Addresses are logically numbered within the grid system in hundreds; for example, addresses on K St. between 17th and 18th Sts. form the 1700 block of K St.

Larger streets crossing the city at angles are called avenues and are named after states. The proximity of each avenue to the Capitol is based on when its state entered the Union, with New Jersey, Delaware and Pennsylvania Aves. intersecting the Capitol grounds, and Alaska and Hawaii Aves. practically in Maryland. Washington Ave. was missing for awhile, mostly to avoid confusion between the city on the East Coast and the state on the West Coast. But finally, in 1989, Washington State was honored by being given a small stretch of concrete near the Capitol.

And now, for a few good complications. Freeways, parkways and roads meander through the District creating havoc out of the basic grid. Some streets are affected by changing traffic patterns twice a day to accommodate the dominant rush-hour traffic into and out of the city. (Refer to the section on Surviving Rush Hour for more specifics.) Street signs can be hard to read and even missing in places, and there isn't an honest local who won't admit to having turned the wrong way down one of DC's many one-way streets. Take these factors into account and you begin to see where confusion arises.

WHERE TO OBTAIN MAPS

• **ADC (Alexandria Drafting Company) puts out a comprehensive series of maps and atlases for both DC and the surrounding counties. You can find them at bookstores, card shops, drugstores, convenience stores and supermarkets.**

• **The Map Store at 1636 Eye St. NW (202-628-2608) recommends** *Station Masters: A Comprehensive Pocket Guide to Metrorail Station Neighborhoods* **and** *The Travel Vision Map of Washington.*

Free maps are available from:

DC Department of Tourism (202-727-4511)

Committee to Promote Washington (202-724-4091)

Maryland Department of Tourism (1-410-333-6611)

Virginia Department of Tourism (202-659-5523)

To complicate matters further, Washington is full of traffic circles, originally introduced as a way of compensating for the intersection of north-south and east-west streets with diagonal avenues, while providing public space in the middle. With today's heavy traffic flows, circles can be difficult to negotiate. Often you have to be in a specific lane of the circle to exit onto a particular street. Unfortunately, these lanes are not always marked. Congestion is alleviated somewhat at several circles by routing the major road through a tunnel underneath the circle. In spite of the challenges of the traffic circles, the avenues are a good way to expedite getting across town. Mastering DC involves getting to know these major routes through, into and out of the city; a little experience and a lot of patience go a long way.

Massachusetts Ave. is the most convenient and potentially the most confusing street in Washington. It is the quickest way to go from the Hill to Dupont Circle, on to the Cathedral, and out to the west side of Bethesda. However, it does not follow a straight line and the unwary driver can quickly get sidetracked around one of the several traffic circles it goes through. The route gets particularly tricky as it jogs around Mount Vernon Place at 7th, 9th and K Sts. NW, just above the Convention Center. Watch carefully for signs and follow them—on faith. After a few side turns, you actually do end up back on track.

During evening rush hour, if you are going north to Bethesda, Chevy Chase or Rockville, the quickest route is Connecticut Ave. Coming from Georgetown, you can also use Wisconsin Ave. to go north to Chevy Chase and Bethesda. Running roughly parallel to 16th St., Georgia Ave. travels up through town and out to Silver Spring.

Stately Pennsylvania Ave. no longer follows a direct route across town, as it once did. Today, its path begins in Georgetown, jogs around the White House on its way to the Capitol, and continues east through the District and on into Prince George's County in Maryland. Recent security precautions in the vicinity of the White House have complicated traffic patterns further by blocking off portions of the avenue.

Most importantly, you should try to familiarize yourself with Rock Creek Parkway. The eccentric parkway winds through Northwest DC with only one light to slow the flow of traffic, making it an excellent north-south route. The major entrances are on K St. near the Kennedy Center, P St. in Georgetown and Massachusetts Ave. near Embassy Row. Along several portions of its route, Rock Creek Parkway has no dividers to separate the two lanes of traffic traveling in opposite directions. This can be disconcerting, even dangerous. Driving there at night, particularly on weekends, can be harrowing. Parts of the parkway are restricted to pedestrian and bicycle traffic on weekends and holidays, creating new traffic patterns and new challenges.

Maryland

In Montgomery County, there are four predominant north-south routes leading into and out of the District. On the western side of the county, Wisconsin Ave. (which becomes Rockville Pike north of Bethesda) is the major route. This road originates at the Potomac River in Georgetown and when you have time for a long, beautiful country drive, you can follow it all the way to the state of Pennsylvania. In central Montgomery County, Connecticut Ave. and 16th St., which merges into Georgia Ave., are options for heading north. On the east side of the county, New Hampshire

Ave. is a straight shot out of town. For rush-hour commuting, Connecticut and Georgia Aves. change from three lanes in each direction to four lanes in the direction of commuter traffic and two the other way.

All four of these routes intersect with the Beltway for moving east and west through the county. Just inside the Beltway, another intersecting thoroughfare is East-West Hwy. (Route 410). This road runs from Bethesda on the west to the Baltimore-Washington Parkway in Prince George's County on the east, intersecting all the north-south avenues mentioned above.

Once you have made your way to the Beltway, several major highways provide access to the more suburban communities. To head northwest, Route 270 is the predominant route, reaching the communities of Rockville, Gaithersburg and Germantown. While traffic can be slow to merge onto 270 from the Beltway, this highway quickly expands to as many as seven lanes in each direction. In the northeast direction, towards Baltimore, you can take either I-95 or the Baltimore-Washington Parkway (whose official name is the Gladys Spellman Parkway). These routes lead to the suburban communities of Greenbelt, Beltsville and Laurel.

The highway that leads directly east out of the District is Route 50. This takes you to Annapolis, the capital of Maryland, and further east to the Maryland and Delaware shores of the Atlantic Ocean. To go south out of the District on the Maryland side of the Potomac, take I-295 then continue onto Indian Head Highway. These routes lead you through or near Suitland, Oxon Hill and Fort Washington.

Virginia

Traffic patterns in the Virginia suburbs closest to DC vary by location, due in part to the way the area developed over the years. Of particular interest are the streets and roads in Arlington and Alexandria.

Newcomers are lucky they do not have to master the pre-1934 Arlington street plan. Back then, residents had to find their way around a hodgepodge of streets, many with identical names. There once were, for example, 10 different streets named Arlington and 11 named Washington. Today, Arlington's streets and roads are still somewhat confusing but much easier to navigate than they once were. Arlington's main east-west thoroughfares are Lee Highway, I-66, Wilson Blvd., Arlington Blvd. (Route 50), Columbia Pike and I-395. Lee Highway runs roughly parallel to I-66 all the way out to Falls Church where the two cross. Lee Highway turns into Washington St. in Falls Church before it heads out to western Virginia.

Wilson Blvd. begins in Rosslyn and travels west through North Arlington. Wilson becomes one-way (heading west) for about two miles through the

Court House and Clarendon sections of Arlington. During this stretch, Clarendon Blvd. provides a parallel route in the eastward direction.

In Arlington, named streets are ordered alphabetically and run north-south, beginning at the Potomac River and extending westward. Street names start with one-syllable names, Ball St. to Wayne St., and progress to two- and three-syllable names and one lonely four-syllable name (Arizona). Numbered streets and boulevards named after historic figures run parallel to Arlington Blvd. in an east-west direction.

One of the most complex interchanges in the area is on the Virginia side of the Arlington Memorial Bridge. In a seemingly random and confusing pattern, this interchange connects several major highways including the George Washington Memorial Parkway and Routes 27 and 110 as well as major access lanes for Arlington Blvd. and I-395. To make matters worse, cars travel through the area at top speed. Keep a sharp eye out for the small signs to direct you and do not get too frustrated if you end up on the wrong road the first couple of times. This one takes a while to learn; practice during non-rush-hour times is strongly recommended.

Following the shores of the Potomac River, the scenic George Washington Parkway starts at Mount Vernon, south of DC, crosses the southern side of the Beltway, continues past Alexandria and National Airport, and ends up at the northwestern side of the Beltway, at the Virginia-Maryland border. Glebe Rd. is the main thoroughfare in western Arlington. Jefferson Davis Highway (Route 1) splits off from I-395 at the Pentagon and carries traffic through Crystal City and on into Alexandria.

The major thoroughfare in Alexandria is Washington St. This street runs parallel to the Potomac River and is the "in-town" stretch of the George Washington Parkway, running north to the District and south to Mount Vernon. King St. and Duke St. are popular east-west routes. These are Old Town's main streets, forming a neat backbone for the grid pattern of the historic center of Alexandria.

Route 1 cuts through Alexandria and splits into two one-way streets in Old Town Alexandria, Patrick St. (Route 1 North) and Henry St. (Route 1 South). During morning rush hour, Patrick St.'s three lanes frequently become grid-locked.

The Beltway and Highways

Washington's most famous highway, the Beltway (I-495/I-95), takes 67 miles to circumnavigate the city and many of its suburbs. Rush-hour traffic reports often refer to the Beltway's "inner" and "outer" loops. The inner

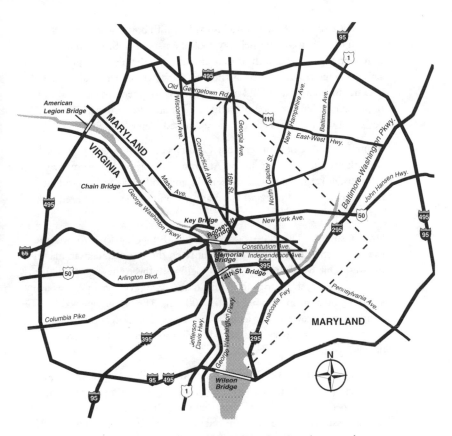

loop is the set of clockwise-traveling lanes circling the city; the outer loop carries traffic in the opposite direction, counterclockwise, outside the inner loop. All highways coming into the area either intersect with or end at the Beltway, which has interchanges approximately every two miles and provides access to all major roads leading to the downtown area. The major interstates connecting DC, Maryland and Virginia with the Beltway are I-270, I-95, I-66 and I-395. Inside the District, interstate and highway routes retain their route markings. Maryland and Virginia highway routes stop at the DC border so be attentive to street names once inside the District line. Note that there is no direct freeway access to the downtown area from the north.

A bit of local history can help you master these highways. When first built, the entire Beltway was called I-495, all the way around the city. It was intersected by I-95, coming up from the south and terminating in the center of DC. Many years later, to make I-95 a contiguous highway through the area, what had been the eastern half of I-495 was renamed

I-95. The east side of the Beltway is marked with both route numbers. The portion of I-95 inside the Beltway took the name I-395. Exit numbers were rearranged along with route numbers, and the orderly logic of the Beltway, originally advertised as the area's first "circumferential highway" became little more than a fond memory among long-term residents. If this bit of bureaucratic history doesn't help you get around on these highways, perhaps it will at least keep you more amused than confused.

Route I-270, one of Montgomery County's main highways, runs north off the Beltway a few miles from the American Legion Bridge (formerly Cabin John Bridge) at the border between Virginia and Maryland, providing direct access to Rockville and Germantown and to the City of Frederick, farther out.

Straight south of DC, the Woodrow Wilson Bridge carries I-95 over the river connecting Prince George's County on the east with Alexandria on the west. One word sums up the problem with this route—drawbridge. To accommodate rush-hour traffic, the Coast Guard prohibits openings from 4:00 to 9:00 a.m. and from 2:00 to 7:00 p.m. The bridge opens on average once a day, causing lengthy traffic delays and occasional serious accidents. Most radio stations keep listeners apprised of scheduled drawbridge activity.

Often the first choice of Virginia commuters on the west side of DC, I-66 stretches 70 miles from Arlington to Front Royal. During morning rush hour, cars traveling eastbound between the Beltway and the District must have at least two people in them; the same is true in the opposite direction during evening rush hour. Shirley Highway (I-395) runs through Arlington County from the Potomac to I-95, providing one of the most direct routes from the District to Crystal City and Alexandria. Three lanes travel in each direction, with a two-lane rush-hour road down the center that changes direction to accommodate the predominant traffic flow.

Surviving Rush Hour

If you are from Los Angeles, Boston or New York, rush-hour traffic in the DC area will not only look familiar, it may be even worse. The entire Washington metropolitan area grew more quickly in the 1980s than the road system could readily accommodate. And rush hour is no longer just about getting into and out of DC. As the suburbs have grown, rush-hour traffic within local areas has become more of a challenge. To compensate, some traffic rules change during rush hour on several of the more well-traveled streets. Rush hour is generally considered to be from 6:30 to 9:00 in the morning and from 4:00 to 6:30 in the evening. If you commute to, from or within the suburbs, you should become familiar with the High Occupancy Vehicle (HOV) lanes in effect on many of the interstates during the morning and evening rush hour. Where posted, you must have a minimum of two (HOV-2) or three (HOV-3) passengers in your vehicle. Take these restrictions seriously. The police do, and fines are steep.

RIDESHARING

DC
202-783-POOL

Maryland
301-593-9291

In Northwest DC, from Woodley Park to the Maryland border, Connecticut Ave. switches from three lanes in each direction to four in the direction of commuter traffic and two the other way. A good portion of Rock Creek Parkway becomes one-way during each rush hour, as does Canal

Virginia
703-783-POOL

Fairfax County
703-324-1111

Road, running parallel to the Potomac River on the DC side. Once a day, 17th St. (in the morning) and 15th St. (in the evening) between Massachusetts Ave. and Eye St. become one-way. All the way from the Maryland border to Adams Morgan, 16th St. has altered traffic patterns. Georgia Ave. between 16th St. and Forest Glen has a middle lane that changes direction during each rush hour.

Like Connecticut Ave. in the District, Colesville Rd. and Georgia Ave. in Maryland change from three lanes in each direction to four lanes going in the prevailing direction of commuter traffic.

During morning rush hour, the three lanes of Patrick St. in Old Town Alexandria (Route 1 North) become grid-locked. One lane is set aside from 6:30 to 9:00 a.m. as a two-person HOV lane. In the afternoon, Henry St. (Route 1 South) supports homebound commuter traffic with a two-person HOV lane in effect from 3:00 to 7:00 p.m. Southbound Route 1 provides access to I-95 South, while northbound Route 1 continues up through Crystal City and branches off to I-395 North.

In Arlington, Columbia Pike switches some of its four lanes to accommodate the flow of traffic. Three lanes carry traffic towards the District in the morning; in the afternoon, three lanes transport cars back out to the suburbs.

The HOV story for I-66 may be in the process of being rewritten. For some time, I-66 has had HOV-3 restrictions for rush-hour traffic. As this book goes to press, a one-year pilot test has just been concluded to evaluate a proposal to change the restriction to HOV-2. The decision has been made to continue the HOV-2 policy unless or until traffic on the 10-mile stretch of highway inside the Beltway increases by 15%. This could occur as soon as 1998, at which time I-66 will revert to HOV-3.

Washingtonians are pretty good about sharing their commuting time and expenses with others. **Ride-Finders** (800-745-RIDE) helps arrange car pools all over the metropolitan area. An informal car pool system has developed in the Virginia suburbs to take advantage of the HOV lanes on I-95 and I-395. Commuters head to the Springfield Plaza parking lot to meet up with drivers willing to take on passengers. At the end of the day, many of these same commuters can be found lined up along 14th St. NW at the Mall, looking to help drivers meet the southbound HOV restrictions.

Parking and Parking Tickets

Drivers face a dual challenge when it comes to parking in the city. Not only do you have to find a space, you have to make sure it is a legal one. Do not take this task lightly. You will quickly learn that the DC traffic enforcement officers spare neither speed nor ink in writing tickets for every possible infraction of the parking laws. They issue over two million expensive parking tickets each year. If you do find a bright-pink ticket prominently displayed on your windshield, it is best to respond as stated on the ticket. Diplomatic status does not exempt you, nor does having out-of-state license plates. If you disregard parking tickets, you may end up having your car booted. If this happens, call the **DC Booted Vehicle Office** at 202-727-5000. In addition, **Dorsey & Associates Inc.** (202-842-2881) helps individuals and businesses handle parking tickets and moving violations in the District. Their fee is $20 per ticket, $50 per moving violation, and $75 if an accident is involved. The amount you save usually exceeds the fee.

The trick here is to recognize that DC has overlapping parking controls and you have to be on the lookout for all of them. On some blocks, parking is free but limited to two hours, unless you are a DC resident and have a current Residential Parking Permit for the particular neighborhood or zone. In other, more commercial blocks, there is metered parking, with most meters accepting only quarters. If you are going to be in one of these neighborhoods for an entire weekday, consider taking the Metro. Or leave your car in an all-day parking garage for around $12 a day. Street parking downtown is illegal in many places during rush hour, no matter how many quarters or parking permits you have. Finally, in 1995, the DC government added a layer of parking restrictions to allow for street cleaning of various blocks on a rotating schedule.

Downtown, Dupont Circle, Georgetown, Adams Morgan, Southwest and Capitol Hill are some of the District's most difficult areas for parking. The trend to more and more parking restrictions—and ticketing—is spreading out into the suburbs as the whole area becomes more densely populated.

For example, parking in Old Town Alexandria can at times be as difficult as it is in DC.

PUBLIC TRANSPORTATION

Metropolitan DC area residents have numerous public transportation options. The Metro system, run by the Washington Metropolitan Area Transit Authority (WMATA) connects neighboring communities with the DC business district. Commuter lines bring people in from suburbs further out. And taxicab service is available throughout the area.

Metrorail and Metrobus

Washingtonians use the term "Metro" to describe both the overall regional transportation system and the rail service that is part of it. Metro—the system—links DC and the Maryland and Virginia suburbs by rapid rail and bus routes. Metrobuses provide feeder service to the Metrorail stations and offer routes and connections in areas where there is no subway (rail) service. While not all rail stations open today are underground, the first ones to open were and the rail system is still sometimes referred to as "the subway."

Each system—bus and rail—has its own operating hours, schedules and fares. These change from time to time and you can keep abreast with information provided at the rail station kiosks, or by contacting Metro directly at 202-637-7000. If you don't see the information you need prominently displayed outside the kiosk, ask the attendants. They keep selected brochures and guides on hand.

Metro has a host of fare options for each of its systems and is always looking for ways to enhance services. There are large-denomination farecards with discounts, various types of Flash Passes for the Metrobus, special fares for senior citizens and riders with disabilities, and a special workplace transit benefit program, MetroPool. Information on these and other options is available from Metro.

Metrorail

At the heart of Washington's public transportation system, Metrorail (Metro) serves as a model to subway systems in other cities. It is safe, clean, convenient and efficient. There are five Metrorail lines, each marked with its own color. The Red Line starts in the Shady Grove/Rockville area to the northwest, travels south through Bethesda, loops down through Northwest and downtown DC, then turns north up to Silver Spring. The Blue Line runs from Alexandria through DC and out to Addison Rd. in Prince George's County. The Orange Line parallels the Blue Line through the District with end points in Vienna, VA and New Carrollton, MD. The

Yellow Line travels through Alexandria and Chinatown to Mt. Vernon Square and the University of the District of Columbia's downtown campus. The Green Line, the newest one and still being built, currently reaches from Anacostia to U St.-Cardoza and from Fort Totten to Greenbelt. There are pockets of the system—on the Blue, Green and Red Lines—still under construction. The entire system is expected to be completed by the year 2001. See the map on the inside back cover.

There are several central transfer points where you can switch lines. The Red, Blue and Orange Lines all converge at Metro Center, the system's busiest station. The Blue, Orange, Green and Yellow Lines meet at another busy station, L'Enfant Plaza. Between the Rosslyn and Stadium-Armory stations, the Blue and Orange Lines run on the same track and transfers can be made at any of the shared stations.

Street entrances to the subway stations are easily identified by the brown pylons capped with the letter M. The horizontal stripes near the top show the color of the lines serving that station. Inside every station, there are large system-wide rail route maps as well as detailed neighborhood street maps, and tall posts on the platform level list the stations on the routes followed by the arriving trains. The key to successful travel on this system is to know the endpoint of the particular line you need, as each line has trains running in opposite directions. Watch out for the trains on Red Line—they do not all go to the last station on the map. Before you board any train, check the color of the line and the destination, displayed above the train's front and side windows.

Many of the Metro stations are equipped with elevators, making access possible for the disabled and those with baby strollers.

Metro starts operating at 5:30 a.m. on weekdays. On Saturdays and Sundays, trains begin running at 8:00 a.m. Although midnight is the official closing time, check the postings at each station for the time the last train passes through. On weekends and holidays, the trains and buses run less frequently. For weekend travel, be sure to consult a schedule, especially if you plan to transfer from Metrorail to Metrobus, which also runs less frequently.

The DC Metro is included in an interactive database of subway systems in cities around the world. You can access it at **http://metro.jussieu.fr:10001/bin/select/english/usa/washington** on the Internet.

Farecards Fares are based on the time of day (peak or off-peak hours) and distance traveled. Currently, one-way fares during peak weekday hours (5:30 to 9:30 a.m. and 3:00 to 8:00 p.m.) range from $1.10 to $3.25, compared with non-peak fares of $1.10 to $2.10.

Farecards, the admission tickets in and out of the Metro system, are sold through machines at the stations. You can buy a higher value farecard for several trips, or by first checking the fare chart posted in the station, you can buy a fare card for the exact amount to get to your destination.

To purchase a farecard, insert bills or coins into the appropriate slot in the Farecard machine. The amount of money you deposit appears in the lighted display above the words, **Select Farecard Value**. To adjust the value of the farecard, use the "–" and "+" buttons. Once you have the display set to the fare you need, press the **Push for Farecard** button to receive the farecard and any change.

To enter the train platforms, insert your farecard into the pass-through gate with the green light and white arrow. The machine records time and location information on the magnetic strip and returns the card to you as the gate opens to let you through. Be sure to take the card with you; you will need it to exit the system. When you reach your destination, follow the same procedure. As you pass through the exit gate, the machine automatically deducts the cost of the trip and prints the remaining value, if any, on your card. Once the card value reaches zero, the machine keeps the card.

If you have insufficient fare to exit the system at your destination, you will need to use the Exitfare machine near the exit gate. Insert your card as instructed on the machine and deposit the amount of change indicated in the display. If you do not realize ahead of time that your farecard is "short," it will be rejected as you try to pass through the exit gate. This happens even to the most veteran rider, and during rush-hour congestion, getting back to the Exitfare machine can remind you of salmon swimming upstream.

FARECARD MACHINES

Change is returned only in quarters and nickels, and the maximum change returned is $4.95. As you can only buy one farecard at a time, if you put a $20 bill into the Farecard machine, you will be the proud owner of a $15.05 farecard, and $4.95 in coins. Unless you intend to buy a large-value farecard, you should carry with you smaller denomination bills and change. There are no bill changers in the subway stations and the attendants are not permitted to supply change.

Farecard machines can be quite finicky. Veteran riders know never to go to the machine closest to the entrance. It always gets the most use and its bill sensors suffer the greatest wear and tear. Luckily, the newer machines are increasingly less sensitive to ragged edged bills.

M Unless you plan carefully, rarely will you use up the value of a farecard exactly. If you find yourself with a drawer full of low-value cards, here are a few options:

Insert your old card into the **Used Farecard Trade-in** slot in one of the Farecard machines at the station entrance (not the Exitfare machines at the exit). Insert the amount you wish to add and press the **Push for Farecard button**. You receive a replacement farecard in the new amount.

To cash in several farecards at once, obtain an envelope at a station kiosk and mail the farecards into Metro headquarters for a replacement card.

For the altruistic, low-value farecards may be donated to help homeless veterans find and keep jobs by helping them get to and from interviews and the job site until they receive their first paycheck. This is handled through a special arrangement in which Metro consolidates the low-value cards into ones of $20 or more and the Veterans Administration distributes them. For further information call the VA Medical Center at 202-745-8313.

Special Features and Transfers Many Metro stations, especially those in the suburbs, have a Kiss & Ride area for dropping off and picking up passengers. Another special feature at many of the suburban stations is Park & Ride. Fees and restrictions vary by lot, although parking in all of the Metro-operated lots is free on weekends and federal holidays. In many of them, weekday parking is also free, as long as you leave the lot before 3:00 p.m. Some lots adjacent to Metro stations are privately owned and do not offer free parking, so be sure to check the rate schedule.

Free bus transfers, available at Metrorail stations, get you a discounted rate on Metrobus travel in DC and Virginia. You still pay some for the bus ride, but less than the normal fare because you started your trip on Metrorail. In Maryland, rail transfers are not valid toward bus fares. Bus transfers are available from machines usually placed next to the escalators or stairs leading to the train platforms. You must get your transfer at the station where you entered the system for your transfer to be valid. There are no transfers from Metrobuses to Metrorail.

Metrobus

The Metrobus system complements Metrorail, extending into the far reaches of the area's neighborhoods with almost 400 routes and some 13,000 bus stops. The buses also link parts of the city not served by the rail system. Like Metrorail fares, the bus fares are determined by time of day and length of trip (number of zones crossed). The base fare is $1.10 and buses accept only exact change. The Bus/Rail Flash Pass, good for a two-week period, allows you to pay a single fee for unlimited bus rides within certain zones or combinations of zones. Depending on the type of Flash Pass you buy, you also get a predetermined amount of Metrorail value. Weekday commuters make only a small amount of money on the deal, benefiting more from the convenience offered. But for those who also use the bus for other reasons, the Flash Pass savings really pile up. Flash Passes can be purchased from the Metro kiosk at the Metro Center

Sales Office and at participating Giant, Safeway and SuperFresh stores. The Metro brochure titled *All About Metro Fares* provides a complete listing of other Metro sales offices where passes are sold.

The Metro system has some buses that are wheelchair accessible. If you need such a bus or want to check on availability at a particular station, call 202-296-1825 for On-Call Metrobus Service or 202-296-1245 for Metro ID Cards for People with Disabilities.

MetroAccess

MetroAccess provides curb-to-curb service for persons with disabilities who cannot use regular public transportation and have been certified eligible to use paratransit service. It is sponsored by the WMATA, local governments and local fixed-route transportation operators. The many sponsors include Montgomery County Ride-On, Prince George's County The Bus, Laurel Connect-A-Ride, Fairfax County Connector, Reston Internal Bus System, Tysons Shuttle, City of Fairfax CUE, City of Alexandria DASH and Arlington County Trolley. People eligible to use MetroAccess are those who (a) are unable, as a result of physical or mental impairments, to get on, ride or get off any vehicle on the transit system; (b) need the assistance of a wheelchair lift or other boarding device to get on, ride or get off an accessible vehicle but find that such a vehicle is not available on the route when they want to travel; or (c) have specific impairment-related conditions which prevent travel to or from a bus stop or rail station. If you or someone you know may qualify for this service, contact MetroAccess at 301-588-8184 (voice) or 301-588-8186 (TDD).

Commuter Lines

To ease the commute from the farthest suburbs, the states of Maryland and Virginia, as well as some local jurisdictions, sponsor special commuter bus and train lines to and from the District.

The **Maryland Rail Commuter System (MARC)** (1-800-325-7245) shuttles nearly 20,000 passengers daily along the three Amtrak lines from as far to the northeast as Baltimore and as far to the west as Harper's Ferry and Martinsburg in West Virginia. The MARC lines intersect with Metrorail stations at various points and all lines terminate at Union Station, the District's Metro and Amtrak station near Capitol Hill. MARC tickets may be purchased on a daily, weekly or monthly basis.

Montgomery County's **Ride-On** (301-217-RIDE) is an extensive bus service, making connections throughout the county at MARC, Metrorail and Metrobus stops. The fare for the Ride-On service is $1.10 for rush hour and $0.90 at other times. Be sure to check out the transfer options as

METRO NUMBERS

Metrorail/Metrobus Information
(Daily, 6:00 a.m.–11:30 p.m.)
202-637-7000
202-638-3780 (TDD)

Events Hotline (recorded info)
202-783-1070

Consumer Assistance
(Weekdays, 8:30 a.m.–4:00 p.m.)
202-637-1328
202-638-3780 (TDD)

On-Call Metrobus Service
202-962-1825

Metro ID Cards for People with Disabilities
202-962-1245
202-628-8973 (TDD)

MetroAccess
301-588-8184
301-588-8186 (TDD)

Lost and Found
202-962-1195

Bike-on-Rail Permits/Bicycle Lockers
202-962-1116

Metro Transit Police (Emergencies)
202-962-2121

a MARC train ticket provides you with free Ride-On service, and transfers may be used between Metrobus and Ride-On.

In Prince George's County, **The Bus** (1-800-486-9797) connects Upper Marlboro County with the Addison Rd. and New Carrollton Metro stations. It runs from 6:00 a.m. until 7:15 p.m. Fares are $0.75 all day; $0.35 for disabled individuals. Transfers to the Metrorail and Ride-On connector service are available for $2.50 during rush hour and $1.50 during non-rush-hour periods.

In Virginia, several options for commuter travel are available as well. The **Virginia Railway Express (VRE)** (703-497-7777) uses the Amtrak lines to ferry passengers from Manassas on the west and Fredericksburg to the south. Both 10-trip and monthly tickets may be purchased at reduced prices. These lines also intersect the Metrorail system, providing optional routes for getting to and from work. For bus lines, the **Fairfax Connector** (703-339-7200) operates in the regions between Springfield Plaza and Mt. Vernon, dropping passengers off at the Huntington, Pentagon and Dunn Loring Metro stations. It also connects Reston with the West Falls Church Metro during rush hour; non-rush-hour service is provided by the **Reston Internal Bus System (RIBS).** The **Tysons Shuttle** connects West Falls Church area with Metro during rush-hour periods only. Information on both these services can be obtained by calling 703-548-4545. Alexandria's **DASH** (703-370-DASH) connects passengers with Metrobus, Metrorail and the Fairfax Connector. The **Fairfax CUE** (703-385-7859) connects most of the city proper to the Vienna Metro station on a daily basis. The fare is $0.50; seniors and students are $0.25.

Taxicabs in DC and the Suburbs

For the past 60-some years, DC taxicabs have run on a rather complicated zone system originally designed to keep legislators' fares cheap. In the 1930s, the DC Public Utilities Commission wanted to replace the traditional ad-hoc method of setting cab fares with a metered system. But the federal government had another idea. Cleverly designed by Congress, the new zone system was based on concentric circles radiating out from the Capitol. Any time you travel to or from the Capitol area, a taxi ride seems like a true bargain and you see for yourself the original motivation for the zone system. According to a recent article in the *Washington Post,* from 1933 to 1986, each DC appropriations bill included language requiring the continuance of the congressionally designed zone system. Taxicabs are in the news at this writing, as the DC Taxicab Commission, the DC Public Utilities Commission and the DC City Council, along with just about everyone else in town, are talking about switching to meters in late 1998.

In the meantime, the zone system continues to be one of the challenges of getting around town. The District is divided into five zones, each with as many as eight subzones. The price of your ride is determined by the number of zones and subzones you cross on the way to your destination. A one-dollar surcharge is added to all trips originating in the District during the evening (4:00 to 6:30 p.m.) rush hours. Get to know the zone map (usually displayed behind the driver's seat) and the correct rates for trips you take on a regular basis. As you become familiar with the city's geography and the zone map, you will find that sometimes a two- or three-block walk can shave a dollar off your fare. The lowest in-town rate is $3.20. At press time, the rates are being reviewed and riders could see a 25% across-the-board increase in zone fares. With the zone system, as you don't pay for time and mileage, the fare is fixed, so you can ask what it will be before getting in the cab. If the amount doesn't sound right to you, the problem just might be with the driver and not the system.

DC cab drivers are allowed to pick up additional passengers en route to your destination and to charge them full fare. They are also allowed to double their fares during a declared snow emergency. If DC-licensed cabs

TAXIS

DC

Capitol Cab	202-546-2400
Clean Air Cab	202-687-7000
Diamond Cab	202-387-6200
Yellow Cab	202-544-1212

Maryland

Tri-County Cab	301-248-2073

Montgomery County

Barwood Cab	301-984-1900
Checker Cab	301-816-0066
Yellow Cab	301-984-1900

Prince George's County

Checker Cab	301-270-6000
Yellow Cab	301-864-7700

Virginia

Red Top Cab	703-522-3333

Yellow Cab

Arlington	703-522-2222
Alexandria	703-549-2500
Fairfax	703-941-4000

are taking you out of the District, they determine fares by using their odometers—currently $2 for the first mile and $0.70 for each additional half-mile. It is a good idea to ask first what the fare is likely to be.

Individuals interested in supporting environmentally friendly ventures will be pleased to know about a local cab company whose vehicles run only on natural gas. As an added attraction, they accept credit cards. **Clean Air Cab Company** provides service throughout the metro area. Call 202-687-7000 to reach their 24-hour dispatch service.

Cab companies in the suburbs are metered. Under a reciprocity agreement with the District, the suburban cab drivers have been allowed to pick up fares in the District after discharging passengers or as part of pre-arranged trips. A recent vote by the Taxicab Commission to end the reciprocity agreement has become a contentious issue and it remains to be seen whether or not the decision will be overturned.

OTHER MODES OF LOCAL TRANSPORTATION

Washington is not just for people with cars, Metro farecards, and bus and cab fare. In fact, you'll find increasing numbers of local residents who get around either on two wheels or on two feet. Some of them won't have it any other way—for work and for play.

Bicycling

Some 480 miles of marked bike routes and 670 miles of paved, off-road bike paths make the Washington area a cyclist's dream. Rock Creek Parkway gives cyclists a quick route from the Connecticut Ave. neighborhoods to Downtown. To get across the Potomac River from Virginia, both Key Bridge and the 14th St. Bridge have wide sidewalks that also make for great bike paths.

Until recently, the paths along the C&O Canal provided an excellent car-free route in from Maryland towns such as Potomac. But following the blizzard of 1996, severe flooding seriously damaged the historic Canal and its Towpath. Reconstruction is expected to require some $20 million and three to four years to complete. The project got underway as early as February 1996, and an active volunteer program has been established to supplement government support of the reconstruction effort. Dedicated bikers, hikers and other nature lovers can get involved by contacting the Rebuild the Towpath Foundation at 1-800-434-9330.

During rush hour, you should avoid the major avenues in town, particularly North Capitol St. and Massachusetts, Pennsylvania,

Connecticut and Wisconsin Aves. Commuters often exceed the speed limit and bikers can easily find themselves in gutters—or worse. Beach Drive, a main part of Rock Creek Parkway, should also be avoided during commuter hours. On weekends and holidays, however, certain sections of Beach Drive are reserved for biking, hiking and in-line roller-skating, making it one of the most popular weekend spots for active Washingtonians.

Metrorail sells passes that allow passengers to bring bicycles on the trains. These passes are good for evenings after 7:00 p.m. and on weekends and holidays, with the exception of the Fourth of July. Bicycle lockers are available at many Metro stations for 3-, 6- or 12-month rental periods. Applications for a Metro **Bike-on-Rail** permit must be made in person at Metro Headquarters, 600 5th St. NW, during designated times. Call 202-962-1116 for information. To obtain a permit, you must complete a written test to demonstrate knowledge of the rules and regulations for transporting bicycles on Metrorail. Bicycles are not permitted on Metro buses.

Walking

The local lifestyle in many parts of DC and in some suburban neighborhoods does not necessarily depend on access to car, train, bus or subway. If you live in one of the more central parts of the District or just across the Potomac River in Rosslyn, Crystal City or Pentagon City—and you love to walk—you can get to many interesting and important locations on your own steam. In these areas, getting to work, shopping, running errands and meeting up with friends and colleagues can all be done on foot. With a scarcity of affordable parking, the benefits of having a car in many DC neighborhoods can often be outweighed by the cost and aggravation. Many Washingtonians can afford to live where they do because they have no car payments, insurance costs or parking and gas expenses. And the flexibility of walking can't be beat. Farther out in Virginia and suburban Maryland, getting around without a car becomes increasingly difficult, even if you live close to a Metro station or bus line. This is one of the many trade-offs offered by the wide variety of approaches to living in and mastering DC.

INTER-CITY TRANSPORTATION

Washington and its suburbs constitute a major hub of activity on the East Coast and a major location with regard to the entire nation—if not the world. Accordingly, the area is not lacking in effective means for inter-city transportation. Metropolitan Washington boasts three major airports as well as Amtrak train and Greyhound bus service.

Airports

The three major airports serving the metropolitan DC area are National Airport on the banks of the Potomac River in Arlington, Dulles International Airport in the far-western suburbs of Virginia, and Baltimore-Washington International Airport in Maryland. Both National and Dulles Airports are undergoing major renovations expected to last until the late 1990s. Traffic patterns and parking situations change frequently and travelers are well advised to allow plenty of extra time getting into and out of these two airports.

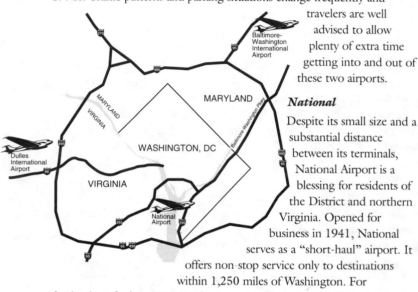

National

Despite its small size and a substantial distance between its terminals, National Airport is a blessing for residents of the District and northern Virginia. Opened for business in 1941, National serves as a "short-haul" airport. It offers non-stop service only to destinations within 1,250 miles of Washington. For destinations farther away, travelers must book connecting flights or use one of the other two major airports. National can be as close as a 15-minute drive from most locations in the District, Arlington and Alexandria, under the very best of traffic conditions. As the only predictable thing about area traffic is its unpredictability, you should test the trip ahead of time so you are well prepared, know where you are going, and have an alternate route in mind.

Metro's Yellow and Blue Lines go to National Airport and a shuttle bus connects the Metro station to the airport terminals. Cabs to National from downtown DC cost approximately $9 to $12. The Washington Flyer (703-685-1400) offers both taxi and shuttle bus service from the airport. The $8 shuttle bus originates at 1517 K St. NW and makes stops at many of the big downtown hotels. The taxi service is metered. To drive from DC, the quickest route is to take 14th St. (south) over the 14th St. Bridge and follow the National Airport signs. From McLean, Arlington or

Alexandria, the George Washington Memorial Parkway is the best option. Travelers from Montgomery County can either cut through DC and take 14th St. or take the Beltway to the George Washington Parkway. The main number for National Airport is 703-685-8000.

Dulles

For cross-country flights, a better option is Dulles International Airport in northern Virginia. Dulles was all the rage when it opened in the mid-1960s, with its Eero Saarinen design. Much larger than National and much farther from DC (26 miles from Downtown), Dulles offers non-stop flights to a long list of domestic and foreign destinations.

Because Dulles is so far from most of the metropolitan region, taxicabs in either direction can cost as much as $40. The Washington Flyer buses and taxis go to Dulles as well as to National. The one-way fare for the bus service, from 1517 K St. NW, is $16. It takes approximately an hour to get to the airport and stops at a number of downtown hotels. You can also take the Orange Line to the West Falls Church station. From there, the Washington Flyer Dulles Express bus provides direct service to the airport every half-hour for $8. For more information, call 703-685-1400. If you are driving, take I-66 west to the 17-mile Dulles Access Road. No matter how you get there, you should budget extra time. The design of the airport requires that you take a shuttle bus, the People Mover, from the gate to the plane. This adds another 10 to 15 minutes. General information about Dulles is available at 703-661-2700.

BWI

The Baltimore-Washington International Airport (BWI), 28 miles from Downtown, has long been considered the area's number three airport. BWI has recently undergone massive renovations to extend runways, enlarge concourses, add passenger gates and build a new parking garage. It now rivals Dulles for international and longer-distance domestic flights. If you are driving, take I-95 or the Baltimore-Washington Parkway to I-195 and follow the signs to BWI. While the Metro system has no direct service to BWI, Amtrak (800-USA-RAIL) provides travelers with access to and from the airport through Union Station in Northeast DC. There is a free shuttle bus from the train station to the airport. You can also get to BWI via the MARC-Penn Line (800-325-RAIL), which connects to Metro Red Line at Union Station and Orange Line at New Carrollton. In addition, Airport Connection (301-261-1091) runs a shuttle between BWI and downtown every 90 minutes from 7:00 a.m. to 8:30 p.m. One-way fares cost $14. BWI's main number is 301-261-1000.

Trains

Amtrak (1-800-USA-RAIL) provides passenger service running in and out of Union Station at 50 Massachusetts Ave. NE. Amtrak also links with the Metrorail system to Washington, DC and the Maryland and Virginia suburbs. Amtrak also runs a daily non-stop auto train from Virginia to Florida. You must accompany your car on this journey. One-way coach fare is $125 per person and $175 per car.

Amtrak welcomes you to its official "station" at **http://www.amtrak.com** on the World Wide Web. Access to Amtrak schedules is provided at **http://www.mcs.net/~dsdawdy/amtrak/amtrak.html** courtesy of an independent service.

Buses

In addition to Metrobus service, the Washington area is served by **Greyhound** at 1005 1st and L Sts. NE (202-289-5154 or 800-231-2222). The line serves Washington and Baltimore from main terminals downtown to satellite terminals in the suburbs. It also provides nationwide and some commuter service, from several passenger stations—in the District at 1005 1st St. NW (202-289-5154), Silver Spring at 8100 Fenton St. and Sligo Ave. (301-588-5110), Arlington at 3860 South Four Mile Run Dr. (703-998-6312), Fairfax County at 4103 Rust Rd. off Lee Hwy. (703-273-7770) and Springfield at 6583 Backlick Rd. off Old Keane Mill Rd. (703-451 5800).

Dealing with the Local Bureaucracy

Most newcomers enjoy looking for an apartment, buying furniture, setting up house and getting to know the place they now call home. These activities are considerably more fun than dealing with the bureaucratic labyrinths you must navigate in order to establish residency. This chapter helps you plan your route as you deal with car ownership— drivers' licenses, registration and insurance—and income and property taxes. Also included are pointers on making sure your four-footed friends are legal residents of the metropolitan Washington area.

THE RESPONSIBILITY OF CAR OWNERSHIP

While some local residents simplify things by living life as pedestrians, most people in the area do own and regularly use a car to get around. For those people, the bureaucratic responsibilities of car ownership must be taken seriously. No matter where you live in the area, you need to acquire a local driver's license, register your vehicle and be sure that it is adequately insured. Traditionally, these activities have consumed the most time and inspired the best horror stories about dealing with local bureaucracies. In recent years, however, a concerted effort has been made to make these types of services more accessible and efficient. While improvements have been made, the District still lags behind the suburban cities and counties. If you don't relish the thought of dealing with these kinds of details, contact the local company, **United States Vehicle Registration Service** at 202-342-2558. For $45 in the District and Virginia ($50 in Maryland), they will obtain a title, registration and parking permit for your car in the District, Maryland or Virginia. Double the fee and you can get your car inspected as well.

Getting Your Driver's License

Regardless of where you live, bring your checkbook, your current license (if you have one) and your social security card (if you can find it). You must also bring one other form of identification bearing your name and birth date. Birth certificates, passports, employer and school IDs are all acceptable, but only the original documents; photocopies will get you nowhere. Take these materials—as well as patience and a sense of humor— to the closest full-service motor vehicle office.

Current out-of-state license holders have a 30-day grace period to get a local driver's license and license plates. If you surrender a valid driver's license from another US state or territory, you do not need to take a

DRIVER'S LICENSE FEES

	Driver's License	Learner's Permit
District of Columbia	$20	$10
Maryland	$30	$30*
Virginia	$12**	$3

*For both learner's permit and license

**Average rate. Virginia is getting residents on a five-year renewal cycle. During this transition period, the driver's license fee will range from $7.20 to $16.80 depending on the individual's month and year of birth.

driving test. Vision tests are mandatory in all jurisdictions. District residents must take a 20-question written test and score 75% or better to pass. Virginia and Maryland both waive written requirements for current license holders.

If you have never gotten a driver's license, you must first apply for a learner's permit and take a written exam. Once you pass, you can sign up for a road test.

Foreign license holders must bring a green card or social security card along with a current passport and proof of a foreign license. Without proof of a foreign license, you will have to apply for a license from scratch—learner's permit and all. Non-US citizens must pass both vision and written tests. They are usually given the same day, so come prepared. The decision to require a road test is handled on an individual basis. If you do have to take it, you will need to make an appointment once you pass the written test.

Registering Your Car

Regardless of where you live in the area, you will need to bring the following items when registering your car—a copy of the title of the car, out-of-state registration (if applicable), proof of auto insurance, proof of address and your checkbook. Other details vary by jurisdiction.

DC

For licenses and car registration, newcomers to the District must go to the Central Office of the city's Bureau of Motor Vehicles (BMV) at 301 C St. NW. The building is open weekdays from 8:15 a.m. to 3:00 p.m. For late-risers, the BMV stays open till 7:00 p.m. on Wednesday. Parking in the neighborhood can be quite difficult, and it is much easier to take the Metro Red Line to Judiciary Square. The building is just across the street from the Metro station.

District residents have been known to spend countless hours in line at the BMV offices. Efforts have been made to make the system more efficient and, while the bureau is much more user-friendly than it used to be, the wait can be lengthy. For quickest results, the BMV suggests visiting during weekday afternoons between 2:00 and 3:00 p.m.

Room 1157 is the single most important room you need to visit. When you have filled out your Application for Certificate of Title for a Motor Vehicle or Trailer, it is time to get in line. BMV uses a concept of moving from one window to another for specific functions. Read the signs and be prepared to move to another window—and often another line—as directed. Expect to pay $20 for the certificate of title, $15 for each recorded lien on your car and a registration fee based on the car's weight—for cars under 3,500 pounds the fee is $65; for heavier cars it is $98. These two fees already include the $10 inspection fee. The District also charges excise taxes based on the fair market ("blue book") value of the vehicle—currently 6% for a small car and 7% for a large one. Be prepared to pay the taxes on the spot.

In addition to the main office at Judiciary Square, there is now a BMV adjunct office in the Community Services Center at 616 H St. NE. This office provides services for registration renewals, residential parking permits, driver's license renewals and non-driver identification cards. The hours are 11:00 a.m. to 7:00 p.m. on weekdays and 8:15 a.m. to 4:00 p.m. on Saturday. No tests are given at this site.

Residential parking permits, required on blocks with residential parking restrictions, are essential in the District. For just $10, the permit allows you to park your car on your neighborhood street during times when parking is limited to two hours for non-residents. To obtain a parking permit, you must present a valid DC vehicle registration along with proof of insurance and residence. You can show proof of residence by bringing along a signed lease, a notarized statement from your landlord or a utility bill.

Full-time students, temporary residents (those living in the District fewer than 180 days), congressional staff and military personnel can keep their home state license plates by applying for a reciprocity sticker. Students must show proof of full-time status (at least nine credit hours) and proof of residence in the District. If you live on a street that has residential parking, you must still pay the $10 parking permit fee.

If you are seeking a **handicapped parking permit**, you should go to Room 1033 to file your application. If you are issued handicapped tags, you will not need a residential parking permit.

Once you leave the BMV, your car still has to be inspected. Safety inspections must be done within 30 days of receipt of your DC registration and all first-time inspections must be done at one of only two inspection stations operated by the District. If the lines are short, your inspection experience can be over in less than 15 minutes. One station is located at

1001 Half St. SW (between Eye and M Sts.) and the other station is at 1827 West Virginia Ave. NE (four blocks south of New York Ave.). Try to avoid visiting these places near the end of the month when lines tend to be longest. These inspections stations are open from 6:00 a.m. to 2:00 p.m. during the summer (June 15-September 15) and from 7:00 a.m. to 3:00 p.m. the rest of the year. You will have already paid the $10 fee for the inspection when you registered your car. After the first year, the District will mail you paperwork for renewing your registration. You still have to have the car inspected, now on a two-year cycle, but the rest of the renewal process can be handled by mail.

If your car fails the inspection, you can go to a District or a private licensed facility for re-inspection. A list of all approved inspection stations is available at the District's Half St. and West Virginia Ave. sites. Private inspection stations will charge a fee for repairs. These places are licensed to give inspection stickers once the car passes the re-inspection.

If you have any questions, you can call the BMV's automated information system (202-727-6680). If the series of recorded messages does not answer your questions, stay on the line and an operator will eventually answer.

Washington, DC Bureau of Motor Vehicles (BMV)

Information	202-727-6680
Central Office	301 C St. NW
Hours	Monday, Tuesday, Thursday and Friday, 8:15 a.m. to 3:00 p.m. Wednesday, 8:15 a.m. to 7:00 p.m.
Adjunct Office	616 H St. NE
Hours	Monday to Friday, 11:00 a.m. to 7:00 p.m. Saturday, 8:15 a.m. to 4:00 p.m.

Maryland

Before you even set foot in a Maryland Motor Vehicle Administration (MVA) office, you should go to an authorized service station and have your car inspected. Vehicles must have been inspected within the 90-day period preceding registration and titling, and proof of passing inspection must accompany the application for title. The inspections are thorough and can take up to two hours. Prices generally range from $40 to $50.

Once your car has passed the safety inspection, you will need to bring your current title, certificate of inspection and all insurance information (company, policy and agent) to a full-service MVA office. MVA charges $15 for titling, $70 for registration (good for two years) and $20 to record each lien (if your car is financed). Marylanders must also pay a one-time excise tax amounting to 5% of the fair market value of the car. If you have paid sales tax on your car in another state, bring your original bill of sale; the previously paid tax will be credited towards the current tax. Maryland has a minimum payment of $100 and although this one-time tax may seem high, Marylanders should consider themselves lucky not to be hit with the annual personal property taxes paid by Virginians.

Most Maryland counties also require an emissions test and inspection with proof of passing required at the time of applying for registration and titling. The fee for emissions inspection is $12 and must be paid in cash. Emissions tests are required every two years. For current inspection station sites near you, check the Yellow Pages under Automobile Inspection Stations.

The MVA has announced plans to test the feasibility of shopping mall self-service terminals, resembling bank ATM machines, at several locations across the state beginning mid-1996. Initially, users will be able only to renew vehicle registrations via the terminals as long as they have a renewal form and a valid automobile insurance form. If the machines prove successful, long-term plans call for expanding the service to allow users to renew driver's licenses and, ultimately, pay taxes.

Maryland Motor Vehicle Administration (MVA)

Full-Service Offices
Information	301-948-3177
Hours	Monday to Friday, 8:30 a.m. to 4:30 p.m. Saturday, 8:30 a.m. to 12:00 p.m. (drivers' licenses only)

Gaithersburg	15 Metropolitan Grove Rd. (off Clopper Rd.)
Frederick	1601 Bowman's Farm Rd. (Exit 56 off I-70)
Largo (Upper Marlboro)	10251 Central Ave. (near Routes 202 and 214)

BIKE OWNERSHIP

For those of you who prefer self-propelled transportation, you will be relieved to know that registering a bicycle in the District is much easier than registering a car. Just take your bike to any District police or fire station. Your bike must be equipped with a night light and a horn. Registration costs just $1 for five years, and proof of ownership is required. For more information, call 202-576-6768. In Maryland, you can simply register your bike for just $1 at any police station. Bicycles in Arlington must be registered at 2100 North 15th St. (703-358-4252). Bring the serial number and $0.50. Alexandria cyclists must also register their bikes and can do so at the Police Department at 2003 Mill Rd., not far from the Metro's Yellow Line Eisenhower Station. As in Arlington, the fee is only $0.50; the police will record your bike's serial number and give you a decal. Fairfax County does not require a bike permit. They do, however, recommend that you etch your social security number on your bike so that you can identify it as yours in the event of theft.

Virginia

Virginians should be prepared for a scavenger hunt and for handling both state and local bureaucracies. First, you have to find a state-registered service station to have your car inspected. Your car must undergo two inspections—for safety and for emissions. The safety inspection is done annually and the emissions inspection is done every other year. Not all places are licensed to perform both tests. Signs at gas stations indicate which tests can be performed there.

With your approved emissions and safety documents in hand, your next stop is a full-service Division of Motor Vehicle (DMV) office to register your car. Blue signs with the letters "DMV" in white let you know you are closing in on one of them. In return for a $10 titling fee and a $26.50 registration fee (for cars weighing under 4,000 pounds), you will receive a Virginia title, a registration card, license plates and current plate decals. Registration cards and decals are valid for one year. Those who have moved to Virginia for the long haul may want to opt for the two-year registration plan—double the registration fee and save yourself some effort next year.

Inspection fees total $23.50 (emissions $13.50 and safety $10). Like doctors who examine their patients from head to toe, inspectors check everything. So, if you are aware of needed repairs, be sure to have the work done before getting the car inspected. If the car fails inspection, don't expect to have the fee refunded. For a current list of inspection stations near you, check the Yellow Pages under Automobile Inspection Stations.

The final stop after getting the safety inspection decal, the registration and the license plates is the local city hall or county courthouse to register for the local personal property tax and to get the license decal for the city or county.

Alexandria   Alexandrians must register to pay the personal property tax in Room 1410 in City Hall at 301 King St. (703-838-4560). Lines here, even during lunch hour, are not that long. The registration office is open weekdays from 8:00 a.m. to 5:00 p.m. You need to bring your driver's license and one of the following—your state vehicle title, state vehicle registration card or bill of sale. The city bills you in August for payment by October 5. If you register your car in Alexandria after October 5, you are given a 30-day grace period to pay your personal property taxes. City stickers, required for on-street parking, cost $25 annually, with residents in zoned areas paying an additional $15.

Arlington County In Arlington County, the Courthouse at 2100 Clarendon Blvd. marks the final stop on your bureaucratic journey. Here you can register your car and while you are at it, register to vote and pick up newcomers' information at the desk right by the main entrance. There is a convenient, inexpensive parking garage on site or you can take the Metro Orange Line to the Court House station.

The Office of Personal Property Tax in Suite 218 (703-358-3135) is where you file your personal property tax forms and pay the Arlington County processing fee. The county charges just under 5% of the current "blue book" value of the car. A wave of relief sweeps over most Arlington residents when they learn that they do not have to pay these taxes on the spot. This tax can amount to a few hundred dollars a year for newer cars. If you register between December 16 and June 15, taxes are due September 15. For those registering between June 16 and December 15, the deadline is March 15.

Fairfax County Fairfax County residents must bring their Virginia registration card to any county office in order to register a vehicle and purchase county tags. Call 703-222-8234 to find the county office closest to you. Tags cost $25 for cars and trucks. The process for paying personal property tax is simple. Just fill out the proper form and you will be billed in late September for payment by December 5. Tax rates are just over 4.5% of the current trading value of your car. Fairfax does prorate its property tax, which is good news if you move to the area halfway through the year.

PET LICENSING

The District requires that residents register their dogs with the local animal control officer. A rabies certificate from a licensed veterinarian is required. Fees are $10 for neutered males and $35 for females and non-neutered males. For information, call 202-727-7100.

The state of Maryland requires that residents register their dogs and cats with the local animal control officer. New residents have 30 days to register their animals. A rabies certificate from a licensed veterinarian is required. For further information, call Montgomery County at 301-279-1095 or Prince George's County at 301-499-8300.

In Virginia, all dogs six months of age and older must be licensed each year. A rabies certificate from a licensed veterinarian is required. Cats are not licensed but are required by law to be inoculated for rabies by four months of age. For information, call Alexandria at 703-838-4777, Arlington County at 703-358-3057, or Fairfax County at 703-830-3310.

Virginia Division of Motor Vehicles (DMV)

Full Service Offices	
Information	703-761-4655
Hours	Monday to Friday, 9:00 a.m. to 6:00 p.m.
	Saturday, 9:00 a.m. to 1:00 p.m.
Alexandria	930 North Henry St.
Arlington	4150 South Four Mile Run Dr.

RENTERS' INSURANCE

Most homeowners have already dealt with the issue of insuring their property, whether they live in a detached house, a townhouse or row house, or a condo. But many renters don't realize that similar protection is available for their belongings as well. If you have an expensive stereo system, computer, large wardrobe or other valuable personal property, you should consider buying renters' insurance. Renters' insurance is usually pretty cheap, relative to the cost of replacing your possessions. A $10,000 policy can cost as little as $100 a year. If you are interested in renters' insurance, ask your car insurance agent for a quote first. You can often obtain a discount if you buy more than one type of insurance from the same agent. If you have any general questions about renters' insurance, the Insurance Helpline at 1-800-942-4242 can answer them.

Fairfax	11215-G Lee Hwy.
Franconia	6308 Grovedale Dr.
Vienna (Tysons Corner)	1968 Gallows Rd.

Insuring Your Car

Car insurance is a necessity, regardless of where you live. Insurance rates are determined by factors that are often out of your control—such as neighborhood (people in the city pay more), age (older is better than younger), sex (women have lower rates) and marital status (married drivers are preferred). Virginians tend to have the lowest auto insurance rates. Residents of the District have the highest annual premiums and Marylanders generally fall somewhere between the two, depending on the specific location.

For buying insurance, you have three options—mail-order, company agents or independent agents. Groups or organizations such as AAA offer insurance by mail. Company agents represent the large insurance companies like Allstate or State Farm. Independent agents sell insurance from various companies and tend to be a little more expensive. Often, the independent agents tend to have close ties with one or two companies and try to push their products. So make sure you call around to a few independent agents and compare their prices and products. Phone book listings of insurance agents and companies tend to be confusing. When calling, you may want to ask if you are talking to a company agent or an independent agent. You can also contact the **Insurance Helpline** at 1-800-942-4242 for assistance.

For the best rates, shop around and ask lots of questions, even if you think the answers are obvious. When you call insurance agents for price quotes, be sure to give each the same information so that you can make accurate comparisons. When applying, honesty is definitely the best policy; the truth comes out eventually, even if it doesn't come from you.

DEALING WITH YOUR TAXES

Everyone knows the line about death and taxes—and the situation is no different in the Washington area. Federal income tax has to be dealt with no matter where you live, and local jurisdictions levy their own income tax as well as personal and real property taxes.

Federal Income Tax

If you do not find the form you need in your mail, at your post office or at other places offering them, you can call the **Internal Revenue Service (IRS)** at 1-800-829-3676. Federal tax information and assistance is available at 1-800-829-1040. For those who like to browse the Net, the IRS has a Website at **http://www.irs.ustreas.gov** featuring tax forms, publications, news on recent developments and other related information. Locally, the *Washington Post* prints a tax guide every February summarizing all of the federal and state tax regulations in the area.

State and Local Income Tax

The District takes the gold medal for the highest income tax rates in the area. Maryland gets the silver and Virginia, the bronze. New Virginia residents accustomed to filing all tax forms by April 15 will be happy to know that Virginia's state income tax deadline is May 1st. District and Maryland residents still have to pay up by April 15.

Before you begin this dreaded ritual, consult the state instruction booklets for information about filing requirements. Unless you arrived on New Year's Day, you should pay special attention to information for part-year residents and non-residents. If you need extra help, each jurisdiction offers assistance.

DC

District of Columbia residents are required to file returns by April 15. Tax rates are progressive and range from 6% to 9.5% on taxable income. Exemptions include a personal exemption of $1,370 for an individual, if single; $2,740 for married filing jointly; and $2,740 for head of family. An additional $1,370 exemption is allowed for taxpayers over age 65 and taxpayers who are blind.

The Income Tax Help office, in Room 550 at 441 4th St. NW, will answer questions about District taxes; you can call them at 202-727-6130. This office keeps extended hours during tax season, January to April. In addition, District residents can pick up tax forms at several locations including the District Building at 1350 Pennsylvania Ave. NW, the Recorder of Deeds Office at 515 D St. NW, Martin Luther King Library at 901 G St. NW, the Potomac Building at 614 H St. NW or the Reeves Center at 2000 14th St. NW. If you would like to have tax forms mailed to you, call 202-727-6170.

Maryland

Maryland imposes a graduated income tax at the current rates of to 6% on taxable income, generally defined the same as federal income taxes. Returns must be filed by April 15.

In addition, the Maryland counties may levy a local "piggy-back" income tax, varying from 50% to 60% of the state tax liability, which is withheld and collected on the same form as the Maryland state income tax.

Maryland income tax forms are available weekdays between 8:00 a.m. and 5:00 p.m. at 2730 University Blvd. in Wheaton (301-949-6030) or can be obtained by mail. If you have any questions while you are preparing your return, try talking to someone in the state tax office at 1-800-638-2937.

Virginia

The Commonwealth of Virginia imposes a graduated income tax at the current rate from 2% to 5.75% on taxable income, generally defined the same as federal income taxes. Virginia returns must be filed by May 1.

Arlington residents can pick up their state income tax forms on the second floor of the Courthouse at 2100 Clarendon Blvd. (703-358-3055) or at any of the seven county public libraries. In Alexandria, forms are available at City Hall at 301 King St. (703-838-4570). If you would like forms mailed to you, call the Richmond Center at 1-804-367-8205. Help can be obtained by calling 1-804-367-8031.

Personal Property Tax

Neither the District of Columbia nor the state of Maryland levies a personal property tax on individuals. In Virginia, such taxes are controlled by the local governments. Counties set a base rate for all unincorporated areas, towns may elect to add a town rate to the county's base rate, and cities set a rate that is paid in lieu of the county tax. Automobiles, boats, mobile homes, motorcycles and business personal property are all subject to tax. Personal effects, household goods, money and securities are not taxed.

Real Property Tax

In DC, all real property is subject to taxation and is assessed at 100% of the estimated market value. Real property tax rates are set in June by the Council of the District of Columbia. There is a $30,000 homestead exemption on owner-occupied residential units; the exemption reduces the assessed value prior to taxing. Application must be made for this exemption, and once granted, is good for five years.

Maryland assesses real property at approximately 40% of fair market value. The state tax rate is $0.21 per $100 of the assessed value. Maryland property is assessed every three years and increases are proportioned over the subsequent three years. Each county, city and district may levy additional taxes which will need to be factored into your planning.

In Virginia, real estate taxes are levied by local governments and not by the state.

Contact one of the following for further information on assessments and taxation.

District of Columbia   202-727-6460

Maryland
Montgomery County   301-279-1431
Prince George's County   301-952-2500

Virginia
Alexandria   703-838-4777
Arlington County   703-358-3090
Fairfax City   703-385-7883
Fairfax County   703-222-8234
Falls Church   703-241-5022

REGISTERING TO VOTE

To receive an application to vote in the District, call the city's 24-hour line at 202-727-2525. You will be asked for your name and address. A few days later you will receive an application in the mail. DC also has a Motor/Voter program. While you are waiting in line at the BMV, you can fill out the voter registration form. In addition, public libraries, police stations and fire stations in the District have voter registration forms.

Virginians can sign up to vote at the local courthouses, city halls or public libraries and even at some shopping centers, including Ballston Common, the Fashion Centre at Pentagon City and Landmark Center. Marylanders can do everything by mail. To receive voter registration materials, Montgomery County residents can call 301-424-4433; in Prince George's County, the number is 301-627-2814.

FEDERAL GOVERNMENT WEBSITES

One of the benefits of living in the Washington, DC area is being within arm's reach of the wealth of information available through the federal government. You can obtain information on virtually any subject through agency public information offices as well as from those federal research libraries that grant public access. You can also obtain information through the Internet without having to leave your home or office. Listed here are Websites that were available for some of the major government offices at the time the book went to press. Watch local publications for announcements of new Websites and check around on the Internet using some of the general addresses listed below.

General Government Information:

The World Wide Web Consortium	http://www.w3.org
FedWorld Information Network	http://www.fedworld.gov
Government Information	http://beta.yahoo.com/government
Federal Information Exchange, Inc.	http://www.fie.com/www/us_gov.htm

Government Agencies:

Census Bureau	http://www.census.gov
Central Intelligence Agency	http://www.odci.gov/cia
Department of Agriculture	http://www.usda.gov
Department of Commerce	http://www.doc.gov
Department of Education	http://www.ed.gov
Department of Energy	http://www.doe.gov
Department of the Interior	http://www.doi.gov
Department of Justice	http://www.usdoj.gov
Department of Labor	http://www.dol.gov
Department of State	http://www.state.gov
Department of Transportation	http://www.dot.gov
Department of Treasury	http://ustreas.gov
Environmental Protection Agency	http://epa.gov
Federal Bureau of Investigation	http://www.fbi.gov
Federal Judicial Center	http://www.fjc.gov
Food and Drug Administration	http://www.fda.gov
Government Printing Office	http://www.gpo.gov
Health and Human Services	http://www.os.dhhs.gov
Housing and Urban Development	http://www.hud.gov
Library of Congress	http://www.loc.gov
Military Services	http://yahoo.com/government/military
National Aeronautics and Space Administration	http://www.nasa.gov
National Institutes of Health	http://www.nih.gov
Postal Service	http://www.usps.gov
Social Security Administration	http://www.ssa.gov
Supreme Court	http://www.uscourts.gov
US House of Representatives	http://www.house.gov
US Senate	Website to be available in Fall '96
Veterans Affairs	http://www.va.gov
White House	http://www.whitehouse.gov

Getting Connected

A big part of getting settled in, no matter where you live, is getting connected to local services. This chapter tells you how to get wired in to the basic utilities and services you will need to run your home—telephone, cable television, natural gas, electricity, trash and recycling, and water and sewer—in the various jurisdictions within the DC metropolitan area. It also helps you connect to the major outlets of information—the other type of power on which Washington runs. Local papers, magazines, newsstands and broadcast media are covered, as well as phone numbers to help to access the Internet.

WIRING IN

There is nothing particularly unusual about the utilities available in the Washington area—other than, perhaps, the fact that setting them up may seem more bureaucratic than elsewhere. The best advice here is to know what you want done and to call early to make the arrangements. Installation of many services tends to be on an "8 to 12" or "1 to 5" schedule and you will most likely have to be at home at least half a day. The companies are working hard to meet customer requirements, but with the area's dense and transient population, there is usually more than enough for them to do.

Telephone Service

To set up residential phone service, call your local **Bell Atlantic** office. If you do not have a credit history you will be asked to give them a deposit. The phone company will generally connect your service within a few business days. Phone numbers, for both English and Spanish, are listed here. You can also reach Bell Atlantic at **http://www.ba.com** on the Internet.

District of Columbia	202-954-6263 (English) 202-392-2146 (Spanish)
Maryland	301-954-6260 (English) 301-595-4652 (Spanish)
Virginia	703-876-7000 (English) 703-280-4652 (Spanish)

LOCAL AREA CODES

Although Washington (202), Northern Virginia (703) and neighboring parts of Maryland (301) have different area codes, all calls within a 30-mile radius of the Washington Monument are local. You do not have to dial "1" but you have to use the area code. Calls to the rest of the states of Maryland (410) and Virginia (804 to the east and 540 to the west) are long distance.

Cable Television

A number of companies, listed here, provide local cable television service, depending on where you live. With the recent changes in legislation governing the telecommunications industry, there could be lots more in the near future.

DC

District Cablevision	202-635-5100

Maryland

Montgomery County

Cable TV Montgomery	301-424-4400

Prince George's County

Metro Vision	301-499-1980
Multivision	301-731-5560

Virginia

Alexandria

Jones Intercable	703-823-3000

Arlington County

Cable TV Arlington	703-841-7700

Fairfax County

Media General Cable	703-378-8411

Natural Gas

If your apartment or house needs gas service turned on or off, call **Washington Gas** at 703-750-1000. The gas company serves all three area jurisdictions.

Electricity

To turn on the electricity, residents in the District and Maryland should call **Potomac Electric Company (PEPCO)** at 202-833-7500. Northern Virginia residents can contact **Virginia Power (VEPCO)** at 703-934-9670. At press time, **PEPCO** and **Baltimore Gas and Electric (BG&E)** have agreed to merge and are awaiting state and federal regulatory approval. The resulting utility, **Constellation Energy Corporation**, will cover DC and Maryland.

Trash

Each jurisdiction handles trash pick-up differently. Based on where your new home is located, contact the appropriate number. In most apartment and condo buildings, trash pick up is handled on a building-wide basis, so check with the management company to find out if you have to do anything on your own.

District of Columbia	202-727-4825

Maryland

Montgomery County	301-217-2410
Prince George's County	301-952-4750

Virginia

Alexandria	703-751-5130
Arlington County	703-358-6570
Fairfax City	703-385-7995
Fairfax County	703-550-3481

Recycling

In the Washington area, both the local governments and private businesses arrange for recycling. This is the best way to dispose of newspapers and plastic and glass containers. The specifics vary by jurisdiction, so call the appropriate number from the list below to find out what is available in your part of town. In condo and apartment buildings, the management company usually arranges for recycling, but there are a number of local residents who—being more "green" than others—go the extra mile.

District of Columbia	202-727-5856

Maryland

Montgomery County	301-217-2870
Prince George's County	301-925-5963

Virginia

Alexandria	703-751-5872
Arlington County	703-358-6570
Fairfax City	703-385-7995
Fairfax County	703-324-5052

Water and Sewer

If you live in a private home, you will have to make arrangements to set up the connection to the water and sewer services. The list here will get you started. Again, for condo and apartment buildings, you probably won't have to make your own arrangements.

District of Columbia	202-727-5696

Maryland

Montgomery County	301-699-4000
Prince George's County	301-206-8000

NEWS BY PHONE

Free telephone information services are available at 202-334-9000, courtesy of the *Washington Post*. Dial the number then enter the extension for type of information you want. A sampling . . .

AP News	5000
Abridged version of the news	5100
Associated Press financial news	3002
Stock Quotations	2000
Sports Scores	4100

Virginia

Alexandria	703-549-7080
Arlington County	703-358-3636
Fairfax City	703-385-7915
Fairfax County	703-698-5800

STAYING INFORMED

As the nation's capital and as a major international city, there is no shortage of sources for news and information in and around the Washington area. The major "local" papers have a global scope and one of them, the *Washington Post* is considered one of the country's major national dailies. On television, it is sometimes hard to tell the local news from the networks' national broadcasts out of New York. In addition to the major print and broadcast media, the number—and quality—of local newspapers, magazines and television and radio stations is increasing. Finally, Washington media and information sources cater to the area's international population, with a number of newsstands that sell local, national and international publications. There also are a number of international television and radio programs—in just about every language and for just about every culture.

Newspapers

In the Washington area there are two major dailies—the *Washington Post* and the *Washington Times*—in addition to a number of regional and specialized newspapers.

The Washington Post

The *Washington Post* is the area's major newspaper and one of the best in the country. It offers its readers a broad perspective on current events both inside and outside the Beltway. Its Federal Page covers the latest news— and scandals—from the Hill. Many area residents rely on Friday's Weekend section for its listings of the city's social, cultural and entertainment events. While the *Post* has a well-deserved reputation for national and political coverage, its neighborhood reporting is not as comprehensive. You may want to consider a local daily or weekly to keep tabs on your community. Subscription rates for the *Post* run approximately $10 a month. To arrange for home delivery call the paper at 202-334-6100. You can also set yourself up to access the *Post* on-line, through their Digital Ink service. For information, call 1-800-510-5104.

The Washington Times

The Rev. Sun Myung Moon's Unification Church funds this newspaper, although most people feel that the paper reflects extreme political conservatism rather than the Rev. Moon's theology. Its layout is flashier and more colorful than its better-known rival (the *Post*) and it offers good coverage of local politics and sports. Subscription rates are about $8 a month; call 202-636-3333 for home delivery.

USA Today

The national newspaper, *USA Today*, is published Monday through Friday by Gannett Co., Inc., headquartered in Arlington, VA. The paper covers news from across the nation in capsule form and in full color. Subscriptions cost about $13 a month. Subscription and general information is available at 1-800-USA-0001.

The Journal Newspapers

The Journal Newspapers, Inc. publishes six county-wide papers in Maryland and Virginia—*Alexandria Journal, Arlington Journal, Fairfax Journal, Montgomery Journal, Prince George's Journal* and *Prince William Journal*. The full-color papers are published Monday through Friday. The minimum three-month subscription costs $17. Call for home delivery at 703-560-4000. You can reach the Journal Newspapers at **http://www.infi.net/journal** on the Internet.

Specialized Newspapers

In an attempt to satisfy the information needs of various constituencies within the local population, a number of independent specialized newspapers are available throughout the area.

Washington's weekly *City Paper* (202-332-2100) does an excellent job covering local news and cultural events, particularly the arts. Well-known for its candid features on Washington phenomena and personalities, the *City Paper* has a steady following. You can pick up the latest *City Paper* on Thursdays at Metro stations and many District stores and less formal restaurants, such as coffee shops and carry outs. Best of all, it is free, and it is a rare example of getting much more than you pay for!

On the Hill, *Roll Call* helps congressional staffers keep up with the latest news. This biweekly newspaper (appearing on Monday and Thursday) covers Congress on much the same level that other community papers cover their neighborhoods. A year's subscription (96 issues) costs $210; call the paper at 202-289-4900.

LIBRARIES

**American University,
Bender Library**
202-885-3200

**Catholic University,
Mullen Memorial Library**
202-319-5077

**George Washington
University, Gelman Library**
202-994-6558

**Georgetown University,
Lauinger Library**
202-687-7452

**Historical Society of
Washington**
202-785-2068

Library of Congress
202-707-5000

**Martin Luther King
Memorial Library**
202-727-1111

National Archives
202-501-5402

**National Geographic
Society Library**
202-857-7783

**University of the District
of Columbia**
202-282-3091

The *Washington Blade*, another free weekly, is the newspaper of Washington's gay and lesbian community. This paper is especially helpful to interested newcomers with its directory of gay professionals and community resources. The *Blade* is available in a number of area shops and restaurants; for more information, call 202-797-7000.

There are many free neighborhood newspapers around to keep residents in touch with community news and issues. Examples include the *Georgetowner, Cleveland Park 20008, Hill Rag*, the *InTowner, Washington Citizen, McLean Providence Journal* and *Arlington Courier.* Check the local phone book for phone numbers and keep an eye out for copies in local shops and restaurants.

Many specialized papers cater to Washington's various ethnic and religious groups. The *Washington Afro-American* (202-332-0080) and *Washington Informer* (202-561-4100) cover news and topics of interest to the African-American community. Washington's sizable Hispanic community is chronicled in the pages of *Tiempo Latino* (202-986-0511) and *El Progonero* (301-853-4504). The *Washington Jewish Week* (301-230-2222) follows the area's Jewish community and the *Korean Times* (202-722-5400) provides news to a growing Korean population.

The monthly *Sports Focus* (301-670-6717) covers amateur and professional sports in the DC area. In addition to several feature articles, the paper includes listings and phone numbers for all area sports organizations and clubs. *Sports Focus* is available at over 1,200 sports-related sites in the Baltimore-Washington area; annual subscriptions are available for $24.95.

Recreation News (202-965-6960) is a monthly recreation publication devoted to providing government employees with the facts on Washington weekend entertainment and road trips. Copies are available at any government building.

Other Print Media

In addition to the national, regional and specialized newspapers, Washington has no shortage of other options for interesting and informative print media. The city is covered in depth in its own city magazine, the *Washingtonian*. This and other magazines—on virtually every topic imaginable—are available at newsstands all over town.

Washingtonian

Washingtonian, a glossy monthly magazine, contains feature articles and in-depth interviews with Washington's movers and shakers as well as restaurant reviews, Washington trivia, the occasional exposé and a gossip column. *Washingtonian* is known for its frequent lists of the area's best restaurants and entertainment. Subscription information is available at 202-331-0715. You can reach *Washingtonian Online*, "the electronic magazine Washington lives by," at **http://www.Infi.net.Washmag** on the Internet.

Area Newsstands

If you are in the mood to read something new, you don't have to go far to satisfy the desire. Newsstands can be found in convenience and grocery stores and pharmacies, and even in some of the area's coffee shops. While these smaller newsstands don't offer as much breadth as the real newsstands, they are certainly readily available.

When you want the real thing, turn to one of the area's larger bookstores, such as **Borders**, **Barnes & Noble** and **Crown**. For a special treat, you can go to one of the major area newsstands offering a wide range of domestic and international newspapers and periodicals. The **Newsroom** (202-332-1489) is the best of its kind. You will find it at the corner of Connecticut Ave. and S St. NW, just north of Dupont Circle. The store offers an array of national and international newspapers as well as magazines, scholarly journals, foreign language textbooks and bilingual dictionaries. There is also the **American International Newsstand** at 1825 Eye St. NW (202-223-2526) and **One Stop News** (202-872-1577) at the corner of Pennsylvania Ave. and 20th St. NW. **Trover Books**, on the Hill at 21 Pennsylvania Ave. SE (202-547-2665), carries a wide selection of domestic newspapers.

Broadcast Media

The Washington area has something for everyone when it comes to broadcast media. Well-connected to national networks and to international sources of information, the local broadcast media seems limitless. Listed here you will find a sampling of the television channels and radio stations available. Tune in to your local papers and flip channels and stations to see what else is around.

Television

In addition to the national networks and Public Broadcasting stations, listed below for easy reference, there is a world of programming available through cable television service providers. Refer to the section on Cable Television earlier in this chapter.

Channel 4	WRC	NBC		Channel 26	WETA	PBS
Channel 5	WTTG	FOX		Channel 32	WHMM	PBS
Channel 7	WJLA	ABC		Channel 56	WNVC	
Channel 9	WUSA	CBS		(International Programming)		
Channel 20	WDCA	UPN				
Channel 22	WMPT	PBS				

Radio

Washington area radio stations have something for every listening taste. Listed here is a selection of the most popular local stations.

570	AM	WGMS	Classical, Sports
630	AM	WMAL	News, Talk, Sports
980	AM	WWRC	Talk
1030	AM	WNTL	International
1120	AM	WUST	New World Radio, International, Multicultural
1500	AM	WTOP	News
1540	AM	WMDO	Latin
88.5	FM	WAMU	National Public Radio
90.1	FM	WDCU	Jazz, Talk, Gospel
90.9	FM	WETA	Classical, National Public Radio, American Public Radio
94.7	FM	WARW	Classic Rock
97.1	FM	WASH	Adult Contemporary
98.7	FM	WMZQ	Country
99.1	FM	WHFS	Modern Rock
99.5	FM	WEBR	Adult Contemporary
101.1	FM	WWDC	Rock
103.5	FM	WGMS	Classical
105.9	FM	WJZW	Jazz
106.7	FM	WJFK	Jazz, Talk
107.3	FM	WRQX	Adult Contemporary

The Information Highway

These days, Washingtonians are increasingly well-connected and well-informed electronically as well as through print and broadcast media. The major on-line services and Internet access companies are becoming part of the local household vocabulary. To help you get connected, or reconnected, here are several names and numbers for the major service providers.

On-Line Services

Several companies offer commercial on-line information services, typically including access to the Internet.

America Online	1-800-827-6364
CompuServe	1-800-848-8990
Digital Ink	1-800-510-5104
Microsoft Network	1-800-386-5550
Prodigy	1-800-776-3449

Internet Service Providers

In addition to using an on-line service to gain access to the Internet, you can travel a more direct route by connecting through an Internet service provider. Some of the major ones are listed here.

AT&T WorldNet Service	1-800-967-5363
GNN	1-800-827-6364
PSiNET	1-800-774-0852
Digital Express Group	1-800-969-9090
Erol's	703-321-8000

There are a number of interesting Internet resources available to give you more information about the Washington area. Listed here are some highlights.

A comprehensive national tourism database includes information about Washington:
http://yahoo.com/Regional/U_S_States/Washington_D_C_/

Washington, DC has its own official website at:
http://www.dchomepage.net

A commercial service provides access to another DC—Digital City:
http://www.digitalcity.com

You can also use these two "launch pads" to see what else is out there in DC cyberspace:
http://dcpages.ari.net/
http://www.washweb.net:8000/

There is also a free local e-zine (electronic magazine), called *dc.story,* published on the Internet. This new media outlet is the largest moderated opinion newsletter in DC, and is a great place to go to find out what your neighbors are thinking about current issues facing the city. It carries event listings and classified ads.

Send an e-mail message to Jeffrey Itell at Story@intr.net to subscribe.

FOR INTERNATIONAL NEWCOMERS

Relocating is an anxiety-producing endeavor, presenting challenges for just about everyone. International newcomers, however, have the extra challenge of making the transition to an entirely new country, with language and cultural differences. As a major world capital, Washington, DC has a vast international community and a wealth of international resources. The key is getting the newcomers in touch with the appropriate resources.

Throughout the book, foreign language phone numbers are included where available. In the chapter on Resources, there is a comprehensive listing of foreign embassies. And here you can read about two special cross-cultural services to help you out.

Hello! America, Inc., a multilingual firm in Washington, DC, provides personal orientation services for international newcomers. They understand the unique requirements of international relocation and can provide information on both public and private resources to assist with housing, transportation, shopping, schools, English instruction, medical care, money matters and much more. Their books, *Hello! Washington* and *Hello! USA*, handbooks on everyday living for international residents, are available through their office or in bookstores, and are provided free to participants in their orientation programs. Contact Hello! America, Inc., 5310 Connecticut Ave. NW #18, Washington, DC 20015 (202-966-9385).

Newcomer's Almanac offers publications by cross-cultural specialists. Their monthly newsletter features information, advice and cultural interpretation for international families, couples and singles. It includes practical tips and thoughtful analysis of American culture; how cross-cultural transitions affect women, men, children and families; what to expect—and what not to expect—from schools and teachers; idioms and language oddities; and much more. For information, contact Newcomer's Almanac, PO Box 1153, Brookline, MA 02146 (1-617-566-2227).

A good suggestion for international newcomers is to make friends soon, and to find one who can serve as your "cultural informant," a person who will take you shopping and help you learn the subtleties of daily life in the Washington metropolitan area.

Shopping

With all the shopping options in the Washington area, you might think that Washingtonians coined the expression, "When the going gets tough, the tough go shopping." At any rate, even during tough economic times, Washington still goes shopping. This chapter clues you into the local shopping scene— with information about everything from buying groceries for tonight's dinner to finding a specialized nut or bolt at an old fashioned hardware store. In between, you will find details on gourmet and specialty food markets—including ones representing a wide range of international cuisines—as well as outlets for furniture, housewares, and new and used books. Special features of Washington shopping are also described, from the freshest piece of fish to the finest 18th century mahogany bureau. And, so you won't get caught wearing the right outfit at the wrong time, major stores for clothes shopping are listed with key locations.

GROCERY, GOURMET AND SPECIALTY FOOD STORES

As you would expect in any large metropolitan area, Washington and the Virginia and Maryland suburbs have all kinds of places for groceries and both gourmet and specialty food items. You can shop at any of a number of major chains, as well as at discount grocery stores. Beyond the main stores, there are several gourmet and specialty chains competing for the attention of local residents. In recent years, a number of bakeries have set up shop throughout the area. Several neighborhoods have food co-ops, usually offering natural foods at reasonable prices and often trading discounts for time spent working in the store. Finally, in keeping with the international flair of the Washington area, there is no shortage of small international markets—representing cuisines from literally all over the world.

Major Grocery Store Chains

For typical every day groceries and staples for the home, you can turn to the two major grocery store chains, Giant and Safeway. Virtually every suburban community has at least one or the other and most have both. In the District, Safeway is more prominent than Giant, but you can find either one if you look. In addition, there are some "discount" grocery stores, such as Shoppers Food Warehouse and Food Lion. To compete with these somewhat lower priced stores, the main chains frequently run sales and coupon book specials. With good planning you can save lots on your monthly grocery bill, without having to run around town for the lowest price on each item.

BUYING BOOZE

Each of the surrounding jurisdictions has its own regulations with regard to the sale of liquor. Here is a brief summary.

DC
Liquor stores are privately owned; beer and wine are available in some grocery stores.

Maryland
Montgomery County: County-owned and operated liquor stores; beer and wine are not available in grocery stores. Montgomery is the only county in the entire country that controls the sale of liquor.

Prince George's County: Privately owned liquor stores; beer and wine are not available in grocery stores.

Virginia
State owned and operated liquor stores (ABC liquor stores); beer and wine are available in grocery stores.

Giant

Giant, one of the two largest grocery chains serving the area, caters mostly to suburbanites. The Gourmet Giants offer a somewhat greater number of specialty items, although at Giant, "gourmet" usually means bigger, not necessarily better. Giant's Someplace Special, in McLean at 1445 Chain Bridge Rd. (703-448-0800), is truly "gourmet." Every Giant has a salad bar and an ATM. Most of the newer stores also have in-store bakeries, pharmacies and seafood departments. Giant's Special Discounts aisles offer bulk items at low prices.

Safeway

If you live in the District, you will probably frequent a Safeway. Several stores are located in the District and many more can be found in the suburbs. The Safeway in Georgetown at 1855 Wisconsin Ave. NW (202-333-3223), known as a place to meet people and hence called the "Social Safeway," boasts the largest sales volume of any Safeway in the country. The "Secret Safeway" hides away just off upper Wisconsin Ave. at 4203 Davenport St. NW (202-364-0290). Like Giant, all stores offer check cashing and ATMs. Two Townhouse stores provide service to the District—in Dupont Circle at 20th and S Sts. NW (202-483-3908) and in the West End at 21st and L Sts. NW (202-659-8784).

Gourmet and Specialty Chains

If you are looking for something special and can't find it at either Giant or Safeway, you have lots of other choices. The Washington area offers a large number of specialty shops, including several gourmet and specialty chains. Each of these chains has its own claim to fame, and you will find that many of them foster a great deal of loyalty among their regular shoppers.

Bread & Circus

Bread & Circus (B&C), owned by the Austin-based Whole Foods chain, opened its first area store in Georgetown at 2323 Wisconsin Ave. NW (202-333-5393) in January 1996, and a second store in Arlington, VA at 2700 Wilson Blvd. (703-527-6596) two months later in March. B&C,

after which Fresh Fields is modeled, features a signature organic produce department occupying 20% of the floor space and an in-store bakery. They also sell naturally raised meat, chicken and fish; specialty cheeses; and wine and beer. The store has an espresso and juice bar and a restaurant area featuring food cooked in a wood-burning oven and rotisserie. B&C offers a large bulk-foods department including culinary and medicinal herbs. Three levels of monitored underground parking are available, with groceries delivered to your car. A new store is planned for Vienna by the fall of 1996, with future sites in both Virginia and Maryland.

Dean & DeLuca

The New York institution, Dean & DeLuca (D&D), has migrated south to Washington. Its flagship location is the Georgetown Market House at 3276 M St. NW (202-342-2500), a historically preserved building that has endured several failed incarnations in recent years. Its overwhelming popularity should ensure that D&D will make a little history of its own, with its great selection of gourmet meats and cheeses, fresh vegetables and bakery items. The 30-minute free parking offered to any customer making over $10 in purchases (not a difficult task) makes D&D especially appreciated in parking-scarce Georgetown. D&D has opened another café in DC in the Warner Theatre building at 1299 Pennsylvania Ave. NW (202-628-8155).

Fresh Fields

One of the area's fastest growing chains, Fresh Fields' supermarkets sell "good-for-you foods." The good-for-you list includes organic produce as well as meat, seafood, dairy products, gourmet and vegetarian prepared foods, natural health care products, and environment-friendly household goods. Prices lower than at other gourmet supermarkets will please your wallet. In early 1996, Fresh Fields opened its first DC store in Tenleytown at 4530 40th St. NW (202-237-5800), where one-hour parking validation is available. In Maryland there are stores in Rockville at 1649 Rockville Pike (301-984-4880), Bethesda at 5225 River Rd. (301-984-4860), and Gaithersburg at 480 N. Frederick Ave. (301-527-1700). In Virginia, you will find Fresh Fields in Tysons Corner at 7511 Leesburg Pike (703-448-1600), Springfield at 8402 Old Keene Mill Rd. (703-644-2500), and Annandale at 6548 Little River Tpk. (703-914-0400), and in Reston's Plaza America at 1160 Plaza America Dr. (703-736-0600).

ETHNIC FOOD STORES

Americana Grocery (Latin American)
1813 Columbia Rd. NW
202-265-7455
8541 Piney Branch Rd., Silver Spring
301-495-0864
6128-30 Columbia Pike, Falls Church
703-671-9625

Assal Middle East Supermarket
118 Maple Ave. W., Vienna
703-281-2248
6039 Leesburg Pike, Falls Church
703-578-3232

Daruma (Japanese)
Talbot Center, 1045 Rockville Pike,
Rockville
301-881-6966

Eden Supermarket (Vietnamese)
6763 Wilson Blvd., Falls Church
703-532-4950

German Gourmet
7185 Lee Hwy., Falls Church
703-534-1908

Indian Spices and Gifts
3901 Wilson Blvd., Arlington
703-522-0149

Litteri's Italian Grocery
517 Morse St. NE, Washington
202-544-0183

Lotte Oriental Supermarket (Korean)
11790 Parklawn Dr., Rockville
301-881-3355
3250 Old Lee Hwy., Fairfax
703-352-1600

Maxim (Chinese)
460 Hungerford Dr., Rockville
301-279-0110

Mediterranean Bakery (Middle Eastern)
352 S. Pickett St., Alexandria
703-751-1702

Merkato Market (Ethiopian)
2116 18th St. NW
202-483-9499

Muskan (Indian)
956 Thayer Ave., Silver Spring
301-588-0331

Red Apple Market (West Indian)
7645 New Hampshire Ave.,
Langley Park
301-434-1810

Marvelous Market

In addition to 12 different types of bread, Marvelous Market sells cheeses, sausages, pastas, homemade jams and other gourmet carry out items. On busy Sunday mornings, be prepared to wait. Marvelous Market has locations at 5035 Connecticut Ave. NW (202-686-4040), 1514 Connecticut Ave. NW (202-986-2222), 4832 Bethesda Ave. in Bethesda (301-986-0555), and 9889 Georgetown Pike in Great Falls (703-759-5666).

Sutton Place Gourmet

Sutton Place Gourmet specializes in the exotic and the esoteric. This chain flies in produce daily from all over the world. Its managers boast that "Sutton Place is the only place you will be able to find fresh, hand-picked raspberries during a snow storm." While only the very well-off can afford to buy all of their groceries here, Sutton Place is great for picking up special ingredients, coffees, cheeses, meats and fish. Sutton Place has three stores in Northwest DC, at 3201 New Mexico Ave. (202-363-5800), at 4872 Massachusetts Ave. (202-966-1740), and at 1647 20th St. NW in Dupont Circle (202-588-9876). There is one in Bethesda at 10323 Old Georgetown Rd. (301-564-3100); and two in Virginia, in Old Town Alexandria at 600 Franklin St. (703-549-6611), and in McLean at 6808 Old Dominion Dr. (703-734-6901). Future sites are planned in McLean and Reston, VA.

Bakeries

Many Washingtonians get their daily bread—and pastries, muffins, cakes and pies—at one of the many relatively new bakeries in the area. Some of the bakeries also offer fresh-brewed coffee and café tables where you can gather with friends for a delicious break.

Bakers Place

Excellent freshly baked breads, scones and muffins are the specialty at Bakers Place. Get there early in the morning for the breakfast items as they sell out early. Stores are located in the District at Union Station-Metro Market Place (202-898-2010) and in Maryland at 15 Wisconsin Cir. in Chevy Chase (301-652-0080), at 3836 International Dr. in Silver Spring (301-598-1100), and in Kentland Square on Great Seneca Hwy. in Gaithersburg (301-417-0797). Virginia residents are served by stores in Herndon at 13340 E. Franklin Farm Rd. (703-742-8405), Fairfax at 9558 Main St. (703-425-2144), McLean at 1386 Chain Bridge Rd. (703-790-1700), and Reston at 1424 Reston Pkwy. (703-904-0401).

Breads Unlimited

The owner of Breads Unlimited at 6914 Arlington Rd. in Bethesda (301-656-2340) oversees the making of his sourdough bread like a brew master caring for his beers. In addition, all the two dozen different breads baked there are fat and cholesterol free. A second location, called the New Yorker Bakery at 8313 Grubb Rd. in Silver Spring (301-585-8585), makes its fresh bagels in front of an appreciative audience.

WHERE TO BUY FISH

The freshest fish in town is available at the Maine Avenue Wharf, down along the Waterfront at 1100 Maine Ave. SW. You can stroll around the market and view the dozens of different fish literally at your feet—most of the stalls are built into large boats on the water and the trays of fish float just a few inches from the sidewalk. At night, this fish market resembles a carnival or small fair, with bright lights illuminating the rows of open stalls as groups of people stroll around and the fish sellers call out to get their attention. The Wharf is open everyday from 7:30 a.m. to 9:30 p.m.

Firehook Bakery and Coffee House

In keeping with the traditional feel of its Old Town Alexandria neighborhood, the Firehook Bakery and Coffee House at 106 North Lee St. (703-519-8020) bakes its breads in a 17-foot-diameter wood-burning oven. The bread is baked with a thick crust much like bread was made 100 years ago. Other special features include twice-monthly poetry readings and complete breakfasts on weekends with quiche, French toast, fresh juice and Italian sodas. The original Old Town location is complemented by a second shop at 1909 Q St. NW in Dupont Circle (202-588-9296).

Reeves

You only need to know two words about Reeves bakery—strawberry pie. This Downtown bakery at 1306 G St. NW (202-628-6350) has operated for more than a century and is famous for many products beyond its delicious pies. Reeves also offers a selection of pastries and other baked goods as well as a two-floor restaurant serving sandwiches and other light fare.

Uptown Bakers

Cleveland Park residents are fortunate to have this bread bakery right in their own neighborhood. From its prolific ovens, Uptown Bakers at 3313 Connecticut Ave. NW (202-362-6262) offers 17 types of bread, including sourdough ficelle, killer toast (perfect for breakfast), and olive bread. They also feature no-fat breads which are excellent.

Food Co-ops—Food for People, Not for Profit

Co-ops are cooperatively owned food stores. In theory, they are owned by their customers, thereby taking away the incentive for profit. While few co-ops in today's economy are truly cooperatively owned, these stores generally do offer lower prices on organic products and bulk foods such as nuts, grains, beans, pasta and flour.

Bethesda Co-op

The Bethesda Co-op at 6500 Seven Locks Rd. (301-320-2530) sells organic and commercial produce, bulk foods, shampoos and household cleaners. Six hours of work at the co-op each month entitles you to a 20% discount. To get there by Metro, take the Red Line to Bethesda and change to a Ride-On bus.

Glut Food Co-op

For over 20 years, the Glut Food Co-op at 4005 34th St. in Mt. Rainier (301-779-1978) has been providing natural food in a not-for-profit setting. On most days, they also have baked breads. Glut opens each day at 10:00 a.m. They close at 7:00 p.m. Saturday through Wednesday, at 8:00 p.m. on Thursday and Friday, and at 5:00 p.m. on Sunday.

Takoma Park Silver Spring Co-op

Takoma Park Silver Spring Co-op at 623 Sligo Ave. in Silver Spring (301-588-6093) packs plenty of products into a small space. Discounts are available in exchange for volunteer work. This co-op can be reached by the Metro Red Line to Silver Spring and from there, the Ride-On bus.

Uncommon Market

The Uncommon Market at 1041 So. Edgewood St. in Arlington (703-521-2667), a co-op in the true sense of the word, is owned by its 3,900 members. You can also become a part-owner for an investment of $200. Owners receive a 5% discount on their groceries, and a 15% discount on case lots. If you work at the co-op, you can get a further discount—three hours a month translates into an additional 15% off.

FURNITURE

Setting up a new home in the Washington area is easy, thanks to the many choices available for furniture and housewares. You can choose the lower-cost option of buying furniture that you have to put together yourself or you can buy ready made furniture in just about any price range. You also have other options, such as selecting from local collections of used furniture, shopping the area and the surrounding countryside for fine antiques, and even renting furniture if you don't want to buy it. In addition to furniture stores, Washington offers a virtually unlimited number of places to shop for housewares and decorative items.

Some Assembly Required

If you are looking to economize on your furniture budget, the "you buy/you build" approach may be just for you. In general, the furniture is relatively simple to assemble and can make for a fun weekend project, especially if you have someone on hand to help out. The largest choices of unassembled furniture are found at Door Store and Ikea, although you will find other places in the phone book.

Door Store

Door Store sells contemporary home furnishings at reasonable prices. Their large selection includes furniture for inside the home as well as outside on the patio or deck. The location in Baileys Crossroads at 5520 Leesburg Pike (703-820-3262) has the largest inventory. A second Virginia store is at Tysons Corner Pike 7 Plaza (703-556-0414). In Maryland, residents can shop at the store in Montgomery Mall (301-365-4425) or in Rockville (301-881-1320). Furniture shoppers without wheels will find convenient store locations in Dupont Circle at 1718 Connecticut Ave. NW (202-232-1322) and in Friendship Heights at 5225 Wisconsin Ave. NW (202-244-0104). If you are looking for bargains, try the Door Store Outlet (202-333-3351)—it's in Georgetown, at the corner of K St. and Wisconsin Ave. NW, just under the Whitehurst Freeway.

Ikea

Most everyone will recommend the warehouse-sized Ikea in Potomac Mills at Exit 156 off I-95, south of Washington. Ikea (703-494-4532) sells a wide range of home furnishings and is best known for its put-it-together-yourself, Scandinavian-style furniture. If you live in the Maryland suburbs, a more convenient Ikea location for you may be the one at White Marsh Mall (410-931-5400) north of Baltimore at I-95 Exit 67B. Ikea receives accolades for prices, not quality or service. If long-term durability is a concern for you, consider looking elsewhere.

Ready Made

For those who want to buy furniture already assembled, many traditional stores can meet your needs. Naturally, major department stores have furniture departments where you can expect to find quality furniture at higher prices. Unless you come across a good sale, though, bargains can be few and far between. If you can afford the time, shop around and watch the newspapers and Sunday circulars for specials.

Scan

While Scan Contemporary Furniture seems to many to be an upscale Ikea, it has in fact been around quite a bit longer. Scan sells some assembly-required furniture at prices competitive with Ikea's, but most of Scan's furniture is well-made, pre-assembled and priced to match. Scan's largest store is in Loehmann's Plaza at 7311 Arlington Blvd (703-573-0100). There is another Virginia store in Springfield (703-644-0500) and Maryland stores in Columbia (410-730-1060), Silver Spring (301-942-0600) and Greenbelt (301-474-8880).

Marlo

Marlo boasts that it sells more furniture in the area than anyone else. They simplify their maze-like showroom by organizing each aisle according to style (traditional, contemporary, Italian, etc.). Beware of their expensive delivery and set-up charges—as much as 7% of the total cost of the furniture, before tax. The District store, at 901 Seventh St. NW (202-842-0100), is within walking distance of the Gallery Pl.-Chinatown Metro. Suburban Maryland stores are located in Laurel at 13450 Baltimore Ave. (301-419-3400), in Forestville at 7801 Marlboro Pike (301-735-2000), and in Rockville at 725 Rockville Pike (301-738-9000). The Virginia store is in Alexandria at Edsall Rd. and I-395 (703-941-0800).

The Hub

The Hub, with its main location at 430 Hungerford Dr. in Rockville (301-762-6164) has a string of 19 stores along the Washington-Baltimore corridor. These furniture centers carry contemporary and traditional styles for living, dining and bedroom areas. Call to find the store nearest you, or check the *Washington Post* for their frequent advertisements.

Other Options

Crate & Barrel, a popular housewares store in the area, features bedroom, dining and living room furniture on the second level of their store at 4820 Massachusetts Ave. NW. (202-364-6500—Furniture Dept.). The **Container Store** specializes in home office furniture, as well as storage solution systems for the entire home including the kitchen and closets. Stores are located at 1601 Rockville Pike (301-770-1800) in Rockville, and at 8508 Leesburg Pike (703-883-2112) in Vienna.

Antique Shops

Antiques are one of the many hidden treasures of the Washington area. Collected from all over the mid-Atlantic states and the Carolinas, beautiful antique furniture and collectibles can be found in local shops. The best buys are traditional, early American style furniture and mahogany pieces from the 1930s and 1940s. You can find solid oak, cherry or mahogany pieces—such as bureaus, tables and desks—that have already withstood the test of time and become more beautiful with age. Even better, they will cost about the same as or only a little more than what you would pay for new pieces, often less well made, at local furniture stores.

Getting the best deals requires time and effort. Be prepared to negotiate, and always turn down the first offered price. Antique shops in the immediate area are generally more expensive than those in the Maryland or Virginia countryside. The farther out you travel, the better the deal.

PUBLICATIONS

Specialized newspapers on mid-Atlantic antiquing events are also available on a complimentary basis at any dealer shop or through paid subscriptions direct from the publisher.

Antiques & Auction News
Route 230 West
PO Box 500
Mount Joy, PA 17552
1-717-653-4300

The Mid-Atlantic Antiques Magazine
PO Box 908
Henderson, NY 27536
1-800-326-3894

The New York Antique Almanac
The New York Eye Publishing Co.
PO Box 2400
New York, NY 10021
1-212-988-2700

Consider combining antique shopping with a leisurely day trip in the country. If you are willing to go as far as some of the small towns in North Carolina or West Virginia, you stand an even greater chance of finding a good piece of furniture at an excellent price—that is where the antique dealers themselves go to shop.

Closer in, you will find that the metropolitan DC area is rich in antiques with both numerous individual shops and several antique malls. In Northwest DC, antique shops can be found on 18th St. in Adams Morgan, along M St. and Wisconsin Ave. in Georgetown, and on Connecticut Ave., starting at Dupont Circle and going north to the Van Ness area. In Maryland, concentrations of antique shops can be found in Kensington, Olney, Hagerstown, Frederick and Columbia. In Virginia, you will find them in Alexandria, Fairfax and Leesburg. Check the Yellow Pages for specific listings. You will also find directories of local antique dealers and announcements about upcoming expositions, fairs, shows and conventions at many shops.

You can also watch the local newspapers for special antique shows at fair grounds, convention centers, shopping malls, high schools, hotels, armories and churches. The Gaithersburg Fair Grounds in Maryland is noted for its many expositions throughout the year, featuring antiques, furniture, toys and dolls, glassware and other collectibles. Antiques can also be bought at estate or house sales. Check the *Washington Post* Home section on Thursdays or the daily classified ads.

Listed here are some of the unique antique villages located in historical settings, both nearby and just far enough away to make a memorable day trip. Call ahead to check hours of operation.

Antiques in the Maryland Suburbs

There are several centralized locations for antique shopping nearby in Maryland. In Old Town Kensington, you can shop at a place called **Antique Row** (301-949-2318). Along five city blocks you will find some 75 shops in historic Kensington's general stores, dating back to the early 1800s. Take the Beltway (I-95/I-495) to Exit #33 North for one and a half miles along Connecticut Ave. to a left turn on Howard Ave.

At **Olney Antique Village**, 16650 Georgia Ave. (301-570-9370) in Olney, some 50 antique dealers can be found in five interconnected buildings spanning across more than three acres. Olney is about 13 miles north of the Beltway and easy to reach. Get off the Beltway at Exit 31 North and follow Georgia Ave. (Route 97) through Wheaton and on to Olney.

You can shop at two antique malls for the travel time of one in Hagerstown, MD. **Antique Crossroads** (301-739-0858) offers 170 dealers and just next door, **Beaver Creek** has another 150. Take I-270 North to I-70 West to Exit 32A and go one mile.

Emporium Antiques (1-301-662-7099) at 112 E. Patrick St. in Frederick offers some 130 dealers under one roof. Take I-270 North to the Market St. Exit (Route 85) at Frederick. Go into downtown historic Frederick, turn right onto South St., then left onto Carroll St. to the parking lot and back entrance for Emporium Antiques.

A special treat is the **Columbia, Maryland Sunday Antique Market** (1-410-329-2188). From late April through October, more than 200 antique dealers come from near and far to display their wares in a free admission market held under the parking deck adjacent to the Columbia Mall, about half way between Washington, DC and Baltimore, MD. Take I-95 North off the Beltway (I-95/I-495) to the exit for Route 175 to Columbia.

Antiques in the Virginia Suburbs

Hundreds of charming small shops can be found in Old Town Alexandria, situated in historic buildings dating back to the 18th century. The shops are mixed in among restaurants and tea rooms, including the historic Gadsby's Tavern, frequented by George Washington and other statesmen of the period. From DC, take the George Washington Memorial Pkwy. past National Airport. The Parkway turns into Washington St. in Old Town. Turn left onto Queen St. and right on Lee St. to reach the general area where most of the shops are located. You can also take the Metro Blue Line to the King St. station.

Thieves Market (703-360-4200) at 8101 Richmond Hwy., in the southern end of Alexandria (well south of Old Town), is a true local landmark. This market advertises itself as the "Nation's Oldest Antiques Mall." Take the Beltway (I-95/I-495) to Exit 1 for Route 1 South, also known as Richmond Hwy. Go five miles and watch for Thieves Market on the left.

In the heart of historic Fairfax City, you will find 40 dealers clustered together in the **Fairfax Antique Mall** (703-591-8883) at 10334 Main St.

Take the Beltway (I-495) to Exit 6, for Route 236, Little River Turnpike, to the University Shopping Center.

The **Shops at Laws** in Manassas (1-703-330-9282) fill two malls at 7208 and 7217 Centreville Rd. Weekend auctions are held directly across the street and admission is free. Take the Beltway (I-495) to I-66 West to Exit 53 for Route 28 South to Centreville. Continue south for three and a half miles.

Day Trips

A popular outing for Washingtonians combines a drive in the local countryside with shopping at one of the area's antique villages. En route to these locations—or during any trip into the outlying counties—watch for signs advertising individual antique shops as well. Many small town and "country" residents sell antiques in a small storefront, out of their home, in a barn or other structure on their property.

Historic **New Market** is a unique 200-year old village nestled in the rolling hills of Maryland offering more than 30 individual antique shops within easy walking distance of each other. The delightful Village Tea Room is a perfect setting for lunch on a day trip to New Market. Take I-270 North to Exit 62 for Route I-70. New Market is about eight miles east of Frederick, MD. Call ahead for details at 1-301-865-3450.

Weaver's Antiques Mall (1-215-777-8535) is located at Antique Row on Route 222 in Sinking Spring, PA. More than 200 dealers feature such items as fine furniture, vintage clothing, linens, toys, jewelry, glasswear and restored lighting. Travel four miles north of the Pennsylvania Tpk., to Exit 21.

Historic **Main Street** in Ellicott City, MD is now occupied by more than 100 antique shops tucked into historic buildings flanking both sides of the street. Ellicott City is located on Route 29 between Washington and Baltimore. Take the Beltway (I-495/I-95) to Exit 29 for Route 29 North. Stay on Route 29 until you get to the Ellicott City Exit and turn right on Rogers Ave. to a dead end on Main St. Call 1-410-461-8700 for more information.

The historic **Savage Mill**, after which the quaint town of Savage Mill, MD is named, is a 19th century cotton mill, lovingly restored and converted into an antiques, art and craft center. Known as Antique Center I, II and III (301-369-4650), the spot offers about 225 dealers and a lunch room, a pleasant spot to rest and relax. Savage Mill, like Columbia and Ellicott City, is located between Washington and Baltimore. Take I-95 north to Route 32 East (Exit 38A) to Route 1 South. Turn right on Gorman Rd. and right again on Foundry St.

Other Options

If you like the low cost aspect of shopping at Door Store and Ikea but don't want to spend your free time assembling furniture, do not despair. There are several other options for furnishing your home in the Washington area. You can find used furniture at thrift shops and floor samples or previously rented items at clearance centers. This type of shopping can be very entertaining, and with a commitment of time and patience, you will be surprised at what you can end up with. In addition, you can rent just about anything, if that approach suits you better than buying.

Thrift Shops

Thrift shops are another great alternative for the truly budget-minded furniture shopper. The selection can be somewhat erratic and it may take time to find the right bargains. It helps to have a car on these shopping expeditions, because many of these shops do not deliver. Since so many people move in and out of the Washington area, the used furniture market is large and constantly replenished. Thrift shops near military bases can be a particularly good starting point.

Thrift Shops for Furniture Items

AMVETS
5944 George Palmer Hwy., Landover
301-925-4668

Columbia Pike Thrift Shop
4101 Columbia Pike, Arlington
703-521-3110

Fort Myer Thrift Shop
224 Forest Cir., Arlington
703-527-0664

Prevention of Blindness Thrift Shop
900 King St., Alexandria
703-683-2558

Salvation Army
6528 Little River Tpk., Alexandria
703-642-9270

St. Coletta Thrift Store
2919 Columbia Pike, Arlington
703-486-2362

Clearance Centers

Clearance centers provide another option, especially for those on tight budgets. Clearance centers sell discontinued furniture and housewares. **Hecht's Clearance Center** (703-354-1900) in Landmark Plaza, just off I-395 at the Duke St. West Exit, sells furniture, televisions and other housewares. All prices are 20% to 50% below retail. Hecht's has an

Some rental companies offer package deals to provide all of the basics for various apartment set-ups. Prices vary, but to give you an idea of what to expect, here is an example—for $99 a month, **Furniture Renters of America** at 2101 L St. NW (202-293-9400) offered to provide a "one-bedroom" package including a sofa, matching chair, cocktail and end tables, dining table with four chairs, bed (box spring, mattress and frame), chest of drawers, night table and two lamps.

automatic price reduction policy where prices are reduced 5% every 30 days.

You can purchase used rental furniture at various clearance centers in the suburbs. The best buys are at **Cort's Clearance Centers** at 3137 Pennsy Dr. in Landover, MD (301-773-3369) and 14130 Sullyfield Cir. in Chantilly, VA (703-818-2678).

Furniture Rentals

If you know that your stay in Washington will be brief, you may want to consider renting your furniture. Renting prevents many hassles, including what to do with your furniture when you move on. Most furniture rental stores have showrooms. Their salespeople can show you samples and discuss the details of price, length of lease, delivery and insurance. Renting furniture creates a pile of paperwork, including a credit application, a lease and insurance papers. Most rental companies require one month's rent as a security deposit and will deliver your furniture within three to five business days. Many places offer student discounts.

Although renting furniture can be enticing, be aware of the pitfalls. Get a quote for the entire price. Unlike rent for an apartment or house, furniture rentals are subject to tax. In addition to this, rental companies often charge for a fire damage waiver. Be sure to include these extras in your budget. If you already have renters' insurance, you do not need to pay the damage waiver fee—just ask your insurance agent to supply you with a certificate of coverage for the full value of the furniture.

Furniture Rental Outlets

AAA Furniture Rentals   703-354-2600
5710 A General Washington Dr., Alexandria

Aaron Rents Furniture   703-941-7195
5720 General Washington Dr., Alexandria

Cort Furniture Rental   202-223-9241
1100 New York Ave. NW

Furniture Renters of America   202-293-9400
2101 L St. NW

Beds and Futons

Its many outlets and aggressive advertising make **Mattress Discounters** easy to find. This local chain gained its prominence not just through advertising, but from its relatively low prices. They offset their $30 delivery charges by including a free frame with each purchase of a mattress and box spring. Call (1-800-666-2344) to find the store nearest you.

Several stores have the same prices as Mattress Discounters, but since they cannot afford the large advertising budgets they often get overlooked. Salespeople at these stores are always willing to make a deal. The **Market** at 3229 M St. NW (202-333-1234) in Georgetown sells mattresses, futons and carpeting. The **Bed Store** at 1100 King St. (703-549-8005) provides an excellent alternative for Alexandria residents.

Getting a futon rather than a bed can add much-needed room, particularly in an efficiency. Futons come in all sizes and you can purchase the mattresses alone or with a variety of adjustable frames. Washington has several futon dealers with very competitive prices. The two most popular ones in the suburbs are **Atlantic Futon** (703-893-9125) in Tysons Corner and **Futons by Shonin** in both Falls Church at 6138-E Arlington Blvd. (703-538-4603) and Takoma Park at 6915 Laurel Ave. (301-270-1036). The prices at **Ginza** in Dupont Circle at 1721 Connecticut Ave. NW (202-331-7991) tend to be slightly higher than the rest, but they do run frequent sales and have the advantage of being in the District close to a Metro station.

Discount Department Stores

Montgomery Ward offers a wide selection of name-brand electronics and furniture at reasonable prices. While they do not have a store in the District, there is one in Falls Church at 6100 Arlington Blvd. (703-241-8700) and another in Wheaton at 11160 Veirs Mill Rd. (301-468-5300).

Wal-Mart made its grand entrance into the Washington area in 1992. Since the opening of the first Wal-Mart in Easton, MD at 8155 Elliot Rd. (410-819-0140), stores have opened in Fairfax at 13059 Fair Lakes Blvd. (703-631-9450), Manassas at 7412 Stream Walk Lane (703-330-5253), Waldorf at 11930 Acton Lane (301-705-7070), Hagerstown at 1650 Wesel Blvd. (301-714-1373), Leesburg at 950 Edwards Ferry Rd. (703-779-0102) and Woodbridge at 14000 Worth Ave. (703-497-2590).

Housewares

Bed, Bath & Beyond at 5810 Leesburg Pike, Falls Church (703-578-3374) sells everything you could want for your kitchen, bathroom and bedroom at reasonable prices. The quality of their merchandise is also superb. The Metro does not stop anywhere nearby, so you will need to get there by car or Metrobus. Marylanders can shop at their location at 12270 Rockville Pike (301-231-7637).

Crate & Barrel carries well-designed and colorful housewares, plus lots of kitchen gadgets. You will find them in DC at 4820 Massachusetts Ave. NW (202-264-6100) and in Bethesda at 7101 Democracy Blvd. (301-365-2600). In Virginia, Crate & Barrel has locations at 1100 Hayes St. in Arlington (703-418-1010) and in Tysons Corner Center in McLean (703-847-8555).

Pier One Imports sells housewares primarily, but they do carry some furniture items. In particular they feature dining room furniture, and you will find a number of wicker and rattan items as well. Pier One has numerous stores throughout the area so check your telephone directories for the location most convenient to you. A few of their addresses include 4477 Connecticut Ave. NW in the District (202-362-4080), 6801 Wisconsin Ave. in Chevy Chase (301-657-9196), and 7253 Arlington Blvd. in Falls Church (703-573-1931).

If you need to do all of your shopping by Metro, try **Kitchen Bazaar**. Two of its stores are right near Metro stops. You can easily reach their Van Ness location at 4401 Connecticut Ave. NW (202-244-1550) by the Red Line or their store at the Fashion Center at Pentagon City (703-415-5545) on the Blue or Yellow Lines. Every store offers cooking classes and you can pick up a course catalog at any store.

Potomac Mills offers lots of choices for housewares. Waccamaw Pottery (703-494-7999), in Neighborhood #1, is an excellent place to start. China lovers should be sure not to miss the Fitz & Floyd Factory Outlet in Neighborhood #2 (703-494-1282).

HARDWARE AND APPLIANCE STORES

Once the furniture is in place, a trip to the hardware store is often the next step in making your home—whether house or apartment—more livable. Hardware stores are few and far between in DC, but are readily available in the suburbs. In the Metropolitan area, you have major chains as well as neighborhood independent stores—some of which are fine reminders of simpler times gone by.

The Big Chains

Washington's largest hardware chains are Hechinger, which has been around for years, and Home Depot, which is relatively new to the area. Both offer wide selections of hardware and appliances, as well as lumber and in some cases even things like kitchen and bathroom cabinets and lawn furniture. Other popular national chain stores, such as Circuit City and Best Buys, can be found in shopping centers throughout the area. Incredible Universe recently located here with facilities in Bailey's Crossroads and Potomac Mills, both in Virginia. Read here about the bigger chains and check the Yellow Pages for locations and other options near you.

Hechinger

For a large selection and one-stop shopping, try Hechinger. Its massive blue and white hardware stores, located throughout the area, contain virtually everything—lumber, electrical supplies, cleaning supplies, garbage cans, file cabinets, fans, door mats, humidifiers, contact paper, paint—you get the idea. The Tenleytown store on Wisconsin Ave. (202-244-0650) is a block north of the local Metro station. A second District location is in Northeast, at Hechinger Mall, 17th St. and Benning Rd. (202-398-7100). Maryland residents can shop at Hechinger's other locations—in Bethesda at Montgomery Mall (301-469-6620), and in Wheaton at the intersection of Randolph Rd. and Georgia Ave. (301-942-8200). The Virginia locations are in Baileys Crossroads at 15516 Leesburg Pike (703-379-0200) and in Alexandria at 3131 Duke St. (703-370-5810).

Home Depot

Home Depot arrived in the area, creating direct competition with the Hechinger chain for the home improvement market. The Home Depot stores are less convenient to DC residents. In Maryland, stores can be found in Gaithersburg at 15740 Shady Grove Rd. (301-330-4900), in Oxon Hill at 6003 Oxon Hill Rd. (301-839-9600), and in Silver Spring at 2330 Broadbirch Dr. (301-680-3500). Virginia Home Depots are found in Alexandria at 400 Pickett St. (703-823-1900), Fairfax at 12275 Price Club Plaza (703-266-9800), Merryfield at 2815 Merrilee Dr. (703-205-1245), and Sterling at 46261 Cranston Way (703-444-2900).

The Independents

In addition to the chains and discount stores, there are many small, independent hardware stores. Typically, these stores have smaller collections than the much larger stores, but the independents can surprise you with their compact storage and knowledgeable staff. If you live near one of these, be sure to stop by to see for yourself.

Candey Hardware at 1210 18th St. NW (202-659-5650) has been dispensing its goods since the beginning of the 20th century and retains the original musty charm just to prove the point. This store's location is ideal for those working in and near Dupont Circle and Downtown. Frager's Hardware at 1115 Pennsylvania Ave. SE (202-543-6157) serves the Hill.

Residents of Arlington can visit their own **Virginia Hardware** at 2915 Wilson Blvd. (703-522-3366), within sight of the Clarendon Metro. In Alexandria, **Smitty's Servistar** at 8457 Richmond Hwy. (703-780-7800) houses a huge lumber yard and will deliver.

In Bethesda, **Strosnider's Hardware** at 6930 Arlington Rd. (301-654-5688) offers all the usual items, from lawn and garden to electrical and housewares. There is also a **Strosnider's Kemp Mill Paint and Hardware** in Silver Spring at 1386 Lamberton Dr. (301-593-5353), but it is unrelated to the one in Bethesda. Zimmerman and Sons Hardware at 8860 Brookville Rd. (301-585-5200) also serves Silver Spring residents.

BOOKSTORES

For many, settling in to a new area involves getting to know the local bookstores. With the number and quality of bookstores in the Washington area, you are never at a loss for reading material. In addition, you can almost always find a book signing or a reading to attend. Such events are publicized twice a month in the Book World section of the Washington Post's Sunday edition. The Washington area has outlets of the major national chains as well as several specialized local stores, including many used book dealers.

New Books

Although the national bookstore chains, **Waldenbooks** and **B. Dalton's**, have numerous locations throughout the area, the largest local chain is **Crown Books**, offering readers discounts on all of its books. Hard cover best sellers are 40% off list price, with succeeding tiers of discounts down to a simple 10% for paperbacks. As the name implies, the **Super Crown** stores offer an even greater selection. There are too many Waldenbooks, B. Dalton's, Crown and Super Crowns to list here; check the phone book for the location most convenient to you.

Borders Books and Music attracts the serious reader and music lover, with a tremendous selection of more esoteric titles, while still providing all the broadly popular items found elsewhere. Borders shops also have cafés in which to sit and enjoy your recent purchases. Their Downtown store is at 1801 L St. NW (202-466-4999). The Rockville store (301-816-1067) is in White Flint Mall; other Maryland stores include Gaithersburg Square (301-921-0990) and Columbia at 9501 Snowden Square (410 290-0062). Northern Virginia residents are served by stores in Arlington at 1201 Hayes St. (703-418-0166), Baileys Crossroads, where Rt. 7 and Columbia Pike meet (703-998-0404), and in Vienna at 8311 Leesburg Pike (703-556-7766).

Barnes & Noble has two superstores in the area. The one at the corner of M and Jefferson Sts. in Georgetown is a three-story facility complete with cathedral ceiling, 220,000 volumes, and an espresso coffee bar featuring Starbucks coffee. A second store is located at Seven Corners at 6201 Arlington Blvd. (703-536-0774), and three other stores are planned for Bethesda, Old Town and Reston.

Olsson's Books and Records, a smaller local chain, sells books and music side by side in each store. Olssons has six locations—Georgetown at 1239 Wisconsin Ave. NW (202-338-9544), Dupont Circle at 1307 19th St. NW (202-785-1133), Downtown at 1200 F St. NW (202-347-3686), and 418 7th St. NW (202-638-7610), Bethesda at 7647 Old Georgetown Rd. (301-652-3336) and Old Town Alexandria at 106 S. Union St. (703-684-0077). They also have a mail order department (202-337-8084).

At 221 Pennsylvania Ave. SE, on Capitol Hill, **Trover Books** (202-547-2665) carries a complete line of Penguin titles and a terrific variety of magazines. Another Trover is located at 1031 Connecticut Ave. NW (202-659-8138).

Chapters Literary Bookstore at 1512 K St. NW (202-347-5495) emphasizes personal service to the serious reader. They will order any book you want and have become one of the main stops for visiting authors, with readings several times each week.

One of Washington's bookstore institutions is **Sidney Kramer Books** at 1825 Eye St. NW (202-293-2685). At its street level location in the International Square Mall, Sidney Kramer has an outstanding selection of nonfiction works and is justifiably proud of its foreign affairs and political science departments. The political-minded will also want to check out **Politics and Prose** at 5015 Connecticut Ave. NW (202-364-1919). In addition to the politics and the prose, there is a coffee house and a staff that could certainly hold its own in any political discussion you may wish to start.

Dupont Circle's top bookstore is **Kramerbooks & Afterwords** at 1517 Connecticut Ave. NW (202-387-1400). Kramerbooks is a good, all-purpose bookstore with strong selections in the current and paperback fiction sections. Just as attractive is the two-tier café located in the rear, and the newer bar and small art gallery in the recent addition. Offering everything from coffee, tea and drinks to sandwiches, full dinners and brunch, Kramer's sunny atrium seating and outdoor area provide a relaxed setting to start enjoying your books.

Lambda Rising at 1625 Connecticut Ave. NW (202-462-6969) specializes in gay books and literature. **Lammas**, in the ground floor at 1426 21st St. NW (202-775-8218), focuses on feminist and lesbian literature.

Bethesda's **Travel Books and Language Center** at 4931 Cordell Ave. (301-951-8533) fills its shelves with thousands of language books, guidebooks, atlases and history books for the well-informed traveler. Downtown, The Map Store Inc. at 1636 Eye St. NW (202-628-2608) stocks up on the obvious—maps—and also has a sizable selection of travel and guidebooks.

Mystery lovers will not want to miss the **Mystery Bookshop** in Bethesda at 7700 Old Georgetown Rd. (301-657-2665) and **MysteryBooks** at 1715 Connecticut Ave. NW (202-483-1600). In addition to wide selections and well-read staffs, these stores offer books on tape, games and other mystery-related items for the aficionado.

Used Books

You can economize on books, and sometimes on music, at some of the local used bookstores. These are also great locations for selling books, whether you are moving or just cleaning out your own overstocked bookshelves.

Cheap books and a broad selection mark the **Lantern Bryn Mawr Bookshop** at 3160 O St. NW (202-333-3222). Several features make this store unique and less expensive than most other used bookstores. Most of the books are donated and the store is run entirely by volunteers. "The Lantern," as it is know by its regulars, is a great place to browse and you can always justify all those book purchases as charity—net proceeds support scholarships at Bryn Mawr College.

Capitol Hill Books at 657 C St. SE (202-544-1621) and **Yesterday's Books** at 4702 Wisconsin Ave. NW (202-363-0581) are two of the area's best used bookstores. **Second Story Books and Antiques** features antiques, international art, and used records, cassettes and CDs in addition to used books at its three locations—at 2000 P St. NW in Dupont Circle (202-659-8884), at 4836 Bethesda Ave. in Bethesda (301-656-0170), and at 12160 Parklawn Dr. in Rockville (301-770-0477).

In Wheaton, **Bonifant Books** at 11240 Georgia Ave. (301-946-1526) is a good, general stock, used bookstore. An added benefit for bookworms without wheels, they are near the Wheaton Metro station.

The **Washington Antiquarian Booksellers Association** (301-460-3700) lists more than 60 member shops. You can pick up one of their directories at any of the above used bookstores.

SHOPPING

Shopping and Outlet Malls

While the predominance of shopping centers and malls is in the suburbs, the District has several spots of note. Many of the DC and suburban malls are accessible by Metro. A number of major outlet malls are within reasonable driving distance of the Washington area. Combining a nice drive with a good deal attracts many Washington shoppers. For directions and other information, call the main numbers listed here.

Shopping Centers and Malls

District of Columbia

Chevy Chase Pavilion
5335 Wisconsin Ave. NW   202-686-5335

Georgetown Park
3222 M St. NW   202-298-5577

Mazza Gallerie
300 Wisconsin Ave. NW   202-966-6644

Shops at National Place
529 14th St. NW   202-783-9090

Union Station Shops
50 Massachusetts Ave. NW   202-371-9441

Maryland

City Place Mall
8661 Colesville Rd., Silver Spring   301-589-1091

Lakeforest Mall
701 Russell Ave., Gaithersburg   301-840-5840

Montgomery Mall
7101 Democracy Blvd., Bethesda   301-469-6000

Wheaton Plaza
11160 Veirs Mill Rd., Wheaton   301-946-3200

White Flint Mall
11301 Rockville Pike, Rockville   301-468-5777

Virginia

Ballston Common
4238 Wilson Blvd., Arlington   703-243-8088

Fashion Centre at Pentagon City
1100 Hayes St., Arlington   703-415-2400

Landmark Center
5801 Duke St., Alexandria   703-941-2582

Reston Town Center
11911 Freedom Dr., Reston   703-742-6500

Springfield Mall Shopping Center
I-95 (Exit 69-Franconia), Springfield   703-971-3000

Tysons Corner Center
Rts. 7 and 123, McLean   703-893-9400

Tysons Galleria
2001 International Dr., McLean   703-827-7700

Outlet Malls

Blue Ridge Outlet Center
315 West Stephen St., Martinsburg, WV   1-800-445-3993

Chesapeake Village Outlet Center
Rt. 50 and 301 East of the Bay Bridge, MD   1-410-827-8699

Potomac Mills
I-95 (Exit 156-Dale City), Woodbridge, VA   1-800-VA-MILLS

Department Stores

Many of the well-known national chains are represented in the area. Listed below is a selection of department stores featuring clothing, and the major malls in which they are located. The listing is not all inclusive, but it will give you some starting points.

Department Stores

Bloomingdale's
White Flint Mall	301-984-4600
Tysons Corner Center	703-556-4600

JC Penney Co.
Ballston Common	703-524-1300
Lake Forest Mall	301-840-0010
Springfield Mall	703-971-8850
Wheaton Plaza (effective July 1996)	

Lord & Taylor
Tysons Corner Center	703-506-1156
White Flint Mall Shopping Center	301-770-9000

Macy's
Pentagon City	703-418-4488
Springfield Mall	703-719-6100
Tysons Galleria	703-556-0000

Neiman Marcus
Mazza Gallerie	202-966-9700
Tysons Galleria	703-761-1600

Nordstrom
Montgomery Mall	301-365-4111
Pentagon City	703-415-1121
Tysons Corner Center	703-761-1121

Discount Apparel

Annie Sez
13875 Outlet Dr., Silver Spring	301-890-3663
12268 Rockville Pike, Rockville	301-816-2100
3512 S. Jefferson St., Falls Church	703-931-6544

Filene's Basement
1133 Connecticut Ave. NW	202-872-8430
5300 Wisconsin Ave. NW	202-966-0208
5840 Crossroads Center, Falls Church	703-578-1551

Frugal Fannie's Fashion Warehouse
2445 Centreville Rd., Herndon	703-713-6000

Loehmann's
Randolph Rd. and Nicholson La., Rockville	301-770-0030
7241 Arlington Blvd., Falls Church	703-573-1510

Nordstrom Rack

Silver Spring Rack, 8661 Colesville Rd.,	
Silver Spring	301-608-8118
Potomac Mills Rack, 2700 Potomac	
Mills Center, Woodbridge	703-490-1440

Syms

11840 Rockville Pike, Rockville	301-984-3335
1000 E. Broad St., Falls Church	703-241-8500
2700 Potomac Mills Circle, Woodbridge	703-497-7332

Membership Clubs

In the past few years, two super discount membership clubs, Price Club and Sam's Club, have proliferated throughout the suburbs. While these stores are particularly well suited to the needs of large families or groups living together, even those who live alone or in couples will find irresistible bargains here. A word of advice, the attractive bulk prices can lead first-time shoppers to overestimate their ability to use bulk sizes of certain items. Watch out for temptation and false economies.

As you might expect from the use of the word "membership," you have to join the club to shop there. While membership is primarily aimed at business owners, credit union members, and hospital and government workers, most everyone is able to qualify for the membership card. Membership usually costs about $35.

Price Club

In Maryland, Price Clubs can be found in Beltsville at the intersection of Route 1 and Powder Mill Rd. (301-595-3400), in Marlow Heights at 4501 Auth Pl. (301-423-6303), and in Gaithersburg at 880 Russell Ave. (301-417-1520). Virginia is served by facilities in Fairfax at 4725 West Ox Rd. (703-802-0372), Pentagon City/Arlington at 1200 S. Fern St. (703-413-2324), in Springfield at 7373 Austin Blvd. (703-912-1200), and in Sterling at 21398 Price Cascades Plaza (703-406-7000).

Sam's Club

Sam's Club has two Maryland locations, one in Gaithersburg at 610 North Frederick Ave. (301-216-2550), the other in Landover at 8511 Landover Rd. (301-386-5577). In Virginia, there is a Sam's Club in Woodbridge at 14045 Worth Ave. (703-491-2662).

Food and Fun

As befits an international city filled with residents, visitors and diplomats from around the world, Washington offers a stunning diversity of dining options as well as many bars and clubs. You will find almost every type of food here— from soft-shell crabs, ribs and jambalaya to Ethiopian injera, Thai lemon grass soup, Vietnamese Bò-Dun and Jamaican jerk chicken. While wine and mixed drinks are available in many restaurants and all the bars, beer is a particularly popular drink, with some local microbreweries appearing on the scene in recent years.

This chapter introduces you to the variety of dining and drinking options available—but in the end, it is up to you to explore some of the more than 1,500 restaurants and bars in the greater metropolitan area and to develop your own list of favorites.

RESTAURANTS

Washington's restaurants run the gamut of type of food, style of dining and expense. The restaurants listed here are classified by type of food and represent some of the more popular and better known ones in each category.

American

American food can mean anything from chili to salads to ribs to burgers, and there are several notable eateries specializing in various types of American dining.

Washington has relatively few restaurants with views, especially views of the water. However, one place that has both, and features a varied menu, is **Sequoia**, right on the Potomac River at 3000 K St. NW (202-944-4200) in Georgetown's Harbour Place. The food is very good, and it is known as a great place to go for early-evening happy hour. Outdoor seating is available during warm weather.

The **Cheesecake Factory**, with sites at 5345 Wisconsin Ave. NW (202-364-0500) in Friendship Heights and 11301 Rockville Pike, and in the White Flint Mall in Bethesda (301-770-0999), is an outpost of a popular Los Angeles chain. The Cheesecake Factory sports a diverse, lengthy menu and serves huge portions. There are plenty of choices here for everyone, including vegetarians. Since the Cheesecake Factory does not accept reservations, you should be prepared for a sometimes lengthy wait on a busy night. Be sure to save room for dessert—there are over 30 types of cheesecake available.

Hard Times Cafe at 3028 Wilson Blvd. in Arlington (703-528-2233) serves three types of chili— Vegetarian, Cincinnati and Texas—from huge vats behind the bar, as well as a terrific selection of beer. Before you order, ask for a chili sampler so you can choose your favorite. Five-way Cincinnati chili and onion rings flavored with chili oil are two special treats. Hard Times has three other locations—in Alexandria at 1404 King St. (703-683-5340), in Rockville at 1117 Nelson St. (301-294-9720), and in Herndon at 394 Elden St. (703-318-8941).

At **Lulu's**, on the corner of 22nd and M Sts. NW (202-861-LULU), you can choose from a variety of New Orleans fare including po'boys, jambalaya, creole and gumbo. Lulu's is connected to Deja Vu, a popular nightclub and dance spot, so happy hour draws a fairly large crowd. Expect lines on Friday evenings.

American Pub Food

Food experts might dispute the existence of American pub food as an official classification, but it effectively describes a typically American style of eating and drinking establishment. These restaurants are essentially up-scale beer and burger joints and Washington is full of them. While they do not offer much in the way of individuality, they do offer the hungry eater a no-surprises, solid meal at generally reasonable prices. The typical menu includes a wide selection of beer and several different types of salads and sandwiches to go with the variously topped, six- to nine-ounce burgers.

Scattered all across town with clusters in Dupont Circle, Georgetown, Capitol Hill and Alexandria, these restaurants are great places for meeting friends after work. In Dupont Circle, your choices include the **Front Page** at 1333 New Hampshire Ave. NW (202-296-6500) and **Timberlake's** at 1726 Connecticut Ave. NW (202-483-2266). Packed together in the 1800 block of M St. are the **Sign of the Whale** at #1825 (202-785-1110), the **Madhatter** at #1831 (202-833-1495) and **Hillary's** at #1827 (202-331-1827). These places are particularly popular for happy hour. Madhatter has drink specials virtually every night and can be very crowded. If you want to eat, you will probably find it more comfortable at lunch time.

More American pub restaurants can be found in Georgetown. Burgers and daiquiris have put **Mr. Smith's** (202-333-3104) on the map, at 3104 M St. NW. Also on M St. you will find the **Guards** at #2915 (202-965-2350), which looks expensive but is not; **Garrett's** at #3003

(202-333-1033), with good seafood chowder; and **J. Paul's** at #3218 (202-333-3450), which has its own house beer and some of the best crab cakes in the District. The **Tombs** at 1226 36th St. NW (202-337-6668), full of crew memorabilia, is a favorite spot for Georgetown students.

A couple of Georgetown establishments have spread out into the suburbs. **Houston's**, in DC at 1065 Wisconsin Ave. NW (202-338-7760), and in Bethesda at 7715 Woodmont Ave. (301-656-9755), has great ribs. **Clyde's** is just plain popular with locations in DC at 3236 M St. NW (202-333-9180), in Chevy Chase at 35 Wisconsin Cir. (301-951-9600), in Tysons Corner at 8332 Leesburg Pike (703-734-1900), and in Reston at 11905 Market St. (703-787-6601).

In the U St. corridor, at 1342 U St. NW, **Polly's Cafe** (202-265-8385) is a neighborhood bar with great food. This small restaurant has some café seating outside, a casual room with tables, and a bar below street level. Polly's offers a selection of sandwiches, burgers, excellent specials and a tasty weekend brunch.

The **Old Ebbitt Grill** at 675 15th St. NW (202-347-4801) attracts the National Theatre crowd and White House staffers. On the Hill, staffers frequent the **Hawk and Dove** at 329 Pennsylvania Ave. SE (202-543-3300). **Bullfeathers** at 410 1st St. SE (202-543-5005), a few steps from the Republican National Club, has half-price burgers on Tuesday nights and scads of staffers every night. A second location is in Old Town Alexandria at 112 King St. (703-836-8088). Former Redskin Joe Theismann's Alexandria restaurant, appropriately called **Joe Theismann's**, is located at 1800 Diagonal Rd. (703-739-0777). The food is typical, but the decor makes you feel as if you are eating in a hotel restaurant.

Planet Hollywood at 1101 Pennsylvania Ave. NW (202-783-7827) is among the galaxy of restaurants started by actors Arnold Schwarzenegger, Bruce Willis and Sylvester Stallone. Positioned near several hotels and across the street from the Post Office Pavilion, this restaurant attracted lots of publicity even before its doors opened in late 1993. Inside, movie memorabilia adorns the walls, including costumes from "Planet of the Apes" and the model of the "Death Star" used in "Return of the Jedi."

For a different planetary dining experience, try **Planet Fred** at 1221 Connecticut Ave. NW (202-331-3773), a restaurant and club that opened in 1994. "It's an Everyman's Planet Hollywood," says a manager. Fred has four sections, each offering a differing view of space and the planet, ranging from ancient man's conception of the sky to Stanley Kubrick's vision of space. The restaurant part gives way to a nightclub at the end of the week, with world beat, reggae and progressive music.

There are several restaurants that you should go to at least once to round out the "Washington experience." **Sholl's Colonial Cafeteria** at 1990 K St. NW (202-296-3065) is a hardy, enduring legacy from Washington's past. In these tough economic times, you will be amazed at how much food your dollar can buy.

The **Well-Dressed Burrito** at 1220 19th St. NW (202-293-0515), a carry-out-only hole in the wall, operates in the alley between 19th and 20th Sts. in Dupont Circle. It is only open on weekdays from 11:45 a.m. to 2:30 p.m. Its menu is limited, but its dishes create enough aroma to help you find your way there.

Barbecue

The Memphis barbecue at **Red Hot & Blue** at 1600 Wilson Blvd. in Arlington (703-276-7427) is among the best in town. If you do not want to wait in line, you can order from the carry-out store about a mile up Wilson Blvd. Red Hot & Blue also has locations in Laurel at 677 Main St. (301-953-1943), Manassas at 8637 Sudley Rd. (703-330-4847) and at 1120 19th St. NW (202-466-6731).

Three Pigs of McLean at 1394 Chain Bridge Rd. (703-356-1700) serves good hickory-smoked barbecue in very informal surroundings. **Hogs on the Hill** at 2001 14th St. NW (202-332-4647) has establishments throughout DC and Alexandria. Ribs, barbecue sandwiches, "greens" and plenty of everything is what you will get here. Its other locations are at 4525 E. Capitol St. SE (202-575-2966), 6209 Georgia Ave. NW (202-726-8332), 732 Maryland Ave. NE (202-547-4553), and 2003 Bladensburg Rd. NE (202-326-2027) in the District; 3414 Mt. Vernon Rd. (703-836-6491) and 828 N. Washington St. (703-836-6966) in Alexandria; and 8694 Liberia Ave. in Manassas (703-361-3500).

At **Old Glory**, 3139 M St. NW (202-337-3406), you can choose among seven sauces to season your ribs. Portions for both appetizers and entrees are large and the frosty-mugged root beer helps wash it down.

Just Burgers

George Washington University students would be lost without **Lindy's Bon Apetit** at the corner of 21st and Eye Sts. NW (202-452-0055), affectionately called "The Bone." In good weather you can sit at one of the couple of outdoor tables, but it is mostly carry out. You can order from the same extensive burger menu upstairs at the **Red Lion Pub**. Capitol Hill's **Li'l Pub** at 655 Pennsylvania Ave. SE (202-543-5526) serves huge burgers (about 11 ounces pre-cooked) for just $3.50. Departing from traditional sit-down burger places, **Five Guys** at 4626 King St. (703-671-1606) in Alexandria sells its bargain burgers ($2.49) and fries ($0.99) for carry out only. These "guys" have another location at 3235 Columbia Pike in Arlington (703-685-1151).

All-Night Diners

If you are prone to the midnight munchies, you have some good options. Georgetown's French café, **Au Pied de Cochon** at 1335 Wisconsin Ave. NW (202-333-5440), is open around the clock. **Bob & Edith's Diner** in Arlington at 2310 Columbia Pike (703-920-6103) offers night owls the regular diner fare—eggs, coffee, waffles, pies, not to mention interesting patrons. You will find a fairly large menu and wonderful desserts at the **Amphora** at 377 Maple Ave. in Vienna (703-938-7877). Each booth comes with an individual juke box. The old suburban stand-by, **Tastee Diner**, is also open 24 hours a day, seven days a week, with locations in Fairfax at 10536 Lee Hwy. (703-591-6720), in Silver Spring at 8516 Georgia Ave. (301-589-8171), in Laurel at 118 Washington Blvd. (301-953-7567) and in Bethesda at 7731 Woodmont Ave. (301-652-3970).

The **Afterwords Cafe** at 1517 Connecticut Ave. NW (202-387-3825) in Dupont Circle can be a perfect place to go for dessert and coffee any night. On weekends, the restaurant, attached to Kramerbooks, stays open all night. Besides the excellent desserts, the Afterwords Cafe offers a selection of vegetarian and southwestern dishes. The **American City Diner** at 5532 Connecticut Ave. NW (202-244-1949) and 7501 Wisconsin Ave. in Bethesda (301-656-3287) is also open around the clock on Friday and Saturday. **Diner-X-Press** at 1101 Clopper Rd. in Gaithersburg (301-330-8700) is part of the Bowl America Gaithersburg. It offers a classic diner menu with breakfast served 24 hours a day and a breakfast buffet on weekends.

Chinese

Washington's Chinatown sits between the DC Convention Center and Capitol Hill. The entrance to Chinatown at 7th and H Sts. NW features the Friendship Archway, a mid-80s joint project between Beijing and the DC government. The neighborhood highlight is the annual Chinese New Year celebration and parade. Reminiscent of the larger Chinatown neighborhoods in San Francisco and New York, this area has a number of its own special treasures. From the Gallery Place Metro station at Chinatown's entrance, you can walk to **Mr. Yung's** at 740 6th St. NW (202-628-1098), which presents customers a list of 30 to 40 different dim sum choices. Close by, the **China Inn** at 631 H St. NW (202-842-0909) serves generous Cantonese and Sichuan dishes. **Hunan Chinatown** at 624 H St. NW (202-783-5858) has won the *Washingtonian's* 50 Best Restaurants Award for at least nine consecutive years. It offers delicious food, an unpretentious atmosphere despite its white tablecloths, and a friendly staff.

Tony Cheng's Mongolian Restaurant at 619 H St. NW (202-842-8669) allows you to concoct your own all-you-can-eat entrees. You choose from a buffet of fresh meats and vegetables and Tony's chefs grill your dishes right in front of you. On Sunday mornings, Tony Cheng's offers an extensive dim sum brunch. **Tony Cheng's Seafood Restaurant** (202-371-8669) is upstairs. You can guess its specialty.

City Lights of China at 1731 Connecticut Ave. NW (202-265-6688) prepares Dupont Circle's best Chinese food. It is so good that its patrons quickly become regulars, although passersby can easily miss it as it is located in the basement of a townhouse.

Charlie Chiang's has maintained high quality and prompt service at each of its locations as it has branched out into the suburbs. The location at 4250 Connecticut Ave. NW (202-966-1916) has an express lunch counter on the ground floor. Other locations are in the District at 1912 Eye St. NW (202-293-6000), in Alexandria at 660 South Pickett St. (703-751-8888) and in the Shirlington area of Arlington at 4060 South 28th St. (703-671-4900).

Top-of-the-line **Mr. K's**, at 2121 K St. NW (202-331-8868), serves Cantonese Chinese food in elegant surroundings. When the Republicans were in the White House, many Washingtonians went to **Peking Gourmet** at 6029 Leesburg Pike (703-671-8088) because it was one of President Bush's favorites. The restaurant looks modest from the outside; inside, the walls of this brightly lit restaurant are covered with pictures of Washington's notables. Peking Gourmet's primary specialty is Peking duck; another is garlic sprouts with chicken, shrimp or pork.

The best strategy when going to **Good Fortune** at 2646 University Blvd. in Wheaton (301-929-8818) is to bring along a group of friends. Its Cantonese menu lists more than 200 dishes begging to be tried. For $78, you and five friends can feast on an eight-course banquet. If you make it there for lunch, you will find dim sum being served.

For Chinese food in less than five minutes and under five dollars, served in carry-out containers, try any one of the several **China Cafes**. Three popular locations in the District draw big lunch crowds—Dupont Circle at 1723 Connecticut Ave. NW (202-234-4053), Downtown at 2009 K St. NW (202-463-2129), and McPherson Sq., 1018 Vermont Ave. NW (202-628-1350). The daily specials are always a good and super-fast choice.

For dim sum in Northern Virginia, you have several options. Clarendon's **Hunan Number One** at 3033 Wilson Blvd. (703-528-1177) serves its dim sum daily between 11:00 a.m. and 3:00 p.m. Weekends offer the best selection. **Fortune Chinese Seafood Restaurant** in Baileys Crossroads at 5900 Leesburg Pike (703-998-8888) has a more extensive daily selection. Despite Fortune's large size, lunch hours can be crowded and you may have to wait.

Ethiopian

Washington is known to have some of the best Ethiopian food in the country. You will quickly discover the best choices are in Adams Morgan. **Red Sea** at 2463 18th St. NW (202-483-5000) and **Meskerem** at 2434 18th St. NW (202-462-4100) are right across the street from each other and are rightfully the most popular Ethiopian restaurants in town. For those who have never eaten Ethiopian food, diners eat the spicy stews with their fingers and injera (something like a moist, doughy tortilla). While you might be tempted to ask for a fork, don't do it. It might be considered impolite and it definitely spoils the experience. In Georgetown, **Zed's** at 3318 M St. NW (202-333-4710) serves Ethiopian cuisine almost on a par with the Adams Morgan favorites.

French

Washington has numerous French restaurants, ranging from casual to expensive. You can find a fixed-price menu at **Le Mistral** at 223 Pennsylvania Ave. SE (202-543-7747), and on winter nights you would be hard-pressed to find a more romantic spot than Le Mistral's front room, with its roaring fireplace and stunning view of Capitol Hill.

For casual French fare, you can eat at one of two adjoining restaurants in Georgetown. **Au Pied de Cochon** at 1335 Wisconsin Ave. NW (202-333-5440) is open 24 hours a day and serves salads and crèpes. Its next door neighbor, **Maison de Crèpes** (202-333-2333), specializes in crèpes and other light fare, and has retained just a few of the fish and seafood specials offered by its long-time predecessor, Aux Fruits de Mer. Just off M St. towards the Potomac is another Georgetown favorite, **Café La Ruche**, at 1039 31st St. NW (202-965-2684). This small café right near the C&O Canal serves lighter fare such as soups, salads and sandwiches as well as not-so-light desserts. When the weather permits, the tables in the garden can provide a peaceful lunch-time interlude.

Le Bistro Français at 3128 M St. NW (202-338-3830) boasts fresh seafood every day and specializes in southern French cuisine. Be sure to ask for a sample of their homemade pâtés when ordering. The chef at Cleveland Park's **Lavandou Cuisine Provençal** at 3321 Connecticut Ave. NW (202-966-3002) also serves dishes from the popular Provence region in the south of France.

For French fare with a view of the Potomac, dine at **Le Rivage**, 1000 Water St. SW (202-488-8111). This waterfront restaurant specializes in seafood, but there are many other choices. Outdoor seating is available during warm weather.

Let the staff at **Maison Blanche** at 1725 F St. NW (202-842-0070) recommend the day's best or suggest a fine wine. Leaving Maison Blanche without sampling their desserts is a "crime de cuisine."

For French wining and dining on the Hill, staffers take to **La Colline** at 400 North Capitol St. NW (202-737-0400) or **La Brasserie** at 239 Massachusetts Ave. NW (202-546-9154). Particularly fine French dining is available at **Jean Louis at the Watergate** at 2650 Virginia Ave. NW (202-298-4488) and **Le Lion d'Or** at 1150 Connecticut Ave. NW (202-296-7972).

Indian

Just across Rock Creek Park from Adams Morgan and Dupont Circle, two Indian restaurants neighbor each other on Connecticut Ave.—**Rajaji** at 2603 Connecticut Ave. NW (202-265-7344) and **Taste of India** at 2623 Connecticut Ave. NW (202-483-1115). Rajaji will satisfy those who enjoy spicy curries, while Taste of India caters to those who prefer milder Indian food. The **Bombay Palace** (202-331-4200) at 2020 K St. NW features some wonderful vegetarian cuisine and is a good choice if you are considering dining with a large crowd. Near K St., you will find **Aroma Indian Restaurant** at 1919 Eye St. (202-833-4700), the area's newest restaurant offering Indian cuisine.

Aditi at 3299 M St. NW (202-625-6825) receives high praise for its Indian food. If you cannot choose among its many Tandoori specialties, try its sample feast for $13.95.

Italian

Arguably the best-valued Italian restaurant in the District, **I Matti** in Adams Morgan at 2436 18th St. NW (202-462-8844) prepares fresh bread, gourmet pizza, innovative pasta, roast meat (including rabbit) and seafood in an up-scale, trendy atmosphere. I Matti is a more affordable, casual and creative version of the three-star Downtown restaurant, **I Ricchi**, at 1220 19th St. NW (202-835-0459), serving excellent authentic Tuscan cuisine. **Galileo** at 1110 21st St. NW (202-293-7197) caters to those who enjoy making deals over some of the finest Italian cuisine anywhere.

A.V. Ristorante Italiano at 607 New York Ave. NW (202-737-0550) is legendary in Washington. This restaurant has the quintessential neighborhood ambiance Italian restaurants are known for—Chianti bottles for candle holders, dark red walls and red-checked tablecloths. Its pizza and pasta dishes are terrific and you will definitely get your money's worth, especially on the meat platters.

Downtown dining received a shot in the arm with the spate of building in the area across from the National Archives. One dining addition is **Bertollini's** at 801 Pennsylvania Ave. NW (202-638-2140). Bertollini's also can be found at White Flint Mall on Rockville Pike (301-984-0004). **Bice** at 601 Pennsylvania Ave. NW (202-638-2423) features Northern Italian cuisine, and serves homemade pastas with a variety of marvelous sauces. Bice's address is on Pennsylvania Ave., but the entrance is around the corner on Indiana Ave.

The two locations for **Il Radicchio**—at 1509 17th St. NW (202-986-2627) and 1211 Wisconsin Ave. NW (202-337-2627)—have excellent pizza and a unique way of serving spaghetti. After you buy the first bowl ($6), you can refill for free and buy just the sauces, ranging from $1 to $4. Not far from Il Radicchio in Georgetown is **Paparazzi** at 1066 Wisconsin Ave. NW (202-298-8000), where the porcini tortellini is reputed to be "outrageous."

Cafe Petitto's at 1724 Connecticut Ave. NW (202-462-8771) is famous for its antipasto bar. A couple of doors away, at 1714 Connecticut Ave., is **Odeon Cafe** (202-328-6228), with its chic neon atmosphere—a great place for a meal or after-dinner drink. The **Italian Kitchen** at 1637 17th St. NW (202-328-3222) has cheap and plentiful pasta dishes better for carry out than eating in.

Paolo's at 1303 Wisconsin Ave. NW (202-333-7353), a trendy, up-scale Italian café, serves delicious pastas, pizzas and salads. If you would like to avoid the crowds, try late lunches or weekend brunches. Paolo's has other locations in Rockville at 1801 Rockville Pike (301-984-2211) and in the Reston Town Center (703-318-8920).

LOCAL DINING WEBSITES

Dining Web
http://diningweb.com
Free on-line database with over 1,700 listings, searchable by name, address, price range, neighborhood or cuisine.

District Area Dining Directory
http://dc.myhouse.com
Database of over 1,600 restaurants including home pages and coupons. Fully searchable by area, cuisine style and delivery service.

Washingtonian Online
http://www.infi.net/washmag
Online version of the monthly magazine; includes lists of best restaurants, reader surveys, a calendar of wine and food events, and a place to leave questions and comments for the magazine's restaurant critic.

Digital City Washington
http://www.digitalcity.com
Electronic database of information about Washington; includes information about restaurants and a link to the National Restaurant Register's Menu-Online, an interactive information service providing actual menus and other restaurant information.

RESTAURANT DELIVERIES

A fast-rising innovation in the food industry is the delivery of food from area restaurants directly to your door. Some of the delivery services covering the metropolitan DC area are listed below. Call for their specific areas of delivery, their rates and the restaurants they serve.

A La Carte Express	202-546-8464
Meals Express	301-565-3030
Waiter on the Way	301-869-0300
Restaurants on the Run	703-527-9000
Takeout Taxi	
DC	202-986-0111
Bethesda and Rockville	301-571-0111
Prince George's County	301-858-0002
Alexandria	703-719-9409
Arlington County	703-578-3363
Fairfax and Loudon Counties	703-204-0002
Herndon, Reston and Sterling	703-435-3663

The budget-minded will enjoy Adams Morgan's **Spaghetti Garden** at 2317 18th St. NW (202-265-6665), especially when you can sit out on its rooftop on a warm summer evening. Dinner for two, including wine, can cost less than $20.

For inexpensive Italian cooking in the suburbs, try any one of the Pines restaurants—each with a different Italian city attached to its name. Some offer only Southern Italian dishes and some only Northern Italian. The best are **Pines of Italy** for Southern Italian (703-524-4969) at 237 North Glebe Rd. in Arlington and **Pines of Rome** for Northern Italian (301-657-8775) at 4709 Hampden La. in Bethesda. Be prepared to wait on weekend nights—these restaurants are popular.

Further out, **Da Domenico Ristorante** at 1992 Chain Bridge Rd. in McLean (703-790-9000) receives rave reviews. Its pork chops and clams come highly recommended and rumor has it that it has the best martinis around.

Japanese

A popular spot for Japanese cuisine is **Perry's** at 1811 Columbia Rd. NW (202-234-6218). Typical of restaurants in Adams Morgan, Perry's offers its diners lots of atmosphere—high-tech in this case. During the spring and summer months, you can eat your dinner on their rooftop deck overlooking the city.

Located at 4050 Lee Hwy. in Arlington, **Tachibana Japanese Restaurant** (703-528-1122) is considered by some to be the best Japanese restaurant in the entire metropolitan DC area.

Tako Grill at 7756 Wisconsin Ave. in Bethesda (301-652-7030) departs from the regular sushi and sake restaurants. Diners can feast on robatayaki (grilled fish, meat and vegetables) and other less common dishes, as well as the more typically Japanese staples (sushi, teriyaki, yosenabe and tempura). Tako Grill is a particularly good place for vegetarians.

Yosaku at 4712 Wisconsin Ave. NW (202-363-4453) offers the best deal on sushi. Take advantage of their regular sushi assortment; it costs $12.50 and includes 16 pieces of sushi.

Pan Asian Noodles at 2020 P St. NW (202-872-8889), a cross between a Japanese noodle shop and a Thai restaurant, serves both spicy and mild noodle dishes.

Asia-Nora at 2213 M St. NW (202-797-4860) features New Asian cooking with all organic ingredients, and offers 20 types of infusion teas. Every detail of the food and decor has been attended to, including the handmade dinner plates.

Kosher

Most of Washington's kosher restaurants are to be found in the area's largest Jewish communities. All of the restaurants listed below are under the supervision of the Vaad of Washington.

The **H St. Hideaway** at 2300 H St. NW (202-452-1161) caters mostly to George Washington University students who are on the Kosher meal plan, but is also open to the public. It serves meat and vegetarian dishes and is open for dinner Monday through Thursday, 5:00 p.m. to 8:30 p.m.

Nuthouse at 11419 Georgia Ave. in Wheaton (301-942-5900) specializes in pizza, falafel and salads and is open until 1:30 a.m. on Saturday nights.

Both the **Royal Dragon** at 4840 Boiling Brook Pkwy. in Rockville (301-468-1922) and **Hunan Gourmet** at 350 Fortune Terrace in Potomac (301-424-0191) serve Glatt kosher Chinese food.

Mediterranean and Middle Eastern

The **Lebanese Taverna** at 2641 Connecticut Ave. NW (202-265-8681) sits among a row of ethnic restaurants across from the Woodley Park Metro station. This restaurant caters to those with larger budgets; dinner can easily cost $20 a person. Still, it is well worth the occasional splurge, particularly during the summer when you can sit outside and watch the world go by. The food is excellent and the service well-timed.

Bacchus at 1827 Jefferson Pl. NW (202-785-0734) also has excellent Lebanese food. This intimate restaurant is neatly tucked away in the basement of a Dupont Circle townhouse. A second, more spacious Bacchus, in Bethesda at 7945 Norfolk Ave. (301-657-1722), promises much of the same.

Kabul Caravan at 1725 Wilson Blvd. (703-522-8394) serves authentic fare in Arlington. Its rather unpretentious exterior disguises the cozy, romantic interior.

The **Calvert Cafe** at 1967 Calvert St. NW (202-232-5431), just over the Calvert St. Bridge in Adams Morgan, looks almost as if it has gone out of business. Nothing could be further from the truth. Venture in and you will find excellent, inexpensive dishes, succulent desserts and Turkish coffee. Long-time Washingtonians know this restaurant by the name Mama Ayesha's.

Many areas in the District have some form of Middle Eastern or Greek food nearby. Inexpensive gyros and falafel are a lunch-time favorite for those working Downtown. In Georgetown, choices include **George's** at the corner of M and 28th Sts. (202-342-2278) and **Fettoosh** at 3277 M St. NW (202-342-1199). Both are great for fast and cheap falafel. George's also makes terrific cheese steaks, proclaiming itself "king of cheese steaks." At **Zorba's Cafe** in Dupont Circle at 1612 20th St. NW (202-387-8555), you can enjoy eating your gyros outside while listening to Greek music played over a loudspeaker. **Pik-a-Pita** (202-842-2438) in the Union Station food court serves a wide range of pita sandwiches and salads (hummus, baba ghannouj and fettoosh). Its roast chicken salad with pita croutons is particularly good. A second Pik-a-Pita (703-415-5630) is in the food court at the Fashion Centre at Pentagon City.

Topkapi Restaurant in Fairfax at 3529 Chain Bridge Rd. (703-273-4310) is a Turkish restaurant in disguise. Camouflaged among entrees such as tortellini and prime rib, the menu lists a banquet of tasty Turkish dishes. Topkapi also has restaurants in Ballston Commons (703-525-8468) and at 5801 Duke St. in Alexandria (703-941-9433).

Mexican and Southwestern

For Mexican food, one of Washington's best deals is **El Tamarindo** at 1785 Florida Ave. NW (202-328-3660). El Tamarindo offers cheap (and good) pitchers of margaritas and solid, no-frills Mexican and Salvadoran dishes. In addition to its primary location on Florida Ave., just around the corner from 18th St. on the Dupont Circle-Adams Morgan border, El Tamarindo has two other locations—4910 Wisconsin Ave. NW (202-244-8888) and 7331 Georgia Ave. NW (202-291-0525). If you are part of a large group, you should go to the Wisconsin Ave. location.

Lauriol Plaza at 1801 18th St. NW (202-387-0035) makes for the most romantic of any Mexican meal. Lauriol Plaza's prices are higher than at El Tamarindo, though not extreme for a nice night out. Besides excellent fajitas, Lauriol Plaza offers a number of offbeat Spanish and Salvadoran dishes. The same owners manage **Cactus Cantina,** near the National Cathedral, at 3300 Wisconsin Ave. NW (202-686-7222). During warm weather, the tables outside the restaurant are a perfect spot for sipping margaritas and sharing nachos and a delicious salsa. Cactus Cantina tends to attract a younger crowd than Lauriol Plaza.

Austin Grill's bar at 2404 Wisconsin Ave. NW (202-337-8080) serves excellent margaritas making it a popular after-work hangout. The menu, like the restaurant space, is somewhat limited. A second restaurant, **South Austin Grill** at 801 King St. in Alexandria (703-684-8969), has more space, a more extensive Tex-Mex menu and more of the excellent margaritas. The newest Austin Grill, in Springfield, is located at 8430A Old Keene Mill Rd. (703-644-3111). Each month, the Austin Grill restaurants donate a portion of dinner proceeds to a local charity. The restaurant and the charity rotate each month.

Enriqueta's at 2811 M St. NW in Georgetown (202-338-7772) serves authentic Mexican food, as opposed to the "north of the border" Tex-Mex version. The brightly painted chairs in this restaurant add to its casual and colorful environment. Enriqueta's Chicken Mole is a winner.

Tex-Mex has been made into big business at **Rio Grande Cafe**. Three extremely popular locations—Ballston, Bethesda and Reston—promise long lines, especially on weekends. Take advantage of their fresh chips and salsa while you wait. In Ballston, Rio Grande is at 4301 North Fairfax Dr. (703-528-3131), just down the street from the Ballston Metro station. The Bethesda location is at 4919 Fairmont Ave. (301-656-2981) and the Reston restaurant is at 1827 Library St. in the Reston Town Center (703-904-0703).

On the Hill, **La Lomita Dos** at 308 Pennsylvania Ave. SE (202-544-0616) serves Mexican food in more typical surroundings. Sombreros and piñatas

SUGGESTIONS

To keep tabs on what is going on in Washington's world of food and fun, you can read "On the Town" in the Friday Weekend section of the *Washington Post*. For specific information about restaurants, nothing beats Phyllis Richman's weekly restaurant review in the Post's Sunday magazine. *Washingtonian* magazine also reviews restaurants and frequently publishes lists of the top ones in various categories.

For the budget-minded as well as the adventurous, the *Entertainment Guide* is a wonderful resource. These coupon books (one for Virginia and DC and another for Maryland and DC) offer discounts at hundreds of restaurants, as well as many area theaters and concert halls. The Entertainment Guide costs about $40, but practically pays for itself with just three restaurant visits. *Entertainment Guides* can be purchased directly from the publisher by credit card (703-207-0770). If you prefer to see the guide before you purchase it, look for it at CVS, Waldenbooks, Brentanos and Drug Emporium stores. Copies are most readily available at these sites following the annual fall publication date.

decorate the small white-stucco dining room. The original **La Lomita** is at 1330 Pennsylvania Ave. SE (202-546-3109).

The tastes of southwestern cuisine are to be found in grand style at the **Red Sage** at 605 14th St. NW (202-638-4444). With its $5 million decor, the Red Sage is a spectacularly fanciful vision of the West. It is under the same ownership as the famous Coyote Cafe in Santa Fe.

Pizza

Over the years, **Armand's** has been recognized as the place to go for pizza. Armand's original pizzeria at 4231 Wisconsin Ave. NW (202-686-9450) serves "Chicago-style" pizza in a casual, family atmosphere. Armand's has now spread throughout the District and the suburbs.

Right next to Armand's original store on upper Wisconsin is rival **Maggie's New York Style Pizzeria** at 4237 Wisconsin Ave. NW (202-363-1447). American University students support this New York pizzeria in droves. It seems odd that two pizzerias, side-by-side, could survive; but they do. A second Maggie's is at 1400 Rhode Island Ave. NW (202-986-9696).

Thin-crust pizza connoisseurs will enjoy **Faccia Luna** at 2400 Wisconsin Ave. NW (202-337-3132) and **Il Forno Pizzeria** at 4926 Cordell Ave. in Bethesda (301-652-7757) and 8941 N. Westland St. in Gaithersburg (301-977-5900). Faccia Luna tops its pies with interesting items such as tuna, eggplant, spinach and pesto. Faccia Luna opened a second location in Arlington at 2909 Wilson Blvd. (703-276-3099). Il Forno bakes its pizza in a wood-burning oven, producing amazing results.

Some locals find that the best pizza in Washington comes out of the wood-burning stove at **Pizzeria Paradiso**, 2029 P St. NW (202-223-1245). The thick, flavorful, chewy crust is truly paradise, particularly when accented by any of the dozen or so fresh, high-quality toppings available. The small dining room fills up quickly, so be prepared to wait for dinner.

Other locals will swear that **Luigi's** makes the best pizza. Luigi's, at 1132 19th St. NW (202-331-7574), is one of the few pizza places in the area that offer a wide range of toppings, including calamari, clam, pineapple and more. Diners can choose to sit inside or in a glassed-in patio out front. Beware of the blue margarita—one is plenty.

Geppetto at 2917 M St. NW (202-333-2602) serves the spiciest and best pepperoni in the District and piles it so high that it tends to form a small mountain in the center of the pizza. The vegetarian pizza, replete with eggplant, provides an excellent alternative. Geppetto's has a second location in Bethesda's Wildwood Shopping Center at 10257 Old Georgetown Rd. (301-493-9230).

Imported from Beverly Hills, the **California Pizza Kitchen** (CPK) has almost 30 different kinds of individual gourmet pizzas. Thai Chicken, Shrimp-Pesto, Barbecue Chicken and Peking Duck are just a few of the imaginative and delicious combinations available. CPK also offers terrific salads to start and desserts to finish. You will find this restaurant located all over town, including 5345 Wisconsin Ave. NW (202-363-6650) and 1220 Connecticut Ave. NW (202-331-4020); in Montgomery Mall at 7101 Democracy Blvd. (301-469-5090); and in Pentagon Center at 1201 S. Hayes St. (703-412-4900) and in Tysons Corner Center, Lower Level (703-761-1473). Their other locations are too numerous to mention, but can be found in any local phone book.

If you are really hungry, try **Generous George's Positive Pizza and Pasta Place** at 3006 Duke St. in Alexandria (703-370-4303). As its name suggests, Generous George's fare is king-sized—enormous pizzas, huge salads and gigantic pasta dishes. Quality does not suffer from the emphasis on quantity. In the Torpedo Factory Food Pavilion in Old Town Alexandria, you will find **Radio Free Italy** (703-836-2151). "Pizza and pasta with frequency" is their motto and Marconi is the house beer.

While pizza is what put **Julio's**, at 1604 U St. NW (202-483-8500), on the map, this restaurant is best known for its Sunday brunches and happy hours. Brunches are all-you-can-eat and there is plenty to choose from, including, of course, pizza. Happy hour, from Monday through Thursday, can easily be turned into dinner—they serve free pizza.

Seafood

Seafood lovers in your crowd will want to take advantage of Maryland's specialty—soft-shell crabs. It may be a little disconcerting at first to eat the whole thing—shells, claws and all—but it is a treat not to be missed. For the freshest crab, make a trip to Maryland's Eastern Shore during the summer months. Just hop on Route 50 East and keep driving. You will know when to stop—when you see corner stands along the highway selling fresh crab and other seafood.

If you want to stay closer to the District, go to the waterfront in Southwest (Metro's Green Line to Waterfront). Along Water St., you will see **Phillips Flagship** at 900 Water St. (202-488-8515), **Hogate's** at 9th St. and Maine Ave. (202-484-6300) and the **Gangplank** at 600 Water St. (202-554-5000). **Le Rivage**, a French seafood restaurant mentioned previously, is also on this street.

Tony & Joe's Seafood Place at 3000 K St. NW (202-944-4545) is farther up the Potomac in Georgetown's Washington Harbour complex. Some prefer its less expensive sister restaurant, the **Dancing Crab** at 4611

STEAK AND BEEF HOUSES

Capital Grille
601 Pennsylvania Ave. NW
202-737-6200

Les Halles de Paris
1201 Pennsylvania Ave. NW
202-347-6848

Morton's of Chicago
3251 Prospect St. NW
202-342-6258

Outback Steakhouse
7720 Woodmont Ave., Bethesda
301-913-0176
4821 North First St., Arlington
703-527-0063
(and other locations)

The Palm
1225 19th St. NW
202-293-9091

The Prime Rib
2020 K St. NW
202-466-8811

Ruth's Chris Steakhouse
1801 Connecticut Ave. NW
202-797-0033
(and other locations)

Sam & Harry's
1200 19th St. NW
202-296-4333

Wisconsin Ave. NW (202-244-1882), at the corner of Wisconsin Ave. and Brandywine St. NW. This restaurant serves all-you-can-eat crab dinners during the summer. During the winter months, the Dancing Crab offers an all-you-can-eat raw bar.

The popular Massachusetts chain, **Legal Seafoods**, has recently opened restaurants at 2020 K St. NW (202-496-1111) and in Tysons Galleria (703-827-8900) in Virginia. An old-time local favorite is **O'Donnell's Restaurant** at 8301 Wisconsin Ave. (301-656-6200), serving seafood for over 70 years, along with tasty, traditional rum buns.

Pesce Trattoria at 2016 P St. NW (202-466-3474), a combination fish market and restaurant, is reported to serve the freshest fish in Washington. It was opened by the same chefs of the four-star restaurants, Jean Louis at the Watergate Hotel and Galileo, as another outlet for their source of supremely fresh fish. You can either take the fish home and cook it yourself or take advantage of two of Washington's finest chefs and have them cook it for you.

Arlington is home to the **Chesapeake Seafood and Crab House and An-Loc Landing Vietnamese Restaurant and Pho** at 3607 Wilson Blvd. (703-528-8896). If the name seems like a mouthful, you should see the menu—a full 15 pages of items ranging from basic seafood to exotic Vietnamese dishes. Despite the incongruity of it all—the menu covers "authentic Vietnamese and Chinese, along with a variety of typically French and American seafood cuisines"—this restaurant pulls it off. The crab and Vietnamese dishes are excellent and plenty of outdoor seating makes the Crab House a must on a summer evening.

Crisfield's (301-589-1306) original location at 8012 Georgia Ave. in Silver Spring is known for its long lines, coffee-shop decor and amazing seafood. To ease the wait, a second Silver Spring location has opened at 8606 Colesville Rd. (301-588-1572).

The **Bethesda Crab House** at 4958 Bethesda Ave. (301-652-3382) serves up crab on long picnic tables under a sprawling awning; the outdoor seating is nice on a warm evening. If you are with a small group, be prepared—the waiters move parties from table to table to make way for the larger groups constantly arriving.

Fish Market at 105 King St. in Old Town Alexandria (703-836-5676) has a double personality—upstairs a lively crowd sings along in a pub-like atmosphere, while downstairs a more sedate group concentrates on eating and drinking. The Fish Market's huge 32-ounce "schooners" of beer make it a popular spot on the weekends, particularly for the 20-something crowd. The **Warehouse Bar & Grill** at 214 King St. (703-683-6868) serves seafood with a New Orleans twist. The soups and seafood chowders should not be overlooked. **Blue Point Grill** at 600 Franklin St. (703-739-0404) in Alexandria is affiliated with Sutton Place Gourmet. The menu starts with more than a dozen varieties of the day's fresh fish.

Thai

One of the newer and more interesting trends in Asian dining is the explosion of restaurants specializing in Thai cuisine. At **Duangrat's**, at 5878 Leesburg Pike (703-820-5775), waitresses in beautiful silk gowns serve some of the area's best Thai food. The whole fried fish and the crying duck come highly recommended at **Bangkok Orchid**, at 301 Massachusetts Ave. NE (202-546-5901). **Xing Kuba** offers authentic Thai cuisine at 2218 Wisconsin Ave. NW (202-965-0665).

Tara Thai in Vienna at 226 Maple Ave. West (703-255-2467) and in Bethesda at 4828 Bethesda Ave. (301-657-0488) is an award-winning restaurant specializing in seafood. Non-seafood eaters will find plenty of choices on their varied menu.

Perhaps the best endorsement for Bethesda's **Bangkok Garden** at 4906 St. Elmo Ave. (301-951-0670) is that it has two menus—one in English for Americans and one in Thai for its many Thai customers. The cook often goes easy on the spices for American customers. If you want the hot stuff, be sure to ask for it.

Vietnamese

If you have never had Vietnamese food, you have been missing something special. Vietnamese food is similar to Chinese food, but tends to be sweeter and more delicate. The Clarendon section of Arlington is absolutely the best place to go—locally—for the exotic flavors of this Asian cuisine. A host of Vietnamese restaurants compete within a several-block radius of the Metro station. **Cafe Saigon** at 1135 North Highland St.

VEGETARIAN EATING

Vegetarian meals are no longer an unusual thing in Washington dining circles. With increased attention being given to healthy eating styles, more and more restaurants are going vegetarian—at least for part of their menu. Traditionally, Chinese and Japanese restaurants have offered good choices for vegetarians. Increasingly, area pizza and pasta restaurants offer all-vegetable dishes and the many other restaurants in the area offer salads and other meat-free dishes. For the more devoted vegetarian, there are a number of specifically vegetarian restaurants in the area. Some of the most popular are listed here. Check with local health food stores for other suggestions.

Berwyn Cafe
5010 Berwyn Rd., College Park
301-345-6655

Food for Thought
1738 Connecticut Ave. NW
202-797-1095

Paru's Indian Vegetarian Restaurant
2010 S St. NW
202-483-5133

Siddhartha
8241 Georgia Ave., Silver Spring
301-585-0550

(703-243-6522), **Nam-Viet** at 1127 North Hudson St. (703-522-7110) and **Queen Bee** at 3181 Wilson Blvd. (703-527-3444). These restaurants all offer fine cuisine at relatively inexpensive prices.

In Georgetown, **Vietnam Georgetown Restaurant** at 2934 M St. NW (202-337-4536) and **Saigon Inn** at 2928 M St. NW (202-337-5588) sit side by side. Eclectic **Germaine's** at 2400 Wisconsin Ave. NW (202-965-1185) offers Pan-Asian and Vietnamese dishes. This restaurant is known for being a good place for star-sightings and is popular among the local press corps.

Etc....

Cities at 2424 18th St. NW in Adams Morgan (202-328-7194) offers a unique approach to the dining experience. Every few months, Cities changes its entire decor and revamps its menu to celebrate the cuisine of a different city. Regional wines are also selected to round out the cultural experience.

Jaleo at 480 7th St. NW (202-628-7949) recreates the taste, feel and atmosphere of a Spanish tapas restaurant. At Jaleo, customers casually linger over the small appetizers with a glass of one of the fine sherries in the restaurant's extensive selection. With a constant crowd in the bar area, Jaleo makes for an appealing night out. Just up the street is **Coco Loco** at 810 7th St. NW (202-289-2626), another popular tapas restaurant. In addition, they offer a fixed-price, all-you-can-eat, traditional Brazilian mixed grill.

The quirky decor of **Andalusian Dog** at 1344 U St. NW (202-986-6364) should not distract you from its excellent food. This tapas restaurant is one of several establishments in the growing U St. corridor that have been designed by area artists. Winged loaves of bread fly across the painted ceiling in the front room and above the bar. A mixture of painting and relief work creates the illusion of a whirlpool sucking bodies into the gaping mouth of a dog. In contrast, the tapas food is simple and really well done, so do not let the wall of human hands distract you.

If you are a hungry art lover, **Utopia** at 1418 U St. NW (202-483-7669) will leave you doubly satisfied. The owner of this restaurant and bar is a painter and the space doubles as an art gallery for his work and the work of other local artists. Utopia's high ceiling (the building used to be a garage) leaves ample wall space for paintings and prints. There is also a full bar with weekday happy hour.

The **State of the Union**—the former Soviet Union that is—at 1357 U St. NW (202-588-8810) offers Russian-American cuisine. The menu even lists a shot of Vodka as an appetizer. Like many of the other restaurants and bars on U St., the owners had local artists decorate the interior. In this case, even the bathrooms are works of art.

Authentic Malaysian food is available at the **Straits of Malaysia** at 1836 18th St. NW (202-483-1483) in Adams Morgan. Enjoy your summer meal on their rooftop restaurant.

Panjshir II at 224 Maple Ave. West in Vienna (703-281-4183) is a family-owned and -operated Afghan restaurant. The menu includes a range of beef, lamb, poultry and vegetarian dishes, with entrees from $10 to $20. One friend says "The kebabs are to die for." On first glance, the decor appears to be formal, but the ambiance is actually comfortable and relaxed. The owners wait on customers and are very entertaining.

For authentic Moroccan cuisine and atmosphere, plan a dinner at **Marrakesh** at 617 New York Ave. NW (202-393-9393). The evening features a fixed-price seven-course meal eaten with the hands using broken bread. Belly dancing is the featured entertainment. This restaurant accepts no credit cards, so be sure to take along cash or your checkbook.

Oodles Noodles at 1010 20th St. NW (202-293-3138) is a Pan-Asian restaurant with an emphasis on Malaysian and Indonesian cooking.

Authentic Jamaican cuisine is available at Adams Morgan's **Montego Cafe** at 2437 18th St. NW (202-745-1002) where reggae music and jerk chicken are only part of the colorful tropical atmosphere. For fine Caribbean dining, **Hibiscus Cafe** at 3401 K St. NW (202-338-0408) in Georgetown specializes in Caribbean fusion cooking.

For That Special Evening

To begin a special evening, start with drinks at the **Terrace at the Hotel Washington** at 515 15th St. NW (202-638-5900), overlooking the Mall and the White House. When you enter the hotel, take the elevator to the top floor. If you are looking for something with a dash of Victorian romance for dinner afterwards, try the nearby **Morrison Clark Inn** at 1015 L St. NW (202-898-1200).

The chic atmosphere at **I Matti** at 2436 18th St. NW (202-462-8844) makes it a great place to begin an evening in Adams Morgan. In Georgetown, **Ristorante Piccolo** at 1068 31st St. NW (202-342-7414) offers intimate candle-lit tables and good Italian cuisine, making it a great spot for dinner before wandering around the neighborhood.

If you are in the mood for French cuisine, try **Le Gaulois Cafe Restaurant** at 1106 King St. in Alexandria (703-739-9494), which has received rave reviews for both food and atmosphere. The fireplace definitely adds to the experience. Be sure to call ahead and make reservations.

Another favorite is Potomac's **Old Angler's Inn** at 10801 MacArthur Blvd. (301-365-2425). This country inn, within walking distance of the C&O Canal Towpath, features regional cuisine with a French accent. In the winter, try to get a spot next to the fireplace. In the summer and spring, take advantage of the outside terrace.

Nora's at 2132 Florida Ave. NW (202-462-5143) is Washington's answer to Chez Panisse, the Berkeley restaurant that started the nouvelle cuisine trend. From appetizers to desserts, everything is freshly made from organic ingredients. They always have one selection from every part of a meal for vegetarians.

The **Iron Gate Inn** at 1734 N St. NW (202-737-1370), a Middle Eastern restaurant in an old carriage house just off Dupont Circle, is another popular favorite. In the summer, take advantage of its wonderful courtyard. Meals are just as romantic in the winter when you can sit indoors in a cozy room with a fireplace.

To cap off an evening out with a drink and a bit of jazz, stop by **Café Lautrec** (202-265-6436) at 2432 18th St. NW in Adams Morgan. You cannot miss the restaurant, thanks to the mural of Lautrec painted on the building. This café has nightly live entertainment and on the weekends, tap dancing on the bar.

If you are in the mood for something a little quieter to finish off the evening, try **Dolce Finale** (202-667-5350). You will have to look closely to find this spot—tucked away under Petitto's restaurant at 2653 Connecticut Ave. NW in Woodley Park. The tiny basement café, with seating for just over a dozen people, has excellent desserts and is open until 1:30 a.m. on weekends.

For the ultimate special evening, slip away to the quiet atmosphere of a warm and inviting French country inn. **L'Auberge Chez François** (703-759-3800) is located at 332 Springvale Rd. in Great Falls and has been rated by the *Washingtonian* reader survey for over 10 years in a row as the area's best place to eat. Reservations at this gem are difficult to get due to its well-deserved popularity.

BARS, PUBS AND CLUBS

When you are out for the evening and want more than just a good meal, you don't have to go far. The metropolitan area is full of evening spots, including traditional bars and Irish pubs, casual and classy coffee bars, and a wide variety of night clubs.

BREW PUBS AND MICROBREWERIES

DC
Capitol City Brewing Company
11th and H Sts. NW
202-628-2222

Dock Street Brewing Company
1299 Pennsylvania Ave. NW
202-639-0403

Maryland
Olde Towne Tavern & Brewing Company
227 E. Diamond Ave., Gaithersburg
301-948-4200

Virginia
Bardo Rodeo
2000 Wilson Blvd., Arlington
703-527-1852

Blue-n-Gold Brewing Company
3100 Clarendon Blvd., Arlington
703-908-4995

Virginia Beverage Company
607 King St., Alexandria
703-684-5397

The Traditional Bars

When Washingtonians want to engage in a friendly game of bar golf or go on a more casual pub crawl, they head for the busy streets of Georgetown. You will find almost every kind of bar here. Prices reflect the neighborhood's trendy status. Old Town's King St. draws much the same crowd. In Dupont Circle, the bars around 19th and M Sts. are the place to go. Below are highlights of some of Washington's many notable bars.

The **Brickskeller** at 1523 22nd St. NW (202-293-1885) boasts over 500 different types of beer from all over the world. The Brickskeller is a better place to go to catch up with a long-lost pal than to meet a new friend. Unlike most bars, no one mills about or dances; instead the host will ask you to choose a table.

On weekdays, the **Bottom Line** at 1716 Eye St. NW (202-298-8488) features free munchies including tacos, buffalo wings and egg rolls, making this a popular watering hole for nearby workers. On the weekends, college students pack this bar to drink and dance. **Quigley's** at 1825 Eye St. NW (202-331-0150) attracts much of the same crowd, with dancing on Tuesday, Friday and Saturday and live entertainment on Thursday. American University students hang out at its second location near Tenleytown at 3201 New Mexico Ave. NW (202-966-0500). Do not mistake the **Third Edition** at 1218 Wisconsin Ave. NW (202-333-3700) in Georgetown for a bookstore. It is a hot spot for the college crowd, especially on weekends, when there is a $5 cover charge.

The area around 19th and M Sts. includes a number of the better-known pick-up spots. Washingtonians and suburbanites flock to **Madhatter** at 1831 M St. NW (202-833-1495), **Sign of the Whale** at 1825 M St. NW (202-785-1110) and particularly **Rumors** at 1900 M St. NW (202-466-7378). Another popular pick-up joint is **Mr. Day's Sports Rock Cafe** at 1111 19th St. NW (202-296-7625), just off 19th St. in the back alley. The **Crow Bar** at 1006 20th St. NW (202-223-2972) attracts a young crowd. **Deja Vu** at 2119 M St. NW (202-452-1966) attracts a slightly older and more international crowd. Just a few blocks away is the **Front Page** at 1333 New Hampshire Ave. NW (202-296-6500). It lacks the reputation of the M St. bars, yet draws large crowds of yuppies and post-yuppies to its happy hour. Another good happy hour spot is **Ha' Penny Lion** at 1101 17th St. NW (202-296-8075), which caters to a slightly younger group.

A lot has been brewing recently at the corner of 11th and H Sts. NW—a lot of beer, that is, since the **Capital City Brewing Company** (202-628-2222) opened. This restaurant and bar serves all kinds of beer, most brewed on the premises. A rotating production schedule ensures that there are lots of new ales, Pilseners and porters to try on a regular basis. The menu ranges from steaks, sausages and burgers to salmon, shrimp and other seafood. The brewery attracts a mostly young, professional crowd and has a popular happy hour.

A wide variety of local talent can be seen at the **Grog & Tankard** at 2408 Wisconsin Ave. NW (202-333-3114). Monday is Grateful Dead night, Tuesday it's the blues, and Wednesday features progressive music. Expect to pay a cover charge of $6 or so.

Bethesda residents hang out at **Slade's** at 7201 Wisconsin Ave. (301-951-9000) and **Nantucket Landing** at 4723 Elm St. (301-654-7979) and shoot pool at **Shootz** at 4915 St. Elmo Ave. (301-654-8288), a pricy billiard hall. Afterwards, they trek out to the **Silver Diner** at 11806 Rockville Pike (301-770-2828) in Rockville for late-night snacking.

In Adams Morgan, the best places to go for a beer without giving up your entire wallet are **Stetson's** at 1610 U St. NW (202-667-6295) and **Millie & Al's** at 2440 18th St. NW (202-387-8131). Stetson's serves Tex-Mex fare and is a popular hangout among young Democrats. At Millie & Al's, you can relive college days in a smoky barroom cluttered with cheap pitchers of beer.

Several bars line Pennsylvania Ave. between 2nd and 7th Sts. SE on Capitol Hill. Among them you will find the **Tune Inn** (202-543-2725) and **Hawk and Dove** (202-543-3300). Both cater to the budgets of congressional staff and interns, who make up the majority of the crowd. Several congressmen are occasionally known to join their staffers at these spots, especially the Tune Inn. Other staffers trek over to **My Brother's Place** at 237 2nd St. NW (202-347-1350). On the Lower Level at nearby Union Station, **Fat Tuesday's** (202-289-6618) serves daiquiris and is a good place to hang out before going to the movies. **Tiber Creek Pub** at 15 E St. NW (202-638-0900) sells beer by the half-yard or yard, which translates into 24 or 48 ounces. People go there for the quantity more than anything else.

Whitey's at 2761 North Washington Blvd. (703-525-9825) is the place to go in Arlington. A young crowd comes to enjoy beer, live music and a large back room with a pool table, pinball machines, dart boards and fooz ball tables, turning this neighborhood bar into a neighborhood traffic jam on the weekends. Whitey's is easy to spot—just look for its neon "EAT" sign out front.

Bardo Rodeo at 2000 Wilson Blvd. (703-527-9399) is located in the old Olmstead Oldsmobile building in Arlington. Bardo never got around to removing the Olmstead sign or the car-jukebox that pokes through the front window. Simply put, this place is huge, occupying both the old showroom and the garage, with tons of outdoor seating to boot. Topping it off is Bardo's on-tap selection of 35 beers, 40 kinds of bottled beer, and root beer and hard cider.

A short distance from Bardo Rodeo, two bars serve a similarly broad selection of beer in much smaller environs. **Strangeways** at 2830 Wilson Blvd. (703-243-5272), adorned with pictures of balding men and imitations of Picasso paintings, is a funky but cozy place to hang out. Check out their dozens of beers on a Sunday night, when the crowd is not so big and there is a better chance of finding the pool table free. You can also visit the **Galaxy Hut** at 2711 Wilson Blvd. (703-525-8646) as an alternative to gigantic Bardo. This bar is similar to Strangeways—a smaller, strangely decorated place with a wide selection of beers on tap. Bring some quarters for the lava-lamp jukebox.

Irish Pubs

Washington has several excellent Irish pubs. The biggest and most popular is **Ireland's Four Provinces**, commonly referred to as the Four Ps, at 3412 Connecticut Ave. NW (202-244-0860), in Cleveland Park. In addition to good folk singers and good food, the Four Ps offers Guinness on draft. On the Hill, staffers and Georgetown law students hang out at the **Dubliner** at 4 F St. NW (202-737-3773) and **Kelly's Irish Times** at 14 F St. NW (202-543-5433). Other favorites include **Murphy's of DC** (202-462-7171) at 2609 24th St. NW, **Murphy's Grand Irish Pub** (703-548-1717) at 713 King St. and **Ireland's Own** (703-549-4535) at 132 N. Royal St., both in Alexandria, and **Flanagan's Irish Pub** (301-986-1007) at 7637 Old Georgetown Rd. in Bethesda.

Gay Bars and Restaurants

The Dupont Circle area is very much the center of Washington's gay community and is home to several of the city's gay restaurants and bars. **JR's Bar & Grill** at 1519 17th St. NW (202-328-0090) attracts the young, preppie crowd. Its popular happy hours draw a regular following. Also on 17th St. you will find several gay-oriented restaurants including **Annie's Paramount Steak House** at #1609 (202-232-0395) and **Trio's** at #1537 (202-232-6305). Around the corner is the popular **Cafe Luna** at 1633 P St. NW (202-387-4005). Capitol Hill has **Two Quail** at 320 Massachusetts Ave. NE (202-543-8030), an excellent restaurant, and **Mr. Henry's** at 601 Pennsylvania Ave. SE (202-546-8412) serving burgers and beer in a relaxed atmosphere. Of all these, Annie's is the place to go to see and be seen. **Trumpets**, a popular bar at 1633 Q St. NW (202-232-4141), is also a great restaurant and features a menu that changes from time to time.

Across Dupont Circle there is dancing at **Badlands** at 1415 22nd St. NW (202-296-0505). If you need more dancing room, try **Tracks** at 1111 1st St. SE (202-488-3320), but you will have to travel to get there. Be careful when you go, Tracks is located in a rough neighborhood.

The Levi/Leather crowd hangs out at **DC Eagle** at 639 New York Ave. NW (202-347-6025) and the **Fireplace** at 2161 P St. NW (202-293-1293). Those looking for country and western bars can go to **Remington's**, on the Hill at 639 Pennsylvania Ave. SE (202-543-3113), one of the friendliest bars in the city. As is true in a number of big cities, gay bashing is no stranger to Washington, so be careful and pay attention to where you walk.

The Coffee Bars

Espresso machines all over town are now busier than ever churning out espresso, latte and cappuccino. San Franciscans who complain that they miss Peet's can get some local coffee satisfaction at Quartermaine Coffee Roasters and can even find Peet's own at all the Au Bon Pain sites. And Seattlites, who used to have to drive to Nordstrom to get their fix, can go to the oh-so-familiar Starbucks. For others, the coffee bar invasion has been a stimulating educational experience.

Since its arrival in the early '90s, **Starbucks** has opened a multitude of shops, too many to mention entirely, but including those at 3430 Wisconsin Ave. NW (202-537-6879), 1501 Connecticut Ave. NW (202-588-1280), 532 King St. in Old Town Alexandria (703-836-2236), 5438 Westbard Ave. in Bethesda (301-718-6339), 10100 River Rd. in Potomac (301-299-9226), 36 Wisconsin Circle in Chevy Chase (301-951-0132), and in the Lyon Village Shopping Center at Lee Hwy. and Spout Run in Arlington (703-527-6506).

Quartermaine Coffee Roasters at 3323 Connecticut Ave. NW (202-244-2676) plans similar growth. Unlike Starbucks, which ships its roasted beans from Seattle, Quartermaine roasts its coffee at their plant in Rockville. Its Bethesda store is located at 4817 Bethesda Ave. (301-718-2853). If you are interested in taking a tour of the roasting plant, just call 301-230-4600.

Hannibal's serves up some of the best cappuccino in DC at its several locations. It has two shops at Dupont Circle, one at 1300 Connecticut Ave. NW (202-822-9800) and another at 1528 Connecticut Ave. NW (202-232-1107), right on the circle. The one on the circle is small inside, but has tables outside for drinking espresso and watching everyone else rush in and out of the Metro. Another location is at 2000 Pennsylvania Ave. (202-822-0040) and others still are at Union Station in the District and in White Flint and College Park in Maryland.

In addition to the larger chains of coffee bars, there are a number of local ones. **Cup'A Cup'A** at 1350 19th St. NW (202-466-6571) is deliciously handy for morning commuters in the Dupont Circle area; no seating, just coffee and pastries to go, half a block from the Metro station. A second location is at 1911 K St. NW (202-466-3378). The **Café des Amis du Café** at 1020 19th St. NW (202-466-7860) is a great choice in the Downtown area.

Dupont Circle hosts **Kramerbooks & Afterwords Cafe** at 1517
Connecticut Ave. NW (202-387-3825), which aims to please the hungry
bookworm. Kramer's is two places in one—a bookstore and a café. Aside
from cakes and pastries, Kramer's offers an eclectic, somewhat pricy dinner
menu and is most known as a late-night hangout after everything else
closes—the café and bookstore are open all night on Friday and Saturday.
A second location recently opened in Arlington at 4201 Wilson Blvd.
(703-524-7227), within sight of the Ballston Metro station. It features an
indoor and outdoor café and stays open until 3:00 a.m. on the weekends.

The **Java House** at 1645 Q St. NW (202-387-6622) stocks over 70 kinds
of beans from all over the world. The beans are roasted and flavored on
the premises. Indoor and outdoor seating is available for those who want
to take advantage of the light sandwich and coffee menu.

Just around the corner is a great place to enjoy your favorite coffee drink
on a cool evening. The storefront at **Cafe Blanca**, at 1523 17th St. NW
(202-986-3476), opens up, blending the interior with the sidewalk. The
decor is inspired by the movie "Casablanca," complete with spinning
ceiling fans and Humphrey Bogart murals.

On the same block, the **Pop Stop** at 1513 17th St. NW (202-328-0880)
offers a more off-beat atmosphere. The walls and floors of this two-story
coffee bar are painted with brightly colored scenes and psychedelic patterns
to offset the mixed bag of old upholstery, chairs and mismatched end
tables. There is plenty of seating inside, but if the decorations are too
much for your eyes, you can join the crowd that is always seated at the
tables in front. In the summer, the iced-coffee drinks are a great choice.

Zig Zag Cafe at 1524 U St. NW (202-986-5949) is perhaps the hippest
coffee bar in town. Located in the up-and-coming U St. corridor, this café
hosts a young artistic crowd. Zig Zag is below street level and crowded
with old tables, chairs and benches. On Fridays and Saturdays, Zig Zag is
open until 4:00 a.m. By contrast, **Jolt 'n Bolt Coffee and Tea House**, at
1918 18th St. NW (202-232-0077), is a quiet neighborhood place. **Soho
Tea & Coffee** at 2150 P St. NW (202-463-7646) is very popular with
Generation Xers and with smokers, with eclectic concerts on Friday nights.

The Clubs
Tracks at 1111 1st St. SE is an institution (202-488-3320). Its three
dance areas—two inside, one outside—add up to over 20,000 square feet.
The outdoor dance area plays a mix of music; indoors, one dance floor
gyrates to techno music while the other plays mostly alternative artists.
Dress down when you go to Tracks—jeans in the winter and shorts in the

summer. Cover charges on Friday and Saturday nights are $5. Tracks is not in the best of neighborhoods; if you drive, it is worth it to pay $3 or so for parking in one of the makeshift parking lots.

The 15th St. corridor, just above the White House, has become a popular ground for new clubs. Within a few blocks, you will find the **Spy Club** at 805 15th St. NW (202-289-1779), **15 Minutes** at 1030 15th St. NW (202-408-1855) and **Zei** at 1415 Zei Alley NW (202-842-2445). The Spy Club's entrance is in an alley off 15th St. By day, 15 Minutes is Rothchild's Cafeteria and at night, this low-key club offers a mix of live and recorded music in its various rooms. The music ranges from progressive and rock to blues and jazz. Cover charges on Friday and Saturday nights ($6) include a free buffet. When you walk into Zei, you are greeted with a jumble of images—a tower of TVs, girls dancing on pedestals and lots of attitude. A $750 membership allows you to skip the line out front and relax in their private club, two floors above the dance floor. This club plays mostly dance and disco.

The **Fifth Column** at 915 F St. NW (202-393-3632), the **Vault** at 911 F St. NW (202-347-8079) and the **Ritz** at 919 E St. NW (202-638-2582) are not far away. Despite their geographic proximity, they offer different types of music and attract different crowds. The Fifth Column is probably the closest thing Washington has to a New York club. A younger, more mixed group frequents its next door neighbor, the Vault. At the Ritz, a fashionably dressed crowd dances on five dance floors to jazz, top 40, reggae, hip hop and Motown.

Adams Morgan, too, has its share of nightclubs. Two spots, **Heaven** and **Hell**, both at 2327 18th St. NW (202-667-4355), are close by. Not surprisingly, Hell is downstairs and Heaven is upstairs. In Heaven, a young crowd dances to progressive music; the dimly lit Hell fosters drinking and talking.

One of Adams Morgan's best-known clubs is **Kilimanjaro** at 1724 California St. NW (202-328-3838). Despite its African name, Kilimanjaro plays a mix of music and concentrates on Caribbean themes. On weekdays before 8:00 p.m., Kilimanjaro offers a happy hour (complete with food). Kilimanjaro carefully controls its two dance floors; the second one opens only when the first is completely packed. This guarantees that you will always experience that club crush, bringing you into close contact with your neighbors. Cover charges for live musical acts start at $15.

Do you want to go out or would you rather eat bugs? Well, the **Insect Club** at 625 E St. NW (202-347-8884) happily caters to both tastes by offering drinks, dancing and edible insects. In addition, the dim lighting and small rooms and hallways give this place the feel of a kind of hive or nest when it's crowded.

On the weekends, there is always a line at **Chief Ike's Mambo Room** at 1725 Columbia Rd. NW (202-332-2211) in Adams Morgan, so consider getting there early if you want to get in at all. Ike's is very casual, very crowded and very dark. The DJ "Stella Neptune" is a big attraction for two reasons—she only plays disco music from the '70s and she is the hottest DJ in town.

For an evening a little outside the mainstream, try the **Black Cat Club** at 1831 14th St. NW (202-667-7960). The Black Cat is owned and operated by musicians and leans toward underground and alternative music, although it also has jazz and blues on certain week nights.

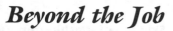

Beyond the Job

*W*hile to some, "Washingtonian" is synonymous with "workaholic," it is really only accurate for the rare and truly stereotypical Washingtonian. In fact, most Washingtonians play just as hard as they work—and in this rich and complex metropolitan area, play takes many different forms. The area has a surprisingly large number of social, cultural, educational, recreational and entertainment resources. You can join any of a multitude of organizations—everything from biking and hiking clubs to volunteer groups to affiliations with the Smithsonian and · Kennedy Center. Organizations provide a great way to meet new friends while taking part in your favorite activities.

ACTIVITIES AND SOCIAL CLUBS

If meeting new people in enjoyable social settings is your free-time preference, you will be glad to know about the many activity and social clubs in the area. Some focus on specific areas of interest, others are more broad-based. Some specialize in creating activities for individuals of certain age groups, others know no limit.

Capital City Dining Club

If you have ever dined alone, wishing for someone to share the experience, the Capital City Dining Club may interest you. The club was formed as a way for busy Washington singles and couples to dine out with others and to make new friends in the process. The club's variety of events is designed to appeal to both the casual and formal diner. Several events are scheduled each month at some of the most popular sites in the Washington area. The emphasis is on meeting people, not matchmaking; they do not pair people up, nor do they give out phone numbers. Individual membership is $85-yr.; $120 for two years; event costs vary depending on the venue. To obtain further information, call 703-971-0284.

Clubhouse

Single individuals in the 24-36 age bracket looking for new activities and friendships may be interested in the opportunities offered by the Clubhouse. Three to five activities, such as parties, movies, rafting trips and biking, are organized each month to appeal to a wide range of interests. Annual membership is $35 for singles, $55 for couples. Contact 301-577-4982 for more information.

POLITICAL ORGANIZATIONS

If you are interested in getting involved with either the Democratic or Republican parties, Washington is certainly the place to be. Call the Democratic National Committee (202-863-8000) or the Republican National Committee (202-863-8500) to find out more. These organizations can also put you in touch with other political groups from their "side of the aisle."

Ski Club of Washington, DC (SCWDC)

Most people do not associate Washington with skiing—the lack of snow during typical winters is one good reason, the lack of nearby mountains is another. However, SCWDC members do not let that slow them down. Over 6,000 members make the Ski Club of Washington the largest year-round ski club on the Eastern Seaboard. The Ski Club offers a host of social and recreational activities, including wine and cheese tastings, swing and ballroom dance lessons, hikes, tennis parties, biking trips and, yes, skiing, both lessons and excursions. Call 703-536-8273 and leave your name and address to receive a membership application and a SKI-O-GRAM (you will have to call to find out what this is). The Ski Club may appeal to individuals slightly older than the Clubhouse crowd. Membership is $35, individual; $55, double. Contact 703-536-8273 for information.

State Societies

Lonely for home and longing to be with people who pronounce the letter "r" just the way you do? Then join your home state society. Nominal membership fees (around $15 a year) guarantee you an invitation to every one of their social events. For more information on your state society, you can call the **National Conference of State Societies** at 301-249-6666.

The Washington Area Party Group

The Washington Area Party Group is a social group for individuals in the 21-40 year age range. They offer a variety of events announced by monthly newsletters and mailed invitations as well as on their Website, **http://www.dyntec.com/partydc** on the Internet. There is no membership fee; however, there is a charge for the events. Further information may be obtained by contacting 703-391-2708, or by calling their events hotline at 202-686-2997.

Wine Tasting Association

This non-profit organization offers such activities as wine tastings and cooking classes, including embassy events to sample the wines of a particular country and an annual international beer and wine festival. Event calendars are distributed to members to announce upcoming events, including information on dates, times and costs. Members receive discounts at area wine shops. Annual membership fees are $50 for an individual and $80 for two people at the same address.

EDUCATION

Washington is a city full of educational resources. With approximately 25 colleges and universities spread among the three jurisdictions, this area is rich in opportunities and deserves the reputation it has earned as a center of education and learning.

Universities

Twelve of the area's leading institutions of higher learning are members of a cooperative venture, the **Consortium of Universities of the Metropolitan Washington Area**, with offices at One Dupont Circle NW (202-331-8080). The Consortium members are the **American University**, the **Catholic University of America**, **Gallaudet University**, **George Mason University**, **George Washington University**, **Georgetown University**, **Howard University**, **Marymount University**, **Mount Vernon College**, **Trinity College**, the **University of the District of Columbia** and the **University of Maryland**. Through the Consortium, students have access to the courses, faculty and libraries of all the member universities.

Founded in 1857, **Gallaudet University** (202-651-5000), is the world's only private educational institution and research center serving deaf and hearing impaired individuals. **Howard University** (202-806-6100), founded in 1867, is the nation's largest and most comprehensive institution of higher learning with a predominantly African-American enrollment.

Non-Degree Classes

Washingtonians can take advantage of having the **Smithsonian Institution** in their backyard. The Smithsonian offers individual lectures, seminars and concerts, most of which are held in the Baird Auditorium at the American History Museum. Their continuing education arm, Campus on the Mall (202-357-3030), offers courses in the arts, humanities, sciences and studio arts, together with a vast offering of lecture series. Many courses include guided tours of local museums and art galleries. Some courses even conclude with receptions at a related embassy. Classes usually meet weekly at one of the Smithsonian museums on the Mall for six to eight weeks. Virtually all locations are easily accessible by Metro.

Georgetown University (202-687-5942) offers some of the best non-credit classes for adults, from Women in Western Political Thought to Screen Writing for Film and Television Movies to Chinese. There are evening and weekend courses in art history, studio arts, theater, music, literature, writing, communication, classics, religion, psychology, philosophy, history, international affairs, languages, economics, personal finance, science, computers and professional development. On-campus parking is available at a discounted rate for registered students.

Another great bargain is the **US Department of Agriculture** (202-720-5885). The USDA offers over a thousand courses per year in 50 subject areas intended to help government and other organizations to increase efficiency and effectiveness. The courses are open to all and most are held week nights at various federal office buildings downtown, accessible by Metro.

Through its Center for Career Education and Workshops (CCEW), **George Washington University** (202-994-5299) also offers non-credit professional training courses. In addition to courses in fields such as desktop publishing and financial planning, CCEW sponsors FSE, GRE, GMAT and LSAT test-prep courses at rates much lower than their commercial competitors. Most CCEW courses cost between $300 and $350. Courses usually last eight weeks and are held in convenient downtown buildings. You can also enroll in regular undergraduate and graduate courses at GWU as a non-matriculating student. The information desk in the lobby of Rice Hall at 2121 Eye St. NW has course catalogs and schedules.

American University (202-885-2500) offers all of its regular undergraduate and graduate courses to qualified non-degree students. All classes are given at the main campus at 4400 Massachusetts Ave. NW. Non-degree students have access to the AU libraries and to the shuttle bus from the AU-Tenleytown Metro station on the Red Line. Once registered, you can purchase a $25 pass to use the sports center's swimming pool, racquetball courts and weight room.

The District's only public university, **University of the District of Columbia** (202-274-5000) offers both academic and non-academic classes at its main campus at 4200 Connecticut Ave. NW. District residents pay at rates substantially below those for non-residents. For professional development and leisure courses, call (202-274-5179).

Residents of Maryland and Virginia get the same advantages at their community colleges. **Montgomery College** has locations at Rockville (301- 279-5000), Takoma Park (301-650-1300) and Germantown (301-353-7700), each offering a wide variety of credit and non-credit courses and seminars. You can pick up catalogs and applications at any of the campuses. **Northern Virginia Community College** has campuses in Alexandria (703-845-6200), Annandale (703-323-3000) and Woodbridge

(703-878-5700). Virginia residents can expect to find course catalogs stuffed in their mailboxes on a regular basis.

First Class (202-797-5102) offers numerous, inexpensive classes that meet anywhere from one to four times. Most of the courses meet at the organization's Dupont Circle office, 1726 20th St. NW. Recent classes have included Bob Levey's Inside Look at Washington, as well as ones featuring New Age and business topics. First Class distributes its brochures in drop boxes at Metro stations, stores and restaurants around town.

ENTERTAINMENT

The Friday Weekend section of the *Washington Post* contains a comprehensive listing of current exhibits, lectures, concerts, plays, performances and movies, and is a valuable resource for beyond the job activities.

Concerts

To find out about upcoming concerts, listen to your favorite radio station or check the newspapers, especially the City Paper. Popular performers, particularly rock groups, play at **RFK Stadium** (202-547-9077), **USAir Arena** (301-350-3400), **George Mason's Patriot Center** (703-993-3033), **Warner Theatre** (202-783-4000) and **Constitution Hall** (202-638-2661).

Smaller concerts play **Lisner Auditorium** at George Washington University (202-994-1500) and the **Bayou** at 3135 K St. NW (202-333-2897). The reputation of Alexandria's **Birchmere** at 3901 Mount Vernon Ave. (703-549-5919) continues to grow even though the space remains small. If you can get in, you will certainly enjoy the live music, ranging from folk to country to blues. Tickets range from $6 to $35; call Ticketmaster at 202-432-SEAT.

During the summer, outdoor concerts and performances are held at **Wolf Trap's Filene Center**, universally known just as Wolf Trap (703-255-1860). Wolf Trap—part of the National Park Service—generally books classical, folk and country performers, as well as storytellers and comedians. If the weather is good you can buy lawn tickets, bring a blanket and some food, and have a picnic while you enjoy the music. The **Barns of Wolf Trap** (703-938-2404), which sponsors indoor concerts

MUSIC REVIEWS

You can listen to excerpts of albums reviewed by the *Washington Post* by calling 202-334-9000. The extension changes daily, so check the Style section of the Post on Sunday and Wednesday and the Weekend section on Friday for the current number.

Read about music, its history and characters at Website **http://www.cdscout.com/cdscout** on the Internet. Recordings ratings are included.

and shows, is their winter site. The **Carter-Barron Amphitheater** (202-426-6837) also holds outdoor concerts. The **Merriweather Post Pavilion** (301-982-1800) in Columbia, MD, is similar to Wolf Trap, but offers a wider variety of performance as it does not have to get Park Service approval for shows.

Classical music lovers will find plenty of opportunities to hear their favorite musicians and orchestras. The **Kennedy Center** (202-467-4600) hosts the National Symphony Orchestra as well as performances ranging from international orchestras to individuals in recital. The **French Embassy** (202-944-6000) and the **Smithsonian** (202-357-3030) both offer subscription series concerts, as do several of the universities in the area.

During the summer, area monuments, various art galleries and churches host free concerts. The Smithsonian (202-357-2700) frequently sponsors classical concerts. Big band aficionados attend performances on the grounds of the **Washington Monument**. If you have time during the day, the **Corcoran Gallery of Art** (202-638-3211) sponsors free summertime jazz. The **Washington National Cathedral** (202-537-6200) hosts free choral and chamber music concerts. From time to time, they also offer lunch-time concerts.

Theater

Washington, once considered a weak theater town, is now a prime pre-Broadway proving ground as well as a regional theater scene in its own right. Stars such as Thomas Hulce, Stacy Keach and Kelly McGillis make regular appearances at the Shakespeare Theatre at the Lansburgh and the Helen Hayes Awards have become an institution honoring local theater.

The **John F. Kennedy Center for the Performing Arts** (202-467-4600), perched along the banks of the Potomac River not far from the Lincoln Memorial, houses many cultural events and programs in its six theaters. Plays and comedies are usually performed in the Eisenhower Theater. The National Symphony Orchestra performs in the Concert Hall, the Washington Opera in the Opera House. The Terrace Theater is reserved for concerts and plays. Theater groups and dance troupes perform experimental works in the Theater Lab. All kinds of movies, from advanced screenings to retrospectives, can be seen at the American Film Institute theater (202-828-4000). Since 1987, the Kennedy Center's Cabaret Theater has performed a comedy whodunit called "Shear Madness." This interactive play, set in DC, lets the audience play armchair detective. The humor is based on local events and people. You can learn about what is on stage at the Kennedy Center at **http://kennedy-center.org/** on the Internet.

The **National Theatre** at 1321 Pennsylvania Ave. NW (202-628-6161), a few blocks from the White House, attracts Broadway previews as well as Broadway hits on tour. The newly renovated **Warner Theatre** at 13th and E Sts. NW (202-783-4000) hosts many musicals and concerts.

Although shows at the National Theatre and Kennedy Center may command the headlines, the irreplaceable gems for Washington theater goers are the Arena and Shakespeare Theaters. Theater-in-the-round is the best-known facet of **Arena Stage** at 6th and Maine Sts. SW (202-488-3300). Arena's own acting company produces a variety of plays, including classics, modern plays and the occasional musical. The Arena complex houses a standard stage, the Kreeger Theatre, and a performance space, the Old Vat Room.

Shakespeare is alive and well at the **Shakespeare Theatre** at the Lansburgh, 450 7th St. NW (202-393-2700). Each season, the company produces three plays by Shakespeare along with one penned by someone other than the Bard. If you were to pick only one theater to subscribe to, the Shakespeare would be an excellent choice. The quality is superb and the price not astronomical. If the performance is sold out, standing-room-only tickets are usually available for $10 and go on sale one hour before the performance. You can look for upcoming events at Website **http://shakespearedc.org** on the Internet.

Each year, the **Ford's Theatre** (202-638-2941), best known as the site of the assassination of President Lincoln, performs big-name, family-oriented shows and musicals. Ford's Theatre is a national monument and the small Lincoln museum in the basement is worth the trip on its own. Website **http://www.fordstheatre.org** will provide you more information on this historic site.

The historic **Lincoln Theatre** at 1215 U St. NW (202-328-6000) was among a number of theaters, cabarets, dance halls and restaurants in what was referred to as "Black Broadway" during the first half of this century. In its heyday, it attracted some of the country's best entertainers. It was restored by the city in 1994 and today hosts musical and comedy acts. Tickets are available through Ticketmaster (202-432-SEAT). The theater is located across from the U St.-Cardoza Metro station.

Studio Theatre at 1333 P St. NW (202-332-3300) offers off-beat comedy and drama on its two small stages. Studio is one of several small theaters in the 14th St. Theater District, an "unofficial" district famous for its daring and experimental theater companies. Along with the Studio Theatre, you will find the **Woolly Mammoth** at 1401 Church St. NW

(202-393-3939) and the **Source Theatre Company** at 1835 14th St. NW (202-462-1073). These theaters attract local thespian groups and occasionally produce the works of local playwrights. In Northern Virginia, **Signature Theatres** at 3806 South Four Mile Run Dr. (703-820-9771) has acquired a terrific reputation for its productions, especially of Stephen Sondheim musicals. This comparatively small company produced the first local staging of Sondheim's offbeat "Assassins." Ticket prices at all of these theaters are generally pretty low.

The award-winning Grupo de Actores Latino Americanos performs at the **GALA Hispanic Theatre** at 1625 Park Rd. NW (202-234-7174). They present three plays a season by Latin American or Spanish authors. One of these productions is performed in both Spanish and English and the others are done in Spanish with simultaneous English translation. There is also a French-American theater group, **Le Néon**, at 3616 Lee Hwy. in Arlington, VA (703-243-NEON).

Each summer, Rock Creek Park and the Shakespeare Theatre sponsor a free play at the **Carter-Barron Amphitheater** at 16th St. and Colorado Ave. NW (202-426-6837). The production is usually a restaging of one of the Shakespeare Theatre's recently produced works. During the rest of the summer, the Carter-Barron is home to a series of free concerts and musical recitals from classical to jazz to pop.

If you are looking for discount theater tickets, half-price tickets can be purchased (cash only) the day of the show at **Ticketplace** at 12th and F Sts. NW (202-842-5387), near Metro Center on the Red, Orange or Blue Lines. Given the high demand, Ticketplace can afford to have limited hours; it is only open Tuesday through Friday from noon to 4:00 p.m. and on Saturdays from 11:00 a.m. to 5:00 p.m. You can also look into standing-room-only tickets or being an usher by checking with the box offices of the individual theaters.

Regular-price tickets can be purchased either at the theater box offices or over the phone through **Ticketmaster** (202-432-7328) or **Telecharge** (1-800-233-3123).

Movies

Washington is a terrific movie town and is, in fact, one of the few places where movie theaters survived the video revolution, although in a relatively diminished state. There are many first-run houses; a sizable collection of theaters specializing in classic, foreign and art films; and an annual local film festival, Filmfest DC.

Each year, hundreds of movies, new and old, from Hollywood and elsewhere are shown at the **American Film Institute** theater in the Kennedy Center (202-785-4601).

The **Uptown Theatre** at 3426 Connecticut Ave. NW (202-966-5400) generally gets the most votes as Washington's best movie theater. It has preserved the old-style seating and balcony. A remnant of the art deco period, the Uptown maintains its original huge screen. The theater shows both first-run movies and, occasionally, classics like "Lawrence of Arabia" and "2001: A Space Odyssey."

The **Avalon**, up the street at 5612 Connecticut Ave. NW (202-966-2600) may turn out to be even better. Renovated in the mid-1980s with a brand new sound system, the Avalon's screen is better for today's movies than the one at the Uptown. The Uptown was built for an old, curved Cinemascope screen. As these screens are no longer made, the Uptown has had to replace the original with a series of one-inch strips running from floor to ceiling. This can be distracting if you sit in the front row.

The **Cineplex Odeon Cinemas** (202-244-0880) is a popular modern multiplex with six screens. Located at 4000 Wisconsin Ave. NW, they show mostly first run commercial movies with an occasional art film that appeals to other tastes. The seats are comfortable and the free parking in the underground garage in convenient.

The **AMC Union Station** at 50 Massachusetts Ave. NE (703-998-4AMC) is the only movie house in the Northeast quadrant of the city. When the idea was first introduced to have a movie theater in the basement of the renovated train station, it was met with some skepticism. Today, nine spacious and popular theaters cater to an otherwise under-served part of the city. Each theater in the complex is named for a famous movie house from Washington's cinema history.

Both the **Arlington Cinema 'n Drafthouse** at 2903 Columbia Pike (703-486-2345) and the **Bethesda Theatre Café** at 7719 Wisconsin Ave. (301-656-3337) serve beer, wine and snacks during movies. Both show second-run movies, and admission is around $4 on the weekends and $3 during the week. Radio station DC 101 sponsors dollar nights on Monday at each. On Sundays during the fall, Redskins games take over the screen and admission is free.

The **Key** at 1222 Wisconsin Ave. NW (202-333-5100) and the **Biograph** at 2819 M St. NW (202-333-2696), both in Georgetown, show independent and foreign films and are ideal places to brush up on your French, Spanish or German. Those who really love serious cinema should

EVENTS AND FESTIVALS

January/February

Martin Luther King Jr.'s Birthday The National Park Service sponsors an annual ceremony at the Lincoln Memorial, the site of Dr. Martin Luther King's 1963 "I Have A Dream" speech.

Chinese New Year Parade Chinatown celebrates the Chinese New Year by watching the fireworks and elaborately costumed parade participants.

George Washington's Birthday Parade Old Town Alexandria hosts a parade; Mount Vernon, George Washington's home, holds special activities.

March/April

St. Patrick's Day Parade Bagpipers, bands and floats parade through Old Town Alexandria and along Constitution Ave. in Washington.

Smithsonian Kite Festival Fly your kite with hundreds of others on the Washington Monument grounds.

Cherry Blossom Festival The local week-long rite of spring celebrates one of the area's most beautiful sights. Short-lived blossoms, concentrated along the Tidal Basin, peak between mid-March and mid-April.

Duke Ellington Birthday Celebration Celebrate the music of this DC-born jazz star with a concert at Freedom Plaza, 13th St. and Pennsylvania Ave. NW.

White House Easter Egg Roll Children aged eight and under, accompanied by adults, gather on the White House South Lawn for this annual event.

May/June

Filmfest DC Over 50 international and American independent films are shown in movie theaters all over town.

Malcolm X Day A day to honor Malcolm X is held each year in Anacostia Park in Southeast DC, featuring speeches, exhibits, music and food.

Gay Pride Day This march to promote gay rights and awareness begins at 16th and W Sts. and ends at 24th and N Sts.

Festival of American Folklife At this annual festival, the Smithsonian presents a slice of American Folklife. The festival is held on the Mall in late June to early July.

Memorial Day Weekend Concert The National Symphony Orchestra performs an outdoor concert on the West Lawn of the US Capitol.

July/August

Fourth of July In the nation's capital, this holiday is a day full of free celebrations—a dramatic reading of the Declaration of Independence, a parade down Constitution Ave., an evening performance of the National Symphony Orchestra, and the main event, a tremendous fireworks display on the Mall.

Latin American Festival For two days at the end of July, the mall comes alive with Latin American music, food, dance and crafts.

September/October

Adams Morgan Day A street festival along 18th St. NW, on the second Sunday in September, celebrates the multicultural flavor of this neighborhood.

Taste of DC Each October, the DC Committee to Promote Washington offers Taste of DC, featuring food from local restaurants, to promote area tourism and benefit local charities.

Marine Corps Marathon In late October, thousands of runners participate in the famous race from the Iwo Jima Memorial in Arlington through downtown DC.

Halloween Georgetown is the place to be for Halloween. Wisconsin Ave. and M St. are closed to traffic as thousands of costumed pedestrians descend upon an eight-block area.

November/December

National Christmas Tree Lighting Join the President—and a few thousand locals and tourists—for this annual ritual on the Ellipse, south of the White House.

look into the Key's Sunday Cinema Club. Members see new, unreleased (mostly foreign) movies on Sunday mornings with free coffee during the showing and a discussion session following. The Biograph, a landmark for 29 years, is being forced to close effective June 30, 1996 due to the loss of its lease. Foreign film aficionados will want to watch for its announced reopening at a new site, away from Georgetown, at some time in the future.

The **Cineplex Odeon Jenifer** at 5252 Wisconsin Ave. NW (202-244-5703) still shows movies for just $1.25. The Jenifer is a great place to catch a movie that you may have missed when it first came out. You can take the Red Line to the Friendship Heights station—the theater is just steps from the Jenifer St. exit. Other than the Jenifer, the other second-run houses are in the suburbs.

Free movies are offered at a number of places including the **National Gallery's East Wing** and the Smithsonian's **Hirschhorn** and **National Air and Space Museums**. The **Mary Pickford Theater** (202-707-5677) in the Madison Building of the Library of Congress is an intimate theater with fewer than 70 seats; reservations are required.

Jazz

While not all that it once was, back in the days of Duke Ellington, Washington's jazz scene is still alive. One of the most popular clubs attracting top musicians is **Blues Alley** at 1073 Wisconsin Ave. NW (202-337-4141). An evening at Blues Alley can be quite expensive; cover charges range from $13 to $31.50, depending on the show, and there is a $7 food and beverage minimum per person. Nearby, **One Step Down** at 2517 Pennsylvania Ave. NW (202-331-8863) is slightly less expensive, with a $5 to $12.50 cover and a two-drink minimum. **Takoma Station Tavern** at 6914 4th St. NW (202-829-1999) features live jazz nightly, charges no cover and has just a two-drink minimum. The **Saloon** in Georgetown at 3239 M St. NW (202-338-4900) features local jazz bands seven nights a week, has low cover charges of only $2 to $3 and reasonable food and drink prices.

Comedy

Washington—particularly the government—is food for thought for many local and national comedians. Who can blame them? Many of the things that go on here can seem pretty outrageous, especially when the story is told just right. A few local comedy clubs and troupes keep Washingtonians in good spirits, even—or especially—when we are laughing at ourselves.

The **Improv** at 1140 Connecticut Ave. NW (202-296-7008) is the local version of the nationally known club. There is a $10 admission charge.

The **Comedy Cafe** at 1520 K St. NW (202-638-JOKE) books a mix of national and local talent. Wednesday and Thursday nights are open-mike nights. Take note, one way or the other—in addition to comedy, there is a strip joint in the basement of this three-story townhouse.

Drawing from local talent, both **Gross National Product** (301-587-4291) and the **Capitol Steps** satirize Washington politics. Gross National Product performs improvisational comedy at the **Bayou** at 3135 K St. NW (202-333-2897). Tickets are $18 per person. The Capitol Steps, a nationally known musical parody group made up of current and former Congressional staffers, can be seen at **Chelsea's** at 1055 Thomas Jefferson St. NW (202-298-8222) most weekends. Tickets for the show and dinner cost $45 per person. If you opt to eat dinner elsewhere, the show is $30 per person. Although an evening with the Steps is a bit pricy, they are terrific and well worth it. For a less expensive dose of the Capitol Steps, watch for one of their frequent specials on PBS, wait for one of their shows on NPR, or buy one of their compact discs.

RECREATION

For those who recreate in a more active format, Washington has a wide range of choices. From park land and trails perfect for hiking and biking to sports and health clubs, from boating and sailing to golf and horseback riding, there are options in the District and the Maryland and Virginia suburbs to suit every preference.

Bicycling

Bicyclists will be glad to know that hundreds of miles of bike trails criss-cross the metropolitan area. Michael Leccesse has written an excellent guide for recreational and serious cyclists alike, entitled *Short Bike Rides In and Around Washington, DC* (Globe Pequot Press; $9.95). The book details bike rides of various lengths and difficulties with maps, pictures and thumbnail descriptions of each.

Many cyclists used to—and some day will again—favor a picturesque 15-mile stretch between Georgetown and Great Falls on the C&O Towpath. Heavy flooding during the winter of 1995-96 destroyed parts of the Towpath, which is expected to be repaired in three to four years. In the meantime, an equally beautiful trail is available on the other side of the Potomac. The paved Mount Vernon Bike Trail rambles 18 miles from Roosevelt Island to George Washington's plantation. The Washington & Old Dominion (W&OD) trail extends from Alexandria to Purcelville.

Rock Creek Park provides another prime location, especially on weekends, when cyclists can enjoy car-free sections of Beach Drive.

One of the largest recreation areas in Maryland is the Beltsville Agricultural Park, just north of Greenbelt. This is a huge tract of government land, criss-crossed by miles of two-lane country roads. It is perfect for bicycling and on weekends you will usually see more bicycle traffic than automobiles. To get there, take the Beltway to the exit for Kenilworth Ave. and go north.

Mountain bikers may not be satisfied with local riverside or park routes. Instead, they can tackle the unrestricted system of challenging trails around Sugarloaf Mountain just outside the northwest corner of Montgomery County. To get to Sugarloaf, take I-270 North to Route 109. Follow Route 109 three miles to Comus Rd., make a right and drive (or ride) another three miles.

Lots of resources are available for people who like to bike. You can rent bikes at **Fletcher's Boathouse** at 4940 Canal Rd. NW (202-244-0461), **Thompson Boat Center** at 2900 Virginia Ave. NW (202-333-4861) or **Swain's Lock** (301-299-9006). The District's **Department of Documents** (202-727-5090) publishes bike trail maps for $3. You can pick them up or order them by mail at Suite 520, 441 4th St. NW. You can also get information from the **Potomac Pedalers Touring Club** (202-363-8687) and the **National Capital Velo Club** (301-588-2087).

Boating and Sailing

The waters of the C&O Canal and the Potomac River (downstream from Chain Bridge) cater to the romantic soul with canoeing and boating from May to October. You can rent both canoes and rowboats ($8/hour or $17/day) at **Fletcher's Boathouse** (202-244-0461). A bit farther downstream near Washington Harbour, **Thompson Boat Center** at 2900 Virginia Ave. NW (202-333-4861) rents canoes ($6/hour) and kayaks ($7/hour). Recreational sculls ($13/hour) are available to individuals providing some type of rowing certification. Thompson's proximity to the Georgetown waterfront and the Mall makes it the best starting point for watercraft tours of the city. If you would like to paddle around the Tidal Basin, you can rent a two-person paddle-boat ($7/hour) at the **Tidal Basin Boathouse** at 1501 Maine Ave. SW (202-484-0206). The **Washington Sailing Marina** (703-548-9027), a mile south of National Airport, gives lessons and rents windsurfers and sailboats. Farther down the George Washington Parkway, the Mariner Sailing School at the **Belle Haven Marina** (703-768-0018) offers sailing lessons and rents canoes, kayaks, windsurfers and sailboats.

HEALTH CLUBS

Aspen Hill Club
301-598-5200

Fit Physique
202-659-5959

Four Seasons Fitness Club
202-944-2022

Olympus Fitness Center
703-241-2255

Sport & Health Centers
703-556-6550

The National Capital YMCA
202-862-9622

Washington Sports Club
202-547-2255

Worldgate Athletic Club
703-709-9100

To meet others with similar interests, you might join the **Washington Canoe Club** (202-333-9749) or **Canoe Cruisers Association of Greater Washington** (301-656-2586). When planning a trip, remember that flooding or severe weather can curtail these water activities. Before you venture out, call 703-260-0505 for the marine forecast.

Golf

Golfers can tee off at **East Potomac Park Golf Course** (202-863-9007). This Hains Point facility has two nine-hole courses and one 18-hole course. Rolling hills and tree-lined fairways characterize the 18-hole golf course in **Rock Creek Park** (202-882-7332), located at Rittenhouse and 16th Sts. NW. Suburbanites can stroll the links closer to home at public courses in Alexandria at 6700 Telegraph Rd. (703-971-6170), in Reston at 11875 Sunrise Valley Dr. (703-620-9333), in Silver Spring at 9701 Sligo Creek Pkwy. (301-585-6006) and in Potomac at Falls Rd. (301-299-5156). If you can afford the fees, Washington's country clubs have some superb golf courses.

Washington has its own bi-monthly golf magazine, *Metro Golf* (202-663-9015). In addition to the usual tips and golf book reviews, *Metro Golf* posts an extensive listing of local tournaments—both open and members-only—so that you can hone your game in competition. A popular group is the Rock Creek Golf Club; call 202-882-7332 for information.

For those who consider the best kind of golf the type where you have to putt up a hill, past the windmill and through Snoopy's dog house, **Hains Point** is the District's only outdoor miniature golf course. At the Post Office Pavilion you can putt through replicas of Washington-area monuments at the indoor **City Golf** in the East Atrium, Bottom Floor, 1100 Pennsylvania Ave. NW (202-898-7888). In the suburbs, miniature golf courses are more numerous. Some of the best include **Uptown Hill Regional Park** at 6060 Wilson Blvd. in Arlington (703-237-4953), **Cameron Run Regional Park** at 4001 Eisenhower Ave. in Alexandria (703-960-0767) and **Putt Putt Rockville** at 130 Rollins Ave. (301-881-1663).

Health Clubs

Most of the national health club chains have facilities in the area and several local entrepreneurs have started their own health clubs. Facilities vary widely in features, but most offer at least exercise rooms and aerobics classes. Hotels, too, have gotten into the act, with most of the larger ones offering exercise rooms and pools to both their guests and local residents. With more HMOs encouraging regular exercise, check to see if your health insurance plan offers a discount at any area health clubs or rebates on premiums for health clubs members.

Hiking

Trails paralleling the Potomac River in Great Falls Park provide great terrain and striking vistas for some of the area's best hiking. Those looking for something closer in should head to Rock Creek Park in the District. Trails also meander through Roosevelt Island, the wildlife sanctuary just across the Potomac from the Lincoln Memorial. Popular hiking clubs include **Sierra Club** (202-547-2326), **Potomac Appalachian Trail Club** (703-242-0965) and **Potomac Backpackers Association** (703-524-1185).

Horseback Riding

City dwellers can enjoy 17 miles of bridle paths in **Rock Creek Park**, winding through some of Washington's best scenery (202-362-0118). The escorted trail rides are $21; lessons are available at all levels. **Wheaton Regional Park** (301-622-3311) offers horseback riding ($20 per person) and guided hour-long trail rides on Sunday afternoon. If you are experimenting with horseback riding, don't forget to wear long pants. For all activities, call ahead for reservations.

Equestrian Enterprises in Great Falls, VA (703-759-2474) offers guided trail rides for adults through Great Falls Park as well as riding lessons for beginners and those with experience. You have to call ahead to book one of the two-hour trail rides ($40 per person). You can also join the **Capitol Hill Equestrian Society**; call 202-828-3035 for more information.

Ice Skating

With the elegant Willard Hotel as a backdrop, ice skaters glide across the ice at the outdoor **Pershing Park Ice Rink** (202-737-6938) at Pennsylvania Ave. and 14th St. NW, just a short stroll from the White House. A few blocks away, winter enthusiasts enjoy skating at the **National Sculpture Garden Ice Rink** at Constitution Ave. and 9th St. NW (202-371-5340) or at the **Reflecting Pool** in front of the Lincoln Memorial. Fees for skating at Pershing Park and the National Sculpture Garden are around $4; skating on the Reflecting Pool is free. Montgomery County has several outdoor rinks including **Wheaton Regional Park Ice Rink** (301-649-2703), the **Bethesda Metro Ice Center** (301-656-0588) and Rockville's **Cabin John Ice Rink** (301-365-2246). Cabin John is open year-round. Virginians can skate year round at the Fairfax Ice Arena (703-323-1131) and at **Reston Town Center** (703-318-7541). If skating means hockey-playing, you can contact Washington's only hockey league, **Hockey North America** (703-471-0400), to join a team.

Running

Thousands of Washingtonians fit a run into their lunch hour along the Mall, East Potomac Park, the Mount Vernon Trail or Rock Creek Park. A few runners even opt for a diabolical sprint up the imposing flight of stone steps featured in "The Exorcist" on M St. in Georgetown near the Key Bridge.

Triathlons take place in Reston, VA and Columbia, MD. The Tri-Maryland Triathlon Club (410-882-6103) plans the "No Frills" Biathlon Series (running/biking and swimming/running) at sites throughout Maryland. *The Running Report*, available at most sports equipment stores, lists upcoming races. Popular clubs are **DC Road Runners** (703-241-0395); **Montgomery County Road Runners Club** (301-353-0200); **National Capital Track Club** (301-948-6905); **Northern Virginia Running Club** (703-644-5364); and **DC Front Runners** (202-628-3223), a running club for gays, lesbians and their friends.

Skiing

During the winter, cross-country skiers pick up where walkers and joggers leave off in Rock Creek Park or on the Mall. Downhill skiing—on the other hand—requires some serious driving to reach the slopes. While Virginia and Maryland have their own ski locations, Eastern Pennsylvania, about 200 miles away, is one of your best bets. Many ski fans—and fans of other kinds of fun activities—join the Ski Club of Washington, DC. Membership is $35, individual; $55, double. Call 703-536-8273 for information. Another number you should know is the *Washington Post's* **Post-Haste Ski Report** hotline. Call 202-334-9000, ext. 4300 for the latest area ski conditions.

Maryland

Wisp, Deep Creek Lake	1-301-387-4911

Virginia

Bryce Mountain, Basye	1-540-856-2121
Massanutten, Harrisonburg	1-540-289-9441
Wintergreen, Wintergreen	1-800-325-2200

Pennsylvania

Blue Knob, Claysburg	1-814-239-5111
Doe Mountain, Macungie	1-610-682-7100
Hidden Valley, Somerset	1-800-458-0175
Seven Springs, Champion	1-800-452-2223
Ski Liberty, Fairfield	1-717-642-8282
Whitetail, Mercersburg	1-717-328-9400

Sports on the Mall

The vast expanse of the Mall, especially around the Washington Monument, is the staging ground for many sports activities. Recreational team sports, particularly softball, have become as vital to politicking and deal-making as power lunches. Interns, legislative aides, partners and associates can be seen battling it out on the Mall grounds, both in and out of uniform. Most teams are co-ed and low-key. You should ask around your office to see about joining a team or contact the **Congressional Softball League** at 202-544-3333.

Swimming

If you do not have access to a pool, relief from Washington's hot, muggy summers can be found in any one of the area's public swimming pools. One of the city's finest pools is just off Wisconsin Ave. in Georgetown, at 34th St. and Volta Pl. NW (202-282-2366). Other public pools are the indoor pool in the **Marie H. Reed Learning Center** at 2200 Champlain St. NW (202-673-7771) or the indoor **Capitol East Natatorium** at 635 North Carolina Ave. SE (202-724-4495).

Arlington's high schools have indoor pools open to the public for lap swimming on a pay-as-you-swim basis. You can try **Washington-Lee** at 1300 North Quincy St. (703-358-6262), **Wakefield** at 4901 South Chesterfield Rd. (703-578-3063) or **Yorktown** at 5201 North 28th St. (703-536-9739). One swim costs $3 (for county residents) and a book of 20 swims can be purchased for $45. Non-residents are welcome but must pay a slightly higher fee.

The **Montgomery Aquatic Center** at 5900 Executive Blvd. (301-468-4211) has a 200-foot-long water slide. Water lovers can also enjoy swimming in the Center's 50-meter pool and relaxing in one of its two hot tubs. For county residents, admission is just $4.50 for adults and $3.50 for senior citizens and children. For non-residents of the county, the fees are $6 for adults and $5 for children.

RECREATION DEPARTMENTS

District of Columbia
202-673-7660

Maryland
Montgomery County
301-217-6800

Prince George's County
301-699-2400

Virginia
Alexandria
703-838-4343

Arlington County
703-358-3322

Fairfax County
703-324-4386

In Silver Spring, the **Martin Luther King Swim Center** at 1201 Jackson Rd. (301-989-1206) has a 42-yard pool, eight 25-yard lanes and a teaching pool. After your swim, you can relax in the hot tub. For residents, swims are $3.25 for adults and $2.75 for children. Nearby the **Fairland Aquatic Center** at 13820 Old Gunpowder Rd. (301-206-2359) boasts a 50-meter Olympic-sized pool and a 20-person jacuzzi. Swims here are also reasonably priced at $2.50 for adults and $1.50 for children.

Nearly every public pool has a Masters Swimming group for adults. You can receive coaching, a private swimming lesson several times a week and, periodically, the chance to compete.

Tennis

Tennis buffs can play on the same courts that have hosted John McEnroe and Martina Navratilova, at the **Washington Tennis Center**, 16th and Kennedy Sts. NW (202-722-5949). A large plastic bubble roof permits winter play on five of the hard courts. Fees for outdoor courts range from $3.25 to $8 an hour. Indoor court fees climb sharply to $15 to $24 per hour. Reservations must be made one week in advance.

Public tennis courts are widely available, both in the District and beyond. **Hains Point's East Potomac Tennis Center** (202-554-5962) has 19 outdoor and five indoor courts. You can also play at the outdoor courts at **Pierce Mill** in Rock Creek Park (202-426-6908). Several courts, on the 3000 block of R St. in Georgetown, are open on a first-come, first-served basis. On the Hill, you can play at Garfield Park, 3rd and Eye Sts. SE. The least well-known public courts in town are on D St. NW, right across from the State Department. Time slots are distributed to employees and the public through a lottery system. You can sign up in person at the **Federal Reserve Bank**, Constitution Ave. and 20th St. NW (202-452-3357). For a list of public tennis courts in your area, call your local recreation department. For the serious tennis player, there is the **Mid-Atlantic Tennis Association** (703-560-9480).

SPECTATOR SPORTS

The Washington area has lots of spectator sports activities, both professional and college. Football, basketball, baseball, hockey, even tennis and ice skating stars bring together avid vans from all around the area.

Professional Sports

Liberal or conservative, Democrat or Republican, the nation's capital has one unifying force—the **Washington Redskins**. Few teams have followers as devoted as Redskin fans. When the local National Football League team plays Dallas, you will hear of little else all week. Chances of seeing a Redskins game at RFK (Robert F. Kennedy Memorial) Stadium are slim at best, unless you go as a guest of a season ticket holder or pay scalpers' exorbitant prices. Tickets are so hot that people fight over them in divorce settlements and pass them along in wills. You may want to get on the waiting list for season tickets. When the proposed new stadium is built there will be increased seating capacity for more season ticket holders. The perennial sell-outs guarantee that all games are televised. But if you still want to be there, tickets can be found. The classified section of the *Washington Post* and *Washington Times* regularly list single game and season ticket packages. If you do plan to see a game, Metro is the best and cheapest way to get to RFK (Orange or Blue Lines to the Stadium-Armory station).

One side benefit to Washington's Redskin-mania is that the stores and shopping malls are fairly quiet during games. For non-football fans, Sunday afternoons can be an excellent time to shop, check out the latest show at the National Gallery of Art, go to the movies or do just about anything unimpeded by the usual crowds.

Washington also hosts professional basketball and hockey teams—the **Bullets** and the **Capitals**. Both teams currently play at the USAir Arena (301-350-3400) in Landover, MD. Seats are easy to come by, except for play-off games. To get to USAir Arena, take the Beltway (I-495/I-95) to Exit 15 or 17 and follow the signs to the arena. Unfortunately, there is no mass transit to the USAir Arena.

A final note about the Bullets—at press time a decision has been made to change the team's name to the Wizards. As with everything else in Washington, the debate is ongoing.

NEW STADIUMS

As this book goes to press, two new football stadiums are being proposed for Washington and Baltimore home teams. The first, estimated for completion by the 1997 season, will be the new home of the Washington Redskins. The proposed site is on the Wilson Farm tract near the Capital Beltway and Route 202 in Maryland. The second is a new stadium to house the NFL's Cleveland franchise, which is relocating to Baltimore. While the construction project awaits approval, the location is expected to be near the Inner Harbor and adjacent to Oriole Park at Camden Yards. Home games would be played there beginning in the 1998 season. Meanwhile, they would be played at Baltimore's existing Memorial Stadium.

Sports fans will be happy to know that the new MCI Arena, scheduled for completion in 1997, will be easier to get to than the USAir Arena, the current location for the popular local teams. The Bullets—likely by then to be playing under their planned new name, the Wizards—and the Capitals will welcome both challengers and fans at the new downtown arena, within a block of the Gallery Place Metro station on 7th St. SW.

Since the Senators left in 1971, Washingtonians have longed for a baseball team they could call their own. They lost their most recent quest, in 1995, to Houston, so it is still Baltimore or bust for major league baseball. The American League **Baltimore Orioles** (1-410-685-9800) play in the wonderful new downtown ballpark, Oriole Park at Camden Yards (or simply Camden Yards). Already Camden Yards is a model for the next generation of stadiums. Even if you are not an Orioles fan, you cannot help but have a great time at this ballpark.

To get to Camden Yards by car, take I-95 North to Baltimore. From I-95 take the I-395 Exit and follow the signs; the new stadium is just off the highway. Since the Stadium is only a short stroll away from Inner Harbor, it is fun to make a day of it. Parking is cheap and you can hang out in Inner Harbor or nearby Little Italy before heading over to the game.

The Orioles regularly sell out, therefore you should plan ahead. Washingtonians (who make up nearly a third of the fans) can go to the convenient **Orioles Baseball Store** at 914 17th St. NW (202-296-2473) for tickets and memorabilia. Players make personal appearances at the store so call and check out when you can do a little "Bird-watching." You can also purchase tickets over the phone through Ticketmaster (202-432-SEAT). If you are unfamiliar with the stadium floor plans and seating, consult the front of the Bell Atlantic Yellow Pages, which contains diagrams of RFK, USAir Arena and Camden Yards.

The **Professional Golfer's Association** (PGA) tour swings through Washington for the **Kemper Open**, traditionally held in late May. The **Tournament Player's Club** at Avenel in Potomac, MD (301-469-3737) hosts the event, which has attracted Greg Norman, Tom Kite, Hale Irwin and many other top pros.

Many of the world's top male tennis players travel here in July for the **Newsweek Classic**. The top women players show up in September for the **Champions' Challenge**. Both events are held at the Washington Tennis Center at the corner of 16th and Kennedy Sts. NW. Tickets can be purchased through Pro Serv (703-276-3030).

Cycling fans await the arrival of the **Tour DuPont** races, with world famous cyclists like Greg Lemond, Alexi Grewal and Davis Phinney participating. The Washington course has yet to be finalized, but it will undoubtedly be a multi-lap race, which means lots of action—several times over—for spectators.

Each February, past and future Olympic medalists assemble at George Mason University for the **Mobil 1 Invitational Track and Field Meet**. It is one of the major events of the competitive circuit. Seating is limited and tickets go quickly. For ticket information, call 703-993-3270.

Serious runners may want to begin training for Washington's biggest marathon. In late October, the **Marine Corps Marathon** tests the mettle of more than a few good men and women. The race begins at the Iwo Jima Memorial in Rosslyn and finishes 26 miles later at the same spot. It attracts thousands of runners each year. The 1996 entrance fee is $27 (it is generally raised annually), and participants must register in advance. For more information, call 703-690-3431.

College Athletics

There are many schools in and around Washington with excellent, nationally competitive athletic programs. The **University of Maryland's** basketball teams play their home games at Cole Field House on the Maryland campus. The **Terrapins** compete in the Atlantic Coast Conference against schools like Duke, North Carolina and Virginia. Tickets for either sport can be ordered in advance by phone (301-314-7070) or mail (PO Box 295, College Park, MD 20741).

The USAir Arena in Landover hosts the **Georgetown Hoyas** men's basketball team (202-687-4692). Contests against Big East Conference rivals sell out quickly. Tickets can be purchased at Georgetown or through Ticketmaster (202-432-SEAT).

George Washington University men's basketball team is the **Colonials** (202-994-DUNK). They play at the Smith Center at 600 22nd St. NW. Tickets to their games are available from Ticketmaster (202-432-SEAT).

VOLUNTEER ACTIVITIES

Whatever your special interest or cause, you are bound to find a way to contribute through one or more of the numerous organizations in the area. The easiest way to get involved is to contact your community's volunteer clearinghouse, which serves as an information bank for prospective volunteers, providing details on hundreds of community service opportunities. Counselors interview you and tell you about projects in your community. They also give you names and numbers of people to contact at various organizations. Most clearinghouses recommend that you come in to browse through their files for ideas and suggestions.

Environmentalists may be interested in helping to rebuild the historic C&O Canal Towpath, which was severely damaged in the blizzard of 1996. Interested parties can get involved with the reconstruction effort by calling the **Rebuild the Towpath Foundation** at 1-800-434-9330.

Two groups, **DC Cares** (202-663-9207 or **http://www.dc-cares.org**) and **DoingSomething** (202-393-5051), bring volunteering right to your doorstep (actually your mailbox). Each month, they mail lists of volunteer projects to members who sign up by contacting the volunteer coordinator of a specific project. Most projects are performed before or after weekday work hours, or on weekends, at locations throughout the District. Projects include working with children, the elderly, the homeless, the disabled and AIDS sufferers, as well as caring for the environment. Both groups will also help you to coordinate your own volunteer project with friends or co-workers.

District of Columbia
DC Volunteer Clearinghouse
1313 New York Ave. NW, Room 303
202-638-2664

Maryland
Montgomery County Volunteer and Community Service Center
401 Fleet St., Room 106, Rockville, MD
301-217-4949

Prince George's County Voluntary Action Center
6309 Baltimore Ave., Room 305, Riverdale, MD
301-779-9444

Virginia
Alexandria Volunteer Bureau
801 North Pitt St., Suite 102, Alexandria, VA
703-836-2176

Arlington County Volunteer Office
2100 Clarendon Blvd., Suite 314, Arlington, VA
703-358-3222

Volunteer Center of Fairfax County
10530 Page Ave.
Fairfax, VA
703-246-3460

Washington Weekends

Washington is a great place for weekend entertainment. As a major world capital set in the midst of an area rich in history, culture and natural beauty, Washington offers an unlimited choice of activities for those seemingly all too rare free weekends. You will find, however, that the tremendous number of attractions—both within the Beltway and throughout the general mid-Atlantic region—just might tempt you to shift your priorities.

Besides word of mouth, one of the best ways to learn about what's going on is to check the Weekend section of the *Washington Post* each Friday. Here you will find details on special events, local exhibits, movie and theater listings, and sports events. Washington's free *City Paper* is also an excellent resource. In addition to its regular column, "City Lights," highlighting the week's best events, the *City Paper* contains numerous ads for some of the area's best night life. Also, remember to peruse the local interest section of your favorite bookstore (see Chapter 6 for ideas) for guide books on various aspects of the metropolitan DC area. While this book directs you to a number of the more prominent sites in the area, no one book can cover a subject as broad and as varied as what to do on a Washington weekend.

DIAL-A-SERVICE
Dial-a-Hike
202-547-2326
Dial-a-Museum
202-357-2020 English
202-633-9126 Spanish
Dial-a-Park
202-619-PARK

THE WEEKEND TOURIST

You would be surprised to find out how many Washingtonians have never been to the top of the Washington Monument or taken a cruise on the Potomac. "It is just for tourists!" claims one Hill staffer, expressing a wide-felt local attitude. Just for tourists, you say? You would be surprised at what you are missing. If you really need an excuse, you can wait for guests or family to arrive for a visit. On the other hand, why not take a break from your routine to see some of the sights on your own. You will end up with a whole new perspective on the city.

Sightseeing Tours

If you aren't sure where to start or you would like to get a good initial overview of the sights, try one of the area's many sightseeing tours, such as the quick, motorized preview provided by **Tourmobile** (202- 554-7950). The red, white and blue Tourmobile cruises through Washington,

GUEST ACCOMMODATIONS

If you wait to entertain family, friends or business colleagues and you need assistance in finding accommodations for them, contact **Capitol Reservations** (1-800-847-4832), a one-stop reservation service offering discount rates at 70 hotels in DC and the nearby Virginia and Maryland suburbs. Through them, you can save $20 to $40 per night off normal rates for hotels throughout the area, including those near Capitol Hill, the Smithsonian and the White House. Even lower rates are available in comfortable hotels in Arlington and Alexandria. In addition, Capitol Reservations offers special rates for weekend and holiday periods at many downtown and suburban properties. Choices range from four-star luxury and corporate class hotels to family-style accommodations.

stopping at its most popular sights—the White House, the Capitol, the Smithsonian, the Bureau of Engraving and Printing, Jefferson Memorial, Lincoln Memorial, Arlington Cemetery and the Kennedy Center. Tours cost $12.00 per person.

If you are looking to take a cruise on the Potomac, there are several companies in the area that will transport you past the monuments and other shoreline attractions while providing dinner and dancing. The **Dandy** (703-683-6090 for information, 703-683-8076 for reservations) sails from Prince St. in Old Town Alexandria for a three-hour dinner cruise past the monuments, the Kennedy Center and Georgetown. Prices range from $47 to $55 and the boat departs at 7:00 p.m. You can float away on a luncheon cruise as well, costing around $30 and departing between 11:30 a.m. and 12:30 p.m.

For a trip with a historical twist, take the **Spirit of Mount Vernon** to George Washington's estate. The captain will point out landmarks along the way and you will have two hours to explore the mansion and gardens at Mount Vernon before the return trip to Washington. The sister ship, **Spirit of Washington**, sails down the Potomac to Alexandria past the monuments and Old Town with either live music from the 1940s through the 1990s or a Cabaret-style show. Both ships are part of the Potomac Spirit fleet (202-554-1542 for information, 202-554-8000 for reservations) and depart from Pier 4 at 6th and Water Sts. SE. Cruises aboard the Spirit of Mount Vernon cost $20 and run daily at 9:00 a.m. and 2:00 p.m. The Spirit of Washington is more expensive, ranging from $25 for a luncheon cruise to $45 dollars for an evening sail. It departs daily at 11:30 a.m. and 6:30 p.m.

The newest, and most unique, Potomac dinner cruise option is Odyssey Cruise Line (1-800-9GO-SAIL) which also has ships in Chicago and Boston. The **Odyssey III**, a $6 million craft constructed specifically to navigate under all the Potomac bridges, is the only ship of its kind in US waters. Its outside decks and glass ceilings offer breathtaking views of the

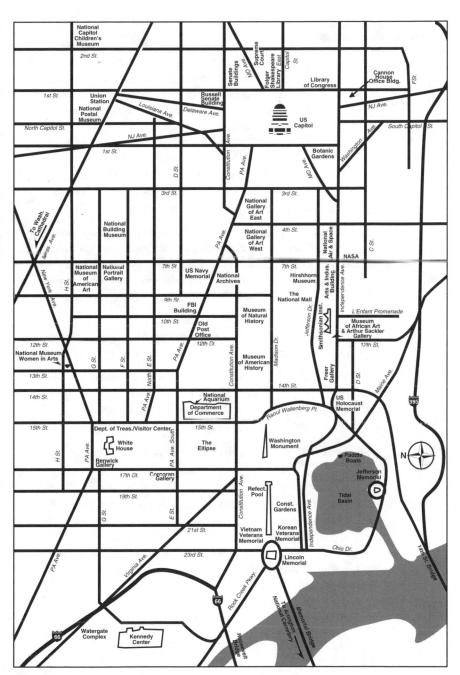

POINTS OF INTEREST

VISITORS CENTERS

Washington DC
202-789-7000

Maryland
1-410-767-3400

Virginia
202-659-5523

Capitol, monuments, Georgetown and the Kennedy Center. The Odyssey departs from the Gangplank Marina at 6th and Water Sts. SW, a short walk from the Green Line Waterfront Metro station. If you drive, complimentary parking is available in the lot across from Hogate's at 7th and Water Sts. SW. Your cruise options include Sunday Jazz Brunch, lunch Monday through Saturday, dinner each night and moonlight cruises.

Ticket prices vary from $27 to $77 depending on the cruise you select. Tax and gratuity are added at the time of reservation, therefore the only on-board cost you have to pay is for drinks from the bar. Departure hours also vary according to cruise choice.

The **Admiral Tilp** takes you on a narrated sight-seeing cruise along Old Town's Waterfront. The several cruises offered by this line sail from behind the Torpedo Factory Arts Center, usually departing every hour on the hour. Reservations are recommended for the short trips, which cost $7 for adults. Call the recording at 703-548-9000 for more information.

Cruise times for all of these ships vary depending upon the time of year and the day of the week. You should probably call ahead to check specific departures for the cruise you want to take.

In addition to tours by bus and by boat, Washington and several of the suburban towns offer pleasant and informative walking tours. Check area parks and recreation departments, the *Washington Post* and the *Smithsonian Associates* for suggestions and schedules.

Museums, Monuments and Memorials

For a quick overview of Washington, start at the Mall, the expansive public space between Constitution and Independence Aves. This sweeping promenade of gardens, museums and famous monuments extends from the **US Capitol** at the east end all the way to the **Lincoln Memorial** at the west end. Along the way, you will find famous sights including the memorials to the **Vietnam** and **Korean War Veterans** as well as the **Washington Monument** and its **Reflecting Pool**. Not far off are the **Tidal Basin** and the **Jefferson Memorial** and two beautiful public spaces, East and West Potomac Parks. On the Mall, between 3rd and 14th Sts., sit some of the city's best museums.

The Smithsonian Institution

You could visit a different museum every day for two weeks and still not have covered all of the **Smithsonian Institution**. With 15 sites today in DC alone, the Smithsonian was founded in 1846 on a bequest from James Smithson, a distinguished English scientist. Today, the Smithsonian is one of the world's great museum complexes as well as a preeminent research institution. All museums are open daily, except Christmas Day. Extended spring and summer hours are established each year. Admission to all museums is free. Many of these facilities have museum shops and cafeterias, so you can make your visit a multi-purpose one. Visitor information is available from 9:00 a.m. to 5:00 p.m. daily, at 202-357-2700 (TDD 202-357-1729, recorded information 202-357-2020, Spanish 202-633-9126). The Smithsonian can be accessed at **http://www.si.sgi.com** on the Internet.

Along the Mall, you can visit several of the Smithsonian facilities, including the main building at 1000 Jefferson Dr. SW. The original Smithsonian Institution Building, known as "The Castle," stands as an icon for the Smithsonian and is recognized across the country and around the world. It houses the Smithsonian Information Center and administrative offices. The Smithsonian facilities on the Mall are easily reached by any of three Metro stations—Smithsonian, Federal Triangle and L'Enfant Plaza. Check the address of the museum, or ask the attendant at the Metro kiosk before boarding the train, to see which one is more convenient.

Arthur M. Sackler Gallery, 1050 Independence Ave. SW. This gallery has a permanent collection of Asian art from ancient times to the present as well as exhibitions of related works of art on loan.

Arts and Industries Building, 900 Jefferson Dr. SW. Arts and Industries features changing exhibitions and the Discovery Theater for children.

Freer Gallery of Art, 12th St. and Jefferson Dr. SW. The Freer, recently renovated, offers Asian and 19th- and early 20th-century American Art.

Hirshhorn Museum and Sculpture Garden, 7th St. and Independence Ave. SW. The focus of the Hirshhorn collection is 19th- and 20th- century painting and sculpture. Changing exhibitions explore the newest trends in modern art.

National Air and Space Museum, 6th St. and Independence Ave. SW. This museum—the most visited in the world—contains exhibits on the history of aviation, space science and space technology. Highlights include shows at the Planetarium and the IMAX theater.

National Museum of African Art, 950 Independence Ave. SW. The focus of this museum is the art and culture of Africa, displayed in both permanent and rotating exhibits.

National Museum of American History, 14th St. and Constitution Ave. NW. Here you will see exhibits on the history of science, technology and culture in America.

National Museum of Natural History, 10th St. and Constitution Ave. NW. The history of the natural world and human cultures is presented in this museum. Highlights include dinosaur skeletons, displays of early man, a living coral reef, an insect zoo and the 45.5-carat Hope Diamond.

In addition to the locations along the Mall, there are several Smithsonian buildings in other parts of town. These include:

National Portrait Gallery, 8th and F Sts. NW. The Gallery is best known for its portraits of distinguished Americans, but it also includes sculptures, paintings, photographs and the Time magazine cover collection. Metro: Gallery Place.

National Postal Museum, 2 Massachusetts Ave. and N. Capitol St. NE. As you might expect, this museum, opened recently, offers a history of postal communication and philately. It features interactive displays and the largest stamp collection in the world. Metro: Union Station.

National Zoological Park, 3000 Connecticut Ave. NW. Washington's zoo is home to some 5,000 animals in a beautiful 163-acre park, right in the midst of town. Exhibits include the world famous giant pandas. Metro: Cleveland Park or Woodley Park-Zoo. You can contact the zoo's Website at **http://www.si.edu/organiza/museums/zoo** on the Internet.

Renwick Gallery, 17th St. at Pennsylvania Ave. NW. The Renwick has a permanent collection and exhibitions of American crafts, design and contemporary arts. Metro: Farragut-West.

Anacostia Museum, 1901 Fort Place SE. In this museum, you will find a collection on African-American history and culture, focusing on the Upper South.

National Museum of American Art, 8th and G Sts. NW. Painting, sculpture, graphics, folk art and photography from the 18th-century to the present are available here, as well as special exhibitions of American art. Metro: Gallery Place.

Private Museums

In addition to the public Smithsonian museums, the Washington area boasts many other fine collections of art and culture, far too numerous to include them all here. One of the most recent is the **US Holocaust Memorial Museum**, located near the Mall at 100 Raoul Wallenberg Place SW, between 14th and 15th Sts. (202-488-0400). This private museum documents the horrors of the Holocaust through artifacts, exhibits, film and photography. On the Internet, use the address **http://www.ushmm.org** to reach the US Holocaust Museum's Website.

The **National Building Museum** in the Pension Building (202-272-2448) fills the block formed by F and G Sts. and 4th and 5th Sts. NW. The collection focuses on major building projects throughout the country. One of its permanent exhibits is on the history of Washington, DC. It includes interactive displays as well as scale models of the major monuments created for the visually impaired to experience through touch. Braille identification signs are attached to each model. Metro: Judiciary Square.

Washington's Many Monuments

With a two-hundred year history, most of it on a national and international scale, Washington has plenty of famous people and events represented by its many public monuments.

The major presidential monuments are those of Lincoln, Jefferson and Washington, all of which are open on weekends. The **Lincoln Memorial** is located at the far west end of the Mall, at 23rd St. The closest Metro is Foggy Bottom-GWU; from there it is an eight-block walk south on 23rd St.

The **Washington Monument** is located on the western half of the Mall, on Constitution Ave. NW between 15th and 17th St. To get there, take the Metro to either the Smithsonian or the Federal Triangle station. It is well worth the wait in line to take the elevator to the top for a panoramic view of the city.

You will find the **Jefferson Memorial** on Ohio Dr., south of the Tidal Basin. There is no direct Metro access to this monument, but in the summer, you can travel there by paddle boat, for rent at the Tidal Basin.

PHOTOGRAPHY

The Library of Congress allows you to make prints from their photography collection (the largest in the world). Photographs of Washington, DC are among those included in the archives of the Prints and Photographs Reading Room in the Madison Building. Take your order to the Photo Duplication Office in the Adams Building. Reprints are only $15 for an 8 x 10 picture. Allow four to six weeks for prints to be ready.

War Memorials

Memorials to wars and military service dot the area. Probably the two best-known are the **Marine Corps War Memorial (Iwo Jima Statue)**, and the **Vietnam Veterans Memorial**. The Iwo Jima Statue, depicting the raising of the American Flag on Iwo Jima during World War II, is located on N. Ft. Myer Dr. and Marshall Dr. in Arlington, VA. It is accessible via Metro's Rosslyn station, then six blocks south on Ft. Myer Dr.

The **Vietnam Veterans Memorial** is on the Mall, between 21st and 22nd Sts. The black granite structure, known as "The Wall," bears the names of the 58,000 soldiers lost in the Vietnam War, listed in chronological order. If you are looking for the name of anyone in particular, check the alphabetical directories along the walkway leading to the wall. The newest war memorial, the **Korean War Veterans Memorial**, is nearby, on the opposite side of the Reflecting Pool.

The **US Navy Memorial** at 8th St. and Pennsylvania Ave. NW features a large map of the world, inlaid in the granite plaza. The "Lone Sailor," a Stanley Bleifeld sculpture, keeps watch. Nearby are two edifices with bronze sculpture panels and a visitors center.

Once you venture outside the District, more sites await nearby, in addition to the Iwo Jima Statue. **Arlington National Cemetery**—a memorial in its own right—rests silently across the Potomac River from the Lincoln Memorial. Originally the home of Robert E. Lee, it was turned into a cemetery for fallen Union soldiers and is now the last resting place for casualties of war, veterans and their spouses. You can wander the grounds and watch the changing of the guard as they keep vigil over the **Tomb of the Unknowns** (commonly referred to as the Tomb of the Unknown Soldier). The eternal flame burns in remembrance at the grave site of President John F. Kennedy and his wife, Jacqueline Kennedy Onassis. His brother Robert rests nearby beneath a simple white cross against a gently sloping, grass-covered hill.

Along the George Washington Memorial Parkway between Memorial Bridge and the 14th St. Bridge is the **Navy-Marine Memorial**. This popular outdoor sculpture of gulls in flight above graceful waves is a monument to American sailors and marines who died at sea during World War I.

Galleries

The **East and West Buildings of the National Gallery of Art** (202-737-4215) face each other at the corner of Constitution Ave. and 4th St. NW. The West Building houses works from the 13th to the early 20th century, including paintings by Raphael, Rembrandt and Monet.

Across the street, I.M. Pei's East Building displays modern art and the museum's special exhibits. An underground tunnel allows you to move easily between the East and West Buildings. Metro: Archives-Navy Memorial or Judiciary Square.

The **Corcoran Gallery of Art** at 17th St. and New York Ave. NW (202- 638-3211) is the area's oldest gallery. It features primarily American paintings and sculpture. Metro: Farragut West.

The **Phillips Collection** at 1600 21st St. NW (202-387-2151) houses European and American masterpieces. Events include workshops, lectures, benefits and opening receptions. The weekly Sunday afternoon concert series in the museum's elegant music room is open to all museum visitors. Metro: Dupont Circle.

The **National Museum of Women in the Arts**, 1250 New York Ave. NW (202-783-5000) is the first museum in the world dedicated to women artists. Ironically, the building is a former Masonic Temple. Metro: McPherson Square or Metro Center.

Gardens and Parks

US Botanic Garden at 245 First St. SW (202-225-8333 or 202-225-7099) is the oldest botanic garden in America. Its first greenhouse was constructed in 1842 and the Conservatory, completed in 1933, houses permanent collections of tropical, subtropical and desert plants, and a world renowned collection of orchids. Located across Independence Ave. from the Conservatory is a beautiful park featuring displays of bulbs, annuals and perennials. The park is named for Frederic Auguste Bartholdi, who designed the fountain that forms the focal point of the park. Metro: Federal Center SW.

Georgetown's **Dumbarton Oaks**, at 1703 32nd St. NW (202-338-8278), maintains spectacular public gardens. Adjacent to the gardens, the Dumbarton Oaks Museum houses, somewhat surprisingly, one of the country's best pre-Columbian and Byzantine collections. If you are visiting the gardens with someone special, you might want to stroll down nearby Lover's Lane (daylight hours only). In the Rose Gardens in Georgetown, at 31st and R Sts. NW (202-342-3200), you can see and smell hundreds of carefully tended rose bushes.

The **Bishop's Garden** is tucked away on the grounds of the Washington National Cathedral at Massachusetts and Wisconsin Aves. NW (202-537-6200). This secluded, contemplative garden features winding stone paths and lush boxwoods.

VIP TOURS

US Congressional offices can assist in arranging VIP tours at a number of federal buildings such as the White House, the Capitol, the Kennedy Center and the Federal Bureau of Investigation (FBI), as well as some non-federal buildings such as Washington National Cathedral. While these VIP tours typically do not provide different views from those available on a public tour, a reservation can minimize the time you have to wait in line.

There are limited numbers of these free tickets and they go quickly, so try to make your request at least several months in advance. You can obtain maps and information on DC sightseeing as well as VIP tour ticket availability by writing the Congressional Representative for your district in care of the US House of Representatives, Washington, DC 20515. Or call the Capitol switchboard at 202-224-3121 and ask for your Representative's office.

You will need to provide a contact name, home address, and both day and evening phone numbers; the size of your party; the tour sites you wish to visit; and your preferred dates. If available, tickets will be mailed a week or two before your scheduled tour.

Hillwood is hidden in the midst of more typical Washington residences, at 4155 Linnean Ave. NW (202-686-5807). The former estate of Marjorie Merriweather Post is especially renowned for its azaleas and rhododendrons. Stroll the wooden paths over Japanese bridges and a waterfall and enjoy a delicious lunch at the lovely café.

The **US National Arboretum** at 3501 New York Ave. NE (202-475-4815) is comprised of 444 acres of trees, shrubs and flowering plants from around the world, and is renowned for its bonsai exhibit.

Brookside Gardens at 1500 Glenallan Ave. in Wheaton, MD (301-949-8230) offers 50 acres of gardens, two conservatories and streams flowing amid its famous azalea gardens.

Last, but certainly not least, is **Rock Creek Park and Nature Center**, on Beach Dr. north of the National Zoo. Its 1,754 acres make it one of the world's largest urban parks. Rock Creek offers golf, exercise courses, jogging paths, bike trails, tennis courts and bridle paths. Enjoy nature exhibits, self-guided trails and a planetarium at the Rock Creek Nature Center, 5200 Glover Rd. NW (202-426-6829).

Other Points of Interest

Washington's two most famous sites are the Capitol and the White House. The **Capitol** building, the seat of the legislative branch of the government, is located at the east end of the Mall at 1st St. between Independence and Constitution Aves. (202-225-6827). **The White House** (202-456-7041), official home of the President of the United States, is almost as well known by its address—1600 Pennsylvania Ave. NW. Tours of both sites make for a fascinating trip through the history of the city and the nation. You can visit the White House without leaving the comfort of your own home; the address is **http://www.whitehouse.gov** on the Internet.

At the **National Archives**, Constitution Ave. at 8th St. NW, you can see the original Declaration of Independence, US Constitution and Bill of Rights. If you are interested in genealogy, you can trace your family history in the Research Room.

The **Washington National Cathedral**, on Wisconsin Ave. about a mile north of Georgetown, dominates the local skyline. It was finally completed as recently as 1990, after 80 years of construction. Wander through the gardens behind the Cathedral and over to St. Albans School next door, where Vice President Gore received his high school education.

Another major facet of Washington is its African-American heritage. The **Frederick Douglass National Historic Site** at 1411 W St. SE (202-426-5960) on Cedar Hill was the last residence of the famous black statesman and abolitionist. Douglass was also the first black US Marshal for the District of Columbia. The **Anacostia Museum** (1901 Fort Place, SE) focuses on African-American art, culture and history; houses permanent and rotating exhibits; and provides lectures, films, workshops and performances.

The historic **Lincoln Theatre** at 1215 U St. NW (202-328-9177) was originally part of the area known as "Black Broadway," and attracted the country's best African-American entertainers. By the 1950s, the theater featured primarily movies, and was, in fact, the first movie theater to offer first-run pictures to black audiences. The theater had closed back in the 1970s but was completely renovated in the early 1990s, replicating its original historical integrity. It is again open for business, featuring live performances in the heart of the revitalized U St. Corridor.

In the Capitol Hill area, you can tour the **Library of Congress**, the **Folger Shakespeare Library** and the **Supreme Court** (only open on weekdays). Round out the day with a trip to **Eastern Market**, Washington's oldest market, at the corner of 7th and C Sts. SE. Eastern Market is particularly fun on weekends, with local artists plying their wares alongside the meat, cheese, fruit and vegetable vendors. Many people on the Hill stroll around Eastern Market on the weekends to pick up food or to have a meal at the Market Lunch. On your way there, you may want to stop at any hotel and pick up *Shaw's Guide to Capitol Hill*. This free pocket guide has an excellent map of the neighborhood.

Farther off the tourist track, **Dupont Circle** houses dozens of small art galleries and interesting museums. The Dupont Circle-Kalorama Museum walk, an informal self-guided tour around the area, stops at the **Phillips Collection**, the **Textile Museum**, the **Woodrow Wilson House**, the **Historical Society of Washington, DC**, the **Anderson House** and the **Fondo del Sol Visual Arts Center**. A brochure mapping out this tour can be obtained at any of these museums. Several of the museums rely on private donations and ask for contributions at the door.

EXPLORING BEYOND THE BELTWAY

For day and weekend trips, you can head out from Washington in just about any direction and not be disappointed. The mid-Atlantic region is full of choices, with some of the most popular ones described here. For more detailed information, you may want to purchase a guidebook for a particular area or get in touch with local chambers of commerce or visitors centers.

The Beach

The Atlantic Ocean beaches are only a few hours from the city and in the summer provide a welcome respite for heat-weary DC residents. Renting beach houses along the coast is a popular summer tradition in Washington, for couples or groups of friends. You can find out about rentals from the chamber of commerce or visitors center in the beach town of your choice, or check the classified section of the *Washington Post* for leads.

If you want to rent a group beach house and find yourself without interested friends, then Beach Night at Rumors restaurant will be a good place to start. Each spring, the restaurant and a publication called the Beach House Directory sponsor a weekly beach night to bring together prospective renters. If you rent a beach house through this route, you will be listed in the Beach House Directory, a "who's who" of the Dewey, Rehoboth, Bethany and Lewes Beaches. To find out more about the directory and to check the schedule for Beach Night, call 202-362-8227.

Ocean City, MD

Ocean City's summer weekend population can swell as high as 200,000 as Washingtonians seek relief from the humidity. Like most beach resorts, Ocean City offers plenty of recreational choices—amusement parks, fishing, sailing, miniature golf and a few movie theaters.

The Coastal Highway (Route 1), Ocean City's main thoroughfare, houses a multitude of hotels, condos and more than 160 restaurants. If you plan to visit during the summer months (May to mid-September), your best bet is to make your reservations early. Many hotels require a minimum stay of two or even three nights during peak season.

Ocean City ends its summer with SunFest, an annual bash held the third weekend after Labor Day. The city sets up four large circus tents filled with food vendors, bands, entertainers, and arts and crafts booths.

Many area high school students participate in "Beach Week" at Ocean City after graduation. Unless you are up to dealing with thousands of newly graduated high school seniors, it is best to avoid Ocean City during the first two weeks of June.

Distance 153 miles
Visitors Center 1-800-62-OCEAN
Directions Take Route 50 East all the way into Ocean City.

Rehoboth Beach and Dewey Beach, DE

Rehoboth is not nearly the size of Ocean City, but offers many of the same activities on a smaller scale. Like Ocean City, the restaurants along Rehoboth's boardwalk keep most beach-goers happy, both in terms of price and variety. The town is filled with interesting shops, ranging from typical beach souvenirs to imported clothing and hand-made arts and crafts.

As Rehoboth is only about a two-and-a-half-hour drive from the District, adventurous Washingtonians sometimes pack a round trip into a one-day excursion. If you opt to do this, leave early (preferably before dawn) to avoid the summer-long traffic jams at the Bay Bridge. If you do plan to stay for just the afternoon, you should bring plenty of quarters. Costly parking meters must be fed every two hours.

BED & BREAKFASTS

Bed and Breakfast establishments (B&Bs) offer weekend escapes from $60 to $150 (and sometimes even more) per night in the myriad small towns and villages within a few hours of the District. To select a weekend B&B, you may want to consult a specialized guidebook. *America's Wonderful Little Hotels and Inns* (St. Martin's Press) reports guests' impressions of local B&Bs, as well as prices, phone numbers and directions. The *Washington Post* runs several pages of B&B ads in the back of its Sunday Magazine. The **Virginia Office of Tourism** (202-659-5523) can provide information on B&Bs in Virginia and can even book your rooms. If you are planning a trip in the fall when the foliage is changing, during apple-picking season, or over a holiday weekend, you should make your reservations at least a few weeks in advance.

Bed and breakfast establishments are becoming more and more popular, and not just beyond the Beltway. Some local families are turning spare rooms into bed and breakfast space, allowing them to earn extra income, as well as make an occasional new friend. If you are interested in this idea— either becoming a B&B host or finding one for your out-of-town visitors—you can call **Bed & Breakfast Accommodations, Ltd.** at 202-328-3510.

Just 10 minutes south of Rehoboth is the two-block-wide community of Dewey Beach. Many visitors choose to rent a cottage in Dewey, as it tends to be much quieter than Rehoboth, and migrate to the Rehoboth boardwalk and beach during the day.

Distance 125 miles
Chamber of Commerce 1-800-441-1329
Directions Take Route 50 East to Route 404 through Delaware to Route 1.

Annapolis, MD

Even though Annapolis is the capital of Maryland, it remains a quaint, small town. Maryland's capitol building, the circular, red-brick **State House** (1-410-974-3400) gives free tours at designated times and is a good place to start learning about the city's past. It is the oldest state house in continuous legislative use in the country. Students of history will be amazed —and appalled— by the prominent statue on the State House grounds, honoring Chief Justice Roger Taney. While Taney accomplished many things in his political and judicial career, many remember him best for his decision in the Dred Scot case, where he ruled that Congress did not have the right to ban slavery in the territories.

The **US Naval Academy** (1-410-263-6933) is also in Annapolis. The **Naval Academy Guide Service** (1-410-267-3363) offers walking tours of the Academy. Visit the Academy Visitors Center at Ricketts Hall, Gate 1, for tour information. Otherwise, just wander past the buildings and along the waterfront on your own.

Annapolis is home to **St. John's College** (1-410-263-2371), a private liberal arts college with only 400 students. For both bachelors and masters degrees, students learn through a unique curriculum based on the reading and study of the great books of the western tradition. On the grounds, in front of McDowell Hall stands the Liberty Tree, a 400-year-old tulip tree. The Sons of Liberty met beneath its branches in the days leading up to the Revolutionary War.

If you saw the television mini-series or read the book, *Roots*, then you should be sure to visit the Kunta Kinte Plaque located at the head of the city dock. The plaque commemorates the 1767 arrival of Alex Haley's famous ancestor.

If shopping is your passion, you can browse in some of Annapolis' upscale stores. Clothing stores compete with antique shops for your business, with several tourist shops thrown in. There are few more relaxing pastimes than spending a lazy spring or summer afternoon feasting on crab cakes and beer in one of the restaurants around the main square. To pursue this pleasure, try the **Old Towne Restaurant** at 105 Main St. (1-410-268-8703) or **Buddy's Crabs & Ribs** at 100 Main St. (1-410-626-1100). For a big date or other special occasion, cap off your visit with dinner at the **Treaty of Paris**, 16 Church Circle (1-410-263-2641), one of Annapolis' finest restaurants. Dinner for two can easily cost around $80. You can also visit the **Fordham Brewing Company**, a local microbrewery, at 33 West St. (1-410-268-4545).

Distance 30 miles
Annapolis & Anne Arundel County Visitors Bureau 1-410-280-0445
Directions Follow US 50 East to Route 70 (Rowe Blvd.) and follow signs to Annapolis.

Baltimore, MD

Located only 45 miles north of the District, Baltimore offers many surprises to the visitor, combining its heritage as a seaport with the bustle of a city revitalized in the 1980s. The **Inner Harbor** is the city's visitor mecca. A brick walkway six blocks long winds along the waterfront past many of Baltimore's tourist attractions, including Harborplace, the **National Aquarium**, the frigate **Constellation**, the **Maryland Science Center** and the **Maritime Museum**.

Most of the food and shopping at Inner Harbor can be found at **Harborplace** at Pratt and Light Sts. (1-410-332-4191) and the **Gallery** at 200 East Pratt St. If you have been to Quincy Market in Boston, South St. Seaport in New York City or Pier 39 in San Francisco, the set-up will probably look familiar. All three Inner Harbor buildings are packed with food kiosks, cafés and specialty stores.

The **Maryland Science Center** at 601 Light St. (1-410-685-5225) is an exciting museum with hands-on or participatory exhibits. The Science Center also boasts a planetarium and five-story IMAX theater. Adult admission is $8.50, for children aged 4-17 it is $6.50.

The modernist, triangular-shaped **National Aquarium** at Pier 3 on Pratt St. (1-410-576-3800) houses over 5,000 aquatic animals and a tropical rain forest exhibit. On weekends, waiting in the ticket line for this popular site can take over an hour, so unless you plan to get there early, you may want to order tickets in advance. Entrance to the aquarium is $11.50 for adults and $7.50 for children. Children under three years of age are admitted free and senior citizens pay $9.50.

The **Baltimore Maritime Museum** (1-410-396-3854), next to the
Aquarium, offers a self-guided tour of the **USS Torsk** submarine, noted
for sinking the last warship in World War II, and the lightship
Chesapeake, which once served as a floating lighthouse. Another nautical
attraction is the frigate **Constellation**. Launched from Baltimore Harbor
in 1797, the Constellation was the US Navy's first commissioned ship.

Also located at Inner Harbor is Baltimore's newest museum. The
American Visionary Art Museum at 800 Key Hwy. (1-410-244-1900)
opened to the public in November 1995. This unique venture features
works of art from visionaries—self-taught artists, the mentally ill, the
disabled, the elderly, all of whom get short shrift in our society but who
have valuable contributions to make. The operating goal is to be as
financially self-sustaining as they can, as soon as possible, and to make
decisions based on what "feels right." For example, they chose to plant an
outdoor garden of wildflowers because it only has to be mowed once a
year. The museum's janitorial contract is with BRACE—Baltimore
Association for Retarded Citizens. Admission is $6 for adults; $4 for
children, students and seniors; and $3 each in groups of 10 or more.

If you are even remotely a baseball fan, you will by now be familiar with
one of the game's gems, **Oriole Park** at Camden Yards (1-410-685-9800).
A short stroll from the Inner Harbor and just off I-95, this park's
convenience is surpassed only by its marvelous ambiance. You do not need
to be a fan of the Orioles, or even of baseball, to have a great time there.

Sports fans can take advantage of the sports bar, **Balls**, at 200 West Pratt
St. (1-410-659-5844) right across from Camden Yards. Baseball fans
might be interested in stopping by the Babe Ruth Birthplace and
Baltimore Orioles Museum (1-410-727-1539) at 216 Emory St. on the
way to the ball game.

Located only five blocks from Inner Harbor, Little Italy has over a dozen
restaurants, ranging from inexpensive pizza parlors to elegant, somewhat
pricey Italian restaurants. President Carter's favorite was **Chiapparelli's** at
237 South High St. (1-410-837-0309). Another highly recommended
restaurant is **Sabatino's** at 901 Fawn St. (1-410-727-9414).

The **World Trade Center** at 401 East Pratt St. (1-410-837-4515) offers a
terrific view of the harbor and most of Baltimore from its 27th floor,
dubbed "The Top of the World." For a different view of the harbor, the
City Clipper, a replica of an 1854 topsail schooner, offers daily (except
Monday) and weekend evening cruises. Call 1-410-539-6277 for tickets.

For a change of pace from Inner Harbor, head for nearby **Fells Point**, one of Baltimore's historic districts. The influence of the area's 200 years of maritime history is visible in every tavern, antique store, restaurant and home. The best taverns and restaurants are often the hardest to find, such as the **John Steven** at 1800 Thames St. (1-410-327-5561), serving some of Baltimore's best seafood. **Bertha's**, at 734 South Broadway (1-410-327-5795), is a favorite for eating mussels and listening to jazz.

In the 19th century, while sailors and shipbuilders were roaming the streets of Fells Point, merchants and shoemakers were busily plying their trade up on **Federal Hill**. This historic neighborhood is only a five-minute walk south on Light St. from Inner Harbor. Cannons were placed on top of Federal Hill during the Civil War to protect the harbor and an observation tower was built to herald arriving ships. Today, the park offers a good view of the harbor and a quiet place to picnic. Dozens of family-owned stalls, some handed down for generations, fill Federal Hill's **Cross St. Market**, each featuring something different—seafood, cheese, bread, barbecue, cookies and pastries.

Another notable Baltimore sight is **Fort McHenry** (1-410-962-4299) at East Fort Ave., where America's successful defense against the British in 1814 inspired Francis Scott Key to write the Star Spangled Banner. Admission to the grounds is free but you pay $2 per adult for the fort.

Baltimore's Art District is located on Charles St., about three-quarters of a mile from the harbor. Among more than a dozen museums and galleries you will find Baltimore's gem, the **Walters Art Gallery** at 600 North Charles St. (1-410-547-9000). This museum houses one of the largest private collections in the world spanning 5,000 years of artistic endeavor. The **Baltimore Museum of Art** (1-410-396-7101), located just off North Charles St., features a collection of French Impressionist paintings and a sculpture garden. Most of the Art District museums and galleries are free to the public; a few charge a nominal admission fee.

Distance 45 miles
Visitors Center 1-410-837-4636 or 1-800-282-6632
Directions Take the Beltway to I-95 North and follow the signs to Inner Harbor, a good starting point for access to other parts of town. If you are headed to a particular spot, call ahead for more specific directions. On weekdays, you can take the MARC commuter train from Union Station to either Camden or Pennsylvania Station in Baltimore. For more information, call 1-800-325-RAIL. Amtrak (1-800-USA-RAIL) will also take you from Union Station to Baltimore's Pennsylvania Station.

Charlottesville, VA

Charlottesville, known by some as Mr. Jefferson's city, is a charming central Virginia town, nestled in the beautiful countryside at the foot of the Blue Ridge Mountains. Nearby, you can visit **Monticello** (1-804-293-6789), which Thomas Jefferson designed as his private home. Here you will quickly learn of Jefferson's wide-ranging interests in science, architecture, philosophy and the arts. The estate sits amidst beautiful gardens on top of a small mountain overlooking Charlottesville and the rolling countryside. Admission to Monticello is $8 and includes a guided tour.

From Monticello, you can see parts of "Mr. Jefferson's University," otherwise known as the **University of Virginia** (1-804-924-7969). Jefferson founded the university, which was chartered in 1819. The grounds (campus) consist mostly of neo-classical buildings, white porticos and carefully manicured grounds. The Lawn (quad) is the focal point of the university and a beautiful architectural site. The school is proud of its strong academic reputation, its major teaching hospital, and its fine athletic teams, particularly in women's basketball and men's soccer and football.

Charlottesville was also home to another president, James Monroe. His estate, **Ash Lawn** (1-804-293-9539), famous for its boxwood gardens and strolling peacocks, has the atmosphere of an early 19th-century working plantation. Jefferson personally selected the site for Monroe's house and, on a clear day, you can see Monticello from the front porch of Ash Lawn. Admission for adults is $7.

If you decide to visit either Ash Lawn or Monticello, you will probably pass by historic **Michie Tavern** (1-804-977-1234), on Route 53 about half a mile from Monticello. The tavern opened in 1784 and still offers native Virginia wine and fine southern cooking.

The highlight of Charlottesville's Historic District is the downtown mall, home to a small collection of antique stores, shops and art galleries and a few good restaurants. The **Old Historic Hardware Store** (1-804-977-1518) is an interesting place to dine, known for its meter-high beers. The **Court Square Tavern** (1-804-296-6111) offers more than 100 imported beers and a tasty Shepherd's Pie.

Central Virginia hosts dozens of festivals and annual celebrations. One of the most famous, the Foxfield Steeplechase, is Charlottesville's pride and joy, attracting people from all over each spring and fall.

Distance 110 miles
Chamber of Commerce 1-804-295-3141
Directions I-66 West to Route 29 South all the way to Charlottesville.

Shenandoah National Park

The Skyline Drive runs through Shenandoah National Park along the crest of the majestic Blue Ridge Mountains. A trip along the 105-mile drive offers breathtaking panoramic views of the Shenandoah Valley to the west and the Virginia Piedmont to the east. Recreational activities in the park include camping, fishing, nature walks and hikes, and horseback riding. Several scenic overlooks provide memorable views and photo opportunities. The *Guide to Skyline Drive* ($4.50) contains information about park accommodations and activities. Call the park at 1-703-999-2229 for more information.

If you stop in Front Royal at the north end of the park, you can replenish yourself with a great meal at **Dean's Steakhouse** at 708 South Royal Ave. (1-703-635-1780). At Dean's you can eat steak the real way—lots of it, served up with very little fuss and a very big baked potato. The warm pecan pie makes for an excellent dessert.

Distance 75 miles
Shenandoah National Park 1-703-999-2229
Directions Take Route 66 West to Front Royal, where you pick up US 340. From there, follow signs to the park.

NATIONAL PARK PASSES

The National Park Service offers several Golden Passports to help you save on entrance fees. If you plan to visit several of the many sites in, around, and within reasonable driving distance of the Washington area, you will be interested in this offer. The passports cover the holder and accompanying private party. Apply in person at any National Park or regional office of the US Park Service or Forest Service for one of the following:

The Golden Eagle Passport
$25/year

The Golden Age Passport
US residents, 62 and older
$10 one-time fee

The Golden Access Passport
Medically blind and permanently disabled
Free

Williamsburg, VA

Williamsburg, originally the capital of Virginia, was also a training ground for the men who led America to independence. In this small city, George Washington, Thomas Jefferson, Patrick Henry and George Mason helped frame the structure of America's government. Here, the House of Burgesses adopted Virginia's Resolution for Independence in May 1776, which led to the adoption of the Declaration of Independence the following July in Philadelphia.

It is easy to picture these events in Colonial Williamsburg, for in a way, life goes on much as it would have nearly 200 years ago. Thanks to generous donations from the late John Rockefeller, Jr., most of the original town was completely restored in the late 1920s and early 1930s. Along its streets you will find all the makings of a colonial town—houses, shops, taverns, gardens and even a church. Costumed actors lend a human dimension as they recreate details of 18th-century daily life. In the historic district, **King's Arms** comes highly recommended for either lunch or dinner. For some 18th-century fun, stop by **Chowning's Tavern** (1-804-229-2141), where you can drink ale, eat peanuts, indulge in their great barbecue sandwiches, and play games from the era including the Most Wonderful Game of Goose and the Game of Life.

To get the most out of this excursion, plan on staying two or three days. A **Patriot Pass** ($33 for adults, $19 for children) allows access to Williamsburg for up to a year. During the summer and the Christmas season, you should call ahead for reservations.

The **College of William and Mary**, the second-oldest college in the United States, has been an integral part of Williamsburg since 1693. The Sir Christopher Wren Building houses the oldest classrooms in the country.

Distance 150 miles
Visitors Center 1-800-HIS-TORY
Directions Take I-95 South to I-64 East.

Civil War Battlefields

Many famous Civil War battle sites, such as **Antietam**, **Manassas** or **Bull Run**, **Fredericksburg** and **Spotsylvania**, are within about an hour's drive of the District. The National Park Service provides excellent guided tours of each site as well as detailed maps for individual walking tours. These battlefields make for great day trips, especially since most of them are now surrounded by quaint towns, many with antique shops selling merchandise at prices lower than anything you could find inside the Beltway. Manassas is an exception, as the area around it has succumbed to fast food restaurants and auto dealers.

Harpers Ferry In West Virginia you can visit Harpers Ferry, the site of John Brown's famous raid. Harpers Ferry perches above the confluence of the Potomac and Shenandoah Rivers where three states meet—Maryland, Virginia and West Virginia. The town remained a strategic location throughout most of the Civil War. Harpers Ferry is a charming museum, shop and tourist town where you can stroll among buildings that appear today much as they would have in the 1850s. There are few better experiences than walking along the Shenandoah River nearby.

Distance A little over an hour from the DC area
Vistors Center 1-304-535-6298
Directions Take I-270 North to Route 340 West.

Gettysburg Visitors to Gettysburg can trace the three-day battle with an organized tour group or through a number of individual walking tours. While you are there, be sure to see the Cyclorama exhibit. This 10-minute film, shown inside a circular auditorium, depicts Pickett's charge with a sound and light program.

Distance 78 miles
Vistors Center 1-717-334-6274
Directions Take I-270 North to Route 15 North.

If you are interested in actually reliving history, a number of local groups regularly recreate Civil War battles, usually on the anniversary dates of the actual battles. Re-enactments are taken seriously in these groups, so if you are interested in participating be prepared to commit many weekends and a fair amount of money to experience the elements and the food as did the soldiers of the day. For information about re-enactments, consult the *Washington Post* Weekend section (on Fridays) or write to Civil War News, PO Box C, Arlington, MA 02174. Civil War News publishes a monthly newsletter that features schedules of re-enactments.

Amusement Parks

Paramount Kings Dominion This theme park boasts five theme areas, similar to the Disney parks, and the infamous Anaconda roller-coaster, curving snakelike through six loops and an underwater tunnel. Admission is $28.95 for adults and $19.95 for children aged three to six.

Distance 75 miles
Vistors Center 1-804-876-5000
Directions Take I-95 South to Doswell, Exit 98.

Hershey Park Chocoholics will think they have reached heaven at Hershey Park in Hershey, PA. Besides its 50 rides, Hershey Park also offers a free narrated tour through the chocolate-making process. Many visitors find the tour disappointing, because you get nowhere near the actual chocolate factory to see the real thing—until the tour ends at a warehouse-sized gift shop devoted entirely to chocolate. Admission to Hershey Park is $26.45 for adults and $15.95 for children three- to eight-years old. Use **http://www.800hershey.com/** to access Hershey Park's Website.

Distance 150 miles
Vistors Center 1-800-HER-SHEY
Directions Take I-95 North to 695 (the Baltimore Beltway). Follow 695 West to Route 83 North. Take 83 to 322 (Harrisburg) and follow it until you see the exit for Hershey Park Dr.

Sesame Place   In historic Bucks County, PA, 30 minutes north of
Philadelphia, you will find the family-oriented theme park, Sesame Place.
Meet your favorite Sesame Street characters, experience water activities
from Runaway Rapids to Little Bird's Birdbath, eat at the Sesame Food
Factory, play in Twiddlebug Land, visit the interactive science and
educational exhibits at Sesame Studio, or be entertained by the Big Bird &
Company Musical Review. Host a children's birthday party, or an all-adult
after-hours group party—there is something for everyone here. The park is
open from early May to mid-October. Admission is $22.95 per person and
free for children under two years old.

Distance Approximately 3 hours from the DC area
Vistors Center 1-215-752-7070
Directions Take I-95 North to Morrisville Exit 29A (Route 1 North) to
the Oxford Valley Exit. Turn right onto Oxford Valley Rd. and right again
at the second traffic light.

Busch Gardens, the Old Country   Finally, you can take a step back
in European history at Busch Gardens in Williamsburg, VA. The park
offers nine re-created hamlets portraying life in Old World Europe, several
roller coasters including the Loch Ness Monster and Big Bad Wolf, and
many other attractions. Adult admission is $29.95, for children aged three
through six it is $22.95.

Distance 165 miles
Vistors Center 1-800-772-8886
Directions Take I-95 South to I-64 all the way to Williamsburg. Follow
signs to Busch Gardens, the Old Country.

Young People

*W*hether entertaining your own children, your nieces and nephews, or your friends' children, you can be assured of an abundance of opportunities to help them pursue their interests, or to introduce them to new ones. The best weekly resource for current exhibits and events can be found in the Saturday's Child column of the Friday *Washington Post* Weekend section. Also, peruse the Local Interest section of area bookstores for books and pamphlets on children and family activities. What follows is just a sampling of places and activities, as well as some resources for learning more. Also included is a Feature Page providing resources for both public and private schools in the metropolitan DC area.

ACTIVITIES

The activity choices in the area are every bit as varied as children's interests. From science exhibits to acting classes, from museums and concerts to nature walks, from the giant pandas at the zoo to the model rockets at NASA, there is truly something for everyone. The challenge for area families is rarely one of not having anything to do . . . and more often one of not being able to decide what to do first. The suggestions here will get you started. And the material in the next section, Resources, will keep you going, at least for a good long while.

Aquariums

National Aquarium, 14th and Constitution Ave. NW (202-482-2825). Over 1,000 specimens of aquatic life are in residence at, of all places, the Department of Commerce building. On specific days of the week, you can watch the feeding of the sharks and piranhas. Admission is charged. Metro: Federal Triangle.

Baltimore Aquarium, 501 E. Pratt St., Baltimore, MD (1-410-576-3810), about a one-hour drive from DC. This aquarium, whose official name is also the National Aquarium, features marine mammals, an Atlantic coral reef, a South American rain forest, and a laser animation exhibit. Admission is charged based on age, day of the week and time of day.

Art Galleries

National Gallery of Art, Constitution Ave. at 6th St. NW (202-737-4215). This major art gallery offers children a free, self-guided tour through the museum's fabulous collection of world-famous art.

PARENTS UNITED

The local media has a tendency to focus only on limitations when covering public education in the District. There are in fact a number of very good District schools that provide strong publication education programs and prepare students for solid academic and professional careers. To find out about the best of DC's public education options, contact **Parents United for the DC Public Schools**. This public advocacy group is committed to gaining appropriate public attention for the many good aspects of city learning. If you would like to find out about the group, the schools in the city, or what you can do to support their efforts, contact them at 202-833-4766 or stop by their office at 1300 19th St. NW.

Walters Art Gallery, 600 N. Charles St., Baltimore, MD (1-410-547-9000). The Walters offers many classes, tours and special events for children. There is a preschoolers program to introduce children to the concept of the art museum. Admission is charged.

Concerts

The **Washington Performing Arts Society**, Arts and Education Program (202-833-9800), performs concerts and cultural enrichment programs at no charge for children, K-12, at schools throughout Washington, DC.

The **Kennedy Center** supports performance and education programs for young people and families. Programs are available for children of all ages, starting at age four. Offerings include an introduction to orchestral instruments with the **National Symphony Orchestra**, theater performances and concerts, storytelling, puppetry and more, available on a subscription or individual ticket basis. Further information on these programs is available at 202-416-8500.

Libraries and Readings

Libraries throughout the area conduct story and poetry readings for children in the general age range of three to six. In addition, several of them are creating new ways to accommodate the many languages spoken by patrons of all ages. The bilingual story hour is becoming more prevalent in several Washington area jurisdictions in an effort both to serve a growing international population and to help English-speaking children learn a second language. Contact your local library to find out about the nearest facility offering such programs.

Museums

Several of the **Smithsonian Institution**'s museums have exhibits of particular interest to children. The free-admission museums listed here are all on the Mall, between Constitution and Independence Aves., close to the Smithsonian, Federal Triangle and L'Enfant Metro stations. If you take the Metro, check with the attendant at your departure station to find out which stop is best for you. You can call the Dial-a-Museum line for daily, 24-hour recorded activity information. Call 202-357-2020 to hear the message in English or 202-633-9126 for Spanish.

The **Arts and Industries** building at 900 Jefferson Dr. SW features the Discovery Theater in addition to its many changing exhibitions for children. The **Museum of Natural History** at 10th St. and Constitution Ave. NW has the popular Dinosaur Hall, and American Indian Life exhibits and the Insect Zoo. A favorite of many children—of all ages—is the **National Air and Space Museum** at 7th St. and Independence Ave. This museum features exhibits on the history of aviation, space science and space technology as well as spectacular movies in its IMAX Theater.

In addition to the Smithsonian, there are a number of private museums of special note, including those listed here.

National Capital Children's Museum, 800 Third St. NE (202-543-8600). This hands-on museum includes a U-TV and Animation Lab where children can play-act in sophisticated picture studios. There is an admission fee. Metro: Union Station.

National Capital Trolley Museum, Bonifont Rd. and New Hampshire Ave., Silver Spring, MD (301-384-6088). This museum features a collection of antique American and European trolleys and streetcars. Admission is charged and includes a trolley ride.

Navy Museum, 901 M St. SE, Navy Yard, Bldg. 76 (202-433-2651). Children can climb on old tanks and cannons in the outdoor playground, operate the periscope, and experience simulated anti-aircraft warfare inside the museum.

Washington Dolls' House and Toy Museum, 5236 44th St. NW (202-244-0024). Here you will find the world's largest collection of antique doll houses, toys and games, most of which are from the Victorian period. Admission is charged. Metro: Friendship Heights.

Nature Centers and Walks

Hiking and biking trails are often either too crowded or simply too treacherous to provide safe and quiet nature experiences for children. There are, however, several stroller-accessible nature walks in the area, a few of which are listed below. Call your state, regional and county parks department for information on fully accessible walks near you. Telephone numbers are listed under Recreation Centers in this chapter.

DC
Rock Creek Nature Center and Planetarium
5200 Glover Rd. NW
202-426-6829

EDUCATIONAL SERVICE

In addition to its other publishing activities, the *Washington Post* runs two important education programs to help parents and teachers use the paper for the benefit of the next generation. The Learning Partners program is for parents and other adults, to help them use the daily paper to build and strengthen children's skills. *Inside the Washington Post* is targeted at teachers, and provides classroom materials for grades 1-12. To obtain information on either of these programs, call 202-334-KIDS and leave your name and address. Or you can call the Post's Educational Services Department at 202-334-4544 or 202-334-7972.

Maryland
Clearwater Nature Center
Cosca Regional Park
11000 Thrift Rd., Clinton
301-297-4575

Locust Grove Nature Center
Cabin John Regional Park
7777 Democracy Blvd., Bethesda
301-299-1990

Virginia
Huntley Meadows Park
3701 Lockheed Blvd., Alexandria
703-768-2525

Riverbend Nature Center
Riverbend Regional Park
8814 Jeffrey Rd., Great Falls
703-759-3211

Of special note is the **Mountain Laurel Trail** at the **National Wildlife Federation's Laurel Ridge Conservation Education Center** (703-790-4437). This trail, at 8925 Leesburg Pike in Vienna, three miles west of Tysons Corner, is perfect for families with strollers, as well as for people with other special needs. The trail includes interpretive signs that are accessible from standing or sitting positions, a specially produced audio cassette tape for the hearing impaired focusing on the nonvisual elements of what might be experienced at each stop, and a large-print version of the brochure and Braille transcriptions of the signs for the visually impaired. Texture and color changes in the asphalt signal the visually impaired that they have reached an interpretive stop.

Points of Interest

Bureau of Engraving and Printing, 14th and C St. SW (202-622-2000). Here you and your children can watch currency being made from start to finish, and view famous coins and currency. Admission is free.

Federal Bureau of Investigation, 9th St. and Pennsylvania Ave. NW (202-324-3447). Look at photographs or drawings of the FBI's Ten Most Wanted individuals, learn how the FBI finds them, and conclude your visit with a marksmanship demonstration. Visits to the FBI are free.

NASA/Goddard Space Flight Center, Visitor Center, Greenbelt and Soil Conservation Rds., Greenbelt, MD (301-286-8981). At this Visitor

Center, you can see models of rockets and spacecraft that have made journeys into space, view the Earth and neighboring stars and planets as seen from space in a stand-up eight-screen theater, and pilot your own manned maneuvering unit and gyrochair. On the first and third Sunday of each month, visitors can also see a model rocket launch. Admission is free.

Recreation Centers

There are plenty of ways for children and families to recreate in the Washington area. In addition to programs run by local schools, each jurisdiction has its own city or county Department of Recreation. These government offices organize, run and publicize all kinds of recreational activities—playgrounds, picnic areas, courses and outings in the vicinity.

Area Departments of Recreation

District of Columbia	202-673-7660
Maryland	
Montgomery County	301-217-6800
Prince George's County	301-669-2400
Virginia	
Alexandria	703-838-4343
Arlington County	703-358-3322
Fairfax County	703-324-4386

Theaters

Arena Stage, 6th and Maine Ave. SW (202-554-9066, TDD 202-484-0247). Arena Stage runs a four-part program called Theater as Discovery, targeting public school teachers and students in grades 9-12. Part One, the Act One Program, allows teachers to participate in activities that focus on the literary, historical and cultural worlds of the plays being performed. Teachers receive study guides and information on effective presentation of materials to students at various levels, allowing them to integrate these activities into their classroom teaching. Part Two, New Discoverers Program, is an intensive one-on-one learning opportunity for Washington metropolitan area high school students. Working with 20 students at a time, the program offers them encouragement and the resources needed to emerge as the next generation of teachers and scholars. Part Three, Student Playwrights Program, is an in-school play-writing program in three area public schools, culminating in a festival of plays by student writers. Part Four, Advanced Student Playwrights, is an extension of Student Playwrights. Plays written in this program are presented at an informal reading in December and are also considered for the Student Playwrights Festival in the spring.

Living Stage, 6th and Maine Ave. SW (202-234-5782, TDD 202-484-0247) is the social outreach company of Arena Stage. Living Stage effects social change through the art of improvisational theater. Working from the fundamental belief that everyone is an artist with the need to create, the company conducts performance workshops in regularly scheduled sessions with children, teens and adults who otherwise lack access to avenues of creative personal development. The company offers summer camps for children and teens in separate two-week sessions by age group, 6-8, 9-12, 13-15 and 16-18.

Kennedy Center Theater Lab at the John F. Kennedy Center for the Performing Arts, New Hampshire Ave. at Rock Creek Pkwy. The theater produces and presents professional performances at the Kennedy Center for youngsters, parents and teachers. It also provides theater training, drama and play-writing workshops, and professional training and performance opportunities for advanced theater students. Call for information at 202-467-4600, 1-800-444-1324 or TDD 202-416-8524.

Adventure Theatre (301-320-5331) and **Puppet Co. Playhouse** (301-320-6668), both located at Glen Echo Park, 7300 MacArthur Blvd., Glen Echo, MD. These are professional children's theaters offering plays, storytelling and puppet shows, among other theater-related activities.

Discovery Theater, at the Smithsonian's Arts and Industries Building, 900 Jefferson Dr. SW (202-357-1500). Discovery theater features live performing arts presentations for young people and their families. The performances range from puppet theater, plays and mime to music, storytelling and dance.

Wolf Trap Farm Park for the Performing Arts, Towlston Rd. and Route 7, Vienna, VA (703-255-1939). This informal story theater offers puppet shows, dance and other child-oriented entertainment.

Zoos and Animal Parks

National Zoological Park, 3001 Connecticut Ave. NW. The National Zoo is home to 5,000 animals including the giant panda Hsing Hsing, Smokey the Bear, American bison, and exotic birds and reptiles. Admission is free. Recorded Zoo information is available at 202-673-4800. Metro: Cleveland Park or Woodley Park-Zoo.

Reston Animal Park, 1228 Hunter Mill Rd., Vienna, VA. This animal park has domestic and exotic animals for children to pet and feed; elephant rides, pony rides and hay rides; educational programs; and playground, pond and picnic facilities. Information can be obtained at 703-759-3636.

RESOURCES

A wide variety of resources exist to help you find out about other activities for young people. Area bookstores include many reference books and local guidebooks on activities for children. Some of the large chain stores include entire children's sections, and there are a number of bookstores that cater solely to children. There are several newsletters and newspapers available either by subscription or for free at various sites in the area. Television and radio also get involved with children's programming. A sampling of these follows.

Books for Washington Area Families

Going Places With Children in Washington is available in most area bookstores. It is a valuable guidebook to museums, historical sights, parks, entertainment, restaurants and shopping and includes a calendar of events particularly suited to family outings. It is also available by mail order from Green Acres School, 11701 Danville Dr., Rockville, MD 20852 (301-881-4100).

The Parent Resource Guide is published in two local editions, one for Northern Virginia and one for Washington, DC and the Maryland suburbs. It is a comprehensive guide to "family-friendly" products and services throughout the metropolitan area. The book is available in area bookstores or by contacting the Parent Resource Guide, 8320 2nd Ave., Vienna, VA 22182 (703-698-8066).

Children's Bookstores

There are a number of fine specialized bookstores in the Washington area, dedicated to the interests of the younger reader. Listed here are a number of favorites.

DC
Cheshire Cat Bookstore
5512 Connecticut Ave. NW
202-244-3956

Fairy Godmother—Children's Books and Toys
319 7th St. SE
202-547-5474

Sullivan's Toy Store
3412 Wisconsin Ave. NW
202-362-1343

Maryland
Bookoo Books for Kids
4923 Elm St., Bethesda
301-652-2794

Virginia
A Likely Story
1555 King St., Alexandria
703-836-2498

Aladdin's Lamp
126 W. Broad St., Falls Church
703-241-8281

Book Nook—A Children's Bookstore
10312 Main St., Fairfax
703-591-6545

Imagination Station
4524 Lee Hwy., Arlington
703-522-2047

Toy Corner Book Department
2918 Chain Bridge Rd., Oakton
703-255-3232

Why Not
200 King St., Alexandria
703-548-4420

Periodicals and Subscriptions

There are a number of local publications in the area focusing on the interests and needs of children. Some are focused more on support for parents and others are published for area children and teenagers. Included here are some of the major ones, but be sure to check your local library, schools and recreation centers for more ideas. Keep in mind, too, that you or your children might have something you would like to share with other families through these media outlets.

The Children's Post
51 Monroe St., Suite 1700
Rockville, MD 20850
Subscription: $17

Dani's News, The Newspaper for Families
PO Box 503
Merrifield, VA 22116-0503
703-560-7722
Subscription: Free to metropolitan DC residents; $18 for others

Parent Weekly, Fairfax County
11701 Bowman Green Dr.
Reston, VA 22090
703-843-1075
Subscription: Free

Washington Families
Publication for Metro Washington Parents
3 Bethesda Metro Center, Suite 750
Bethesda, MD 20814
301-656-0901
http://family.com
and
3326 Fern Hollow Pl.
Herndon, VA 22071
703-648-3281 (VA/Metro)
Subscription: $25; free at 1,500 area locations

Washington Parent
The Parent Connection, Inc.
5606 Knollwood Rd.
Bethesda, MD 20816
301-320-2321, Subscription: $10

Young DC
2025 Pennsylvania Ave. NW, #321
Washington, DC 20006
202-429-5292
Subscription: Free at 100 area locations

Television and Radio Programs

Several television channels and radio stations feature programs just for children and their families. In addition to the standard fare of the networks, you will find great shows on the three local Public Broadcasting channels—WMPT, WETA and WHMM. If you have cable, you can also tune into the Discovery Channel, Family Channel, Learning Channel, Nickelodeon and the USA Network. Across these options, you will find programming of all types for children and teenagers alike. Radio Zone is a children's program broadcast on three different AM frequencies—in Washington, DC on 1050, in Northern Virginia on 1460, and out of Baltimore, MD on 1570.

OF SPECIAL NOTE

While $10 gets you a subscription to Washington Parent, for only $20, you can become a member of the Parent Connection. Membership entitles you to a one-year subscription to the newspaper as well as discounts on parenting workshops, special events, project SHARE—a computer database that matches families whose child care needs are compatible, and member discounts including a $10 gift certificate from Turtle Park Toys.

Young DC is an independent newspaper written exclusively by and for Washington DC area teens, aged 14 to 19. The publication reflects the cultural, economic and racial diversity of the Washington community and seeks to reduce the isolation between the area's urban and suburban teens. *Young DC* is a great outlet for aspiring teen writers, editors, artists, photographers and cartoonists, giving them a chance to be seen and heard. It is distributed to more than 100 high schools and retail outlets in DC, Maryland and Virginia, including typical teen "hangouts," such as coffee shops and laundromats. The paper is particularly popular in that it covers subjects of interest to teens in a way that teens can truly appreciate.

Cyber-surfing families might want to look at **http://www.family.com** on the Internet. This Family World site gives you access to information from more than 40 regional parenting publications across the United States. Information at this Web site covers feature articles from the participating publications, events calendars, forums and other resources. Of particular interest to "connected" families are the links to other Internet resources including the Children's Literature Web Guide; Parents Helping Parents network to support children with special needs; a Missing Children Database; and other sports, museum and science sites.

WASHINGTON AREA SCHOOLS

The Washington metropolitan area schools are among the best in the nation. In addition to the extensive public school systems in DC, Maryland and Virginia, there are a substantial number of excellent independent, private and international schools. Several publications with comprehensive listings of private schools can be found in local bookstores. Each November, *Washingtonian* publishes an updated list of area private schools.

For further information on public schools, contact the Boards of Education for the jurisdiction where you live.

District of Columbia
415 12th St. NW
Washington, DC 20004
202-724-4044

Maryland
Montgomery County
850 Hungerford Dr.
Rockville, MD 20850
301-279-3167

Prince George's County
14201 School La.
Upper Marlboro, MD 20772
301-952-6000

Virginia
Alexandria City
2000 N. Beauregard St.
Alexandria, VA 22311
703-824-6660

Arlington County
1426 N. Quincy St.
Arlington, VA 22207
703-358-6000

Fairfax County
10700 Page Ave.
Fairfax, VA 22030
703-246-3646

Falls Church
210 E. Broad St.
Falls Church, VA 22046
703-241-7600

For information on independent and private schools, contact one of the following:

Association of Independent
Schools of Greater Washington
PO Box 9956
Washington, DC 20016
202-537-1114

Association of Independent
Maryland Schools
PO Box 802
Severna Park, MD 21146
301-621-0787

Virginia Council for
Private Education
Department of Education
PO Box 6Q
Richmond, VA 23216-2060
804-740-9052

Resources

EMERGENCY NUMBERS

Ambulance, Fire, Police	**911**
National Capital Poison Center, Georgetown University Hospital	**202-625-3333**

USEFUL NUMBERS

Automobile and Truck Rental

Alamo	1-800-327-9633
Avis	1-800-331-1212
Budget	1-800-527-0700
Hertz	1-800-654-3131
National	1-800-227-7368
Thrifty	1-800-367-2277

City and County Governments

District of Columbia	202-727-1000

Maryland

Bethesda-Chevy Chase Government Center	301-986-4325
Montgomery County	301-217-6500
Prince George's County	301-350-9700

Virginia

Alexandria City	703-838-4000
Arlington County	703-358-3000
Fairfax County	703-246-2000
Falls Church City	703-241-5001

Consumer Information

Talking Yellow Pages	703-237-1001
Better Business Bureau	202-393-8000
Washington Consumers' Checkbook	202-347-9612

Embassies (see pages 221-232)

Gay and Lesbian Resources

General

Gay and Lesbian Hotline	202-833-3234

Gay and Lesbian Switchboard	202-628-4667
	202-628-4669 (TDD)
Directory of Services: *The Other Pages*	202-265-5073

Religious and Spiritual Organizations

Affirmation (Methodist)	202-462-4897
Bet Mishpachah (Jewish)	202-833-1638
Church of the Disciples (MCC)	202-387-5230
Dignity (Catholics)	202-332-2424
Integrity (Episcopalians)	301-953-9421
Lutherans Concerned	703-971-4342
Presbyterian	301-345-0324
Quakers	202-483-3310
Unitarians for	
Lesbian/Gay Concerns	301-776-6891

Hospitals

District of Columbia

DC General Hospital	202-675-5000 (English)
Massachusetts Ave. and 19th St. SE	202-675-7655 (Spanish)
Capitol Hill	202-675-0400
700 Constitution Ave. NE	202-547-9729 (TDD)
Children's Hospital National Medical Center	202-884-5000
111 Michigan Ave. NW	202-884-3444 (TDD)
Columbia Hospital for Women Medical Center	
2425 L St. NW	202-293-6500
George Washington Medical Center	
901 23rd St. NW	202-994-1000
Georgetown University Hospital	202-687-2000
3800 Reservoir Rd. NW	202-687-4639 (TDD)
Greater Southeast Community Hospital	
1310 Southern Ave. SE	202-574-6000
Howard University Hospital	
2041 Georgia Ave. NW	202-865-6100
Providence Hospital	
1150 Varnum St. NE	202-269-7000
Psychiatric Institute of Washington	202-965-8400
4228 Wisconsin Ave. NW	202-965-8403 (TDD)

Sibley Memorial Hospital
5255 Loughboro Rd. NW   202-537-4000

Washington Hospital Center
110 Irving St. NW   202-877-7000

Maryland
Doctor's Hospital of PG County
8118 Good Luck Rd., Lanham   301-552-8118

Holy Cross Hospital   301-905-0100
1500 Forest Glen Rd., Silver Spring   301-905-1414 (TDD)

NIH - Clinical Center
9000 Rockville Pike, Bethesda   301-496-2563

PG Hospital Center
3001 Hospital Dr., Cheverly   301-618-2000

Suburban Hospital
8600 Old Georgetown Rd., Bethesda   301-530-3100

Washington Adventist Hospital
7600 Carroll Ave., Takoma Park   301-891-7600

Virginia
Alexandria Hospital
4320 Seminary Rd., Alexandria   703-504-3000

Arlington Hospital
1701 N. George Mason Dr., Arlington   703-558-5000

Fair Oaks Hospital
2960 Sleepy Hollow Rd., Falls Church   703-391-3600

Fairfax Hospital
3300 Gallows Rd., Falls Church   703-698-1110

Lawyers Referral Service

District of Columbia   202-626-3499
Montgomery County   301-279-9100
Prince George's County   301-952-1440
Northern Virginia   1-800-552-7977

Medical Referral Services
Dentist Referrals
District of Columbia   202-547-7615
Montgomery County   301-460-0500

Prince George's County	301-731-7333
Northern Virginia	703-642-5297
Doctors' Referral (Metro area)	202-362-8677

Medical and Health Services

AIDS Hotline	202-332-AIDS
HIV Testing	202-332-3926

Planned Parenthood Clinic

District of Columbia	202-483-3999
Silver Spring	301-588-7933
Northern Virginia	703-820-3335

Rape Crisis Hotline

District of Columbia	202-333-7273
Montgomery County	301-738-2255
Northern Virginia	703-527-4077

Suicide Hotline

District of Columbia	202-223-2255
Montgomery County	301-738-2255
Northern Virginia	703-527-4077

Whitman-Walker Clinic	202-797-3500

Police Non-Emergency Calls

Alexandria	703-838-4444
Arlington	703-558-2222
Bethesda-Chevy Chase	301-652-9200
District of Columbia	202-727-4326
Falls Church	703-241-5054
Prince George's County	301-336-8800
Silver Spring	301-565-7744

Pharmacies, 24-Hour CVS/Pharmacies

District of Columbia

Dupont Circle, 6-7 Dupont Circle, NW	202-785-1466
14th St. Area, 1121 Vermont Ave. NW	202-628-0720

Maryland

Bethesda-Chevy Chase, 6917 Arlington Rd.	301-656-2522
Gaithersburg Square, Gaithersburg	301-948-3250
Langley Park Shopping Center	301-434-3121

Virginia

Arlington, 3133 Lee Highway	703-522-0260
Greenbriar Shopping Center, Fairfax	703-378-7550
Falls Church, 8124 Arlington Blvd.	703-560-7280
Springfield, 6436 Springfield Plaza	703-451-1400

Postal Service Answer Line (24 hour)   202-526-3920

Religious Organizations

Buddhist	202-829-2423
Catholic Information Center	202-783-2062
Episcopal Diocese of Washington	202-537-6560
Friends Meeting of Washington	202-483-3310
Islamic Center	202-332-8343
Jewish Information and Referral Service	301-770-4848
Lutheran (Washington, DC Synod)	202-543-8610
Methodist (District Superintendent's Office)	1-800-251-8140
Presbyterian (National Capitol)	202-244-4760
Unitarian Church of Arlington	703-892-2565
Catholic Young Adults Club	703-841-2759
Jewish Information and Referral Service	301-770-4848

Time (no area code required)   844-1212

Travel Resources (International)

Passport Applications or Renewals
Washington Passport Agency
1425 K St. NW   202-647-0518

Immunizations/Testing
Travelers Medical Service of Washington
2141 K St. NW   202-466-8109

Foreign Currency
The American Express Travel Service Offices

1150 Connecticut Ave. NW	202-457-1300
1776 Pennsylvania Ave. NW	202-289-8800
1001 G St. NW	202-393-0095
5300 Wisconsin Ave. NW (Mazza Gallerie)	202-364-4000

Riggs National Bank
17th and H Sts. NW   202-835-6000

Ruesch International
825 14th St. NW   202-408-1200

Thomas Cook Currency Services
1800 K St. NW   202-872-1427

Travel Advisories
US State Department
Office of Overseas Citizens Services
Telephone   202-647-5225
Computer Bulletin Board   202-647-9225
Automated Fax Service   202-647-3000

US Capitol Switchboard   202-224-3121

Veterinarians/Animal Hospitals (24 Hour)
DC
Friendship Hospital for Animals
4105 Brandywine St. NW   202-363-7300

Maryland
Chevy Chase Veterinary Clinic
8815 Connecticut Ave., Chevy Chase   301-656-6655

Virginia

McLean Animal Hospital
1330 Old Chain Bridge Road, McLean   703-356-5000

Virginia-Maryland Veterinary Emergency Service
2660 Duke St., Alexandria   703-823-3601

Washington, DC Convention and
Visitors Association   202-789-7000

Weather (no area code required)   936-1212
National Weather Service Forecast Line:
Local and Extended   703-260-0307
Selected US Cities   703-260-0806

Weather-related Websites
Weather   http://www.nws.noaa.gov

Earthquakes   http://quake.wr.usgs.gov

Hurricanes   http://thunder.atms.purdue.edu/hurricane.html

Zip Codes   202-682-9595

EMBASSIES

Country	Embassy	Phone/Fax
AFGHANISTAN	Embassy of the Republic of Afghanistan 2341 Wyoming Ave. NW, 20008	202-234-3770, 3771 202-328-3516 (fax)
ALBANIA	Embassy of the Republic of Albania 1511 K St. NW, Suite 1010, 20005	202-223-4942, 8187 202-628-7342 (fax)
ALGERIA	Embassy of the Democratic and Popular Republic of Algeria 2118 Kalorama Rd NW, 20008	202-265-2800
ANGOLA	Embassy of the Republic of Angola 1819 L St. NW, Suite 400, 20036	202-785-1156 202-785-1258 (fax)
ANTIGUA AND BARBUDA	Embassy of Antigua and Barbuda 3216 New Mexico Ave. NW, 20016	202-362-5211, 5166, 5122 202-362-5225 (fax)
ARGENTINA	Embassy of the Argentine Republic 1600 New Hampshire Ave. NW, 20009	202-939-6400 to 6403
ARMENIA	Embassy of the Republic of Armenia 1660 L St. NW, 11th Floor, 20036	202-628-5766 202-628-5769 (fax)
AUSTRALIA	Embassy of Australia 1601 Massachusetts Ave. NW, 20036	202-797-3000 202-797-3168 (fax)
AUSTRIA	Embassy of Austria 3524 International Court NW, 20008	202-895-6700 202-895-6750 (fax)
AZERBAIJAN	Embassy of the Republic of Azerbaijan Temporary: 927 15th St. NW, Suite 700, 20005	202-842-0001 202-842-0004 (fax)
BAHAMAS	Embassy of the Commonwealth of the Bahamas 2220 Massachusetts Ave. NW, 20008	202-319-2660 202-319-2668 (fax)
BAHRAIN	Embassy of the State of Bahrain 3502 International Dr. NW, 20008	202-342-0741, 0742 202-362-2192 (fax)
BANGLADESH	Embassy of the People's Republic of Bangladesh 2201 Wisconsin Ave. NW, 20007	202-342-8372 to 8376

BARBADOS	Embassy of Barbados 2144 Wyoming Ave. NW, 20008	202-939-9200 to 9202 202-332-7467 (fax)
BARBUDA	See Antigua and Barbuda	
BELARUS	Embassy of the Republic of Belarus 1619 New Hampshire Ave. NW, 20009	202-986-1604 202-986-1805 (fax)
BELGIUM	Embassy of Belgium 3330 Garfield St. NW, 20008	202-333-6900 202-333-3079 (fax)
BELIZE	Embassy of Belize 2535 Massachusetts Ave. NW, 20008	202-332-9636 202-332-6888 (fax)
BENIN	Embassy of the Republic of Benin 2737 Cathedral Ave. NW, 20008	202-232-6656 to 6658 202-265-1996 (fax)
BOLIVIA	Embassy of the Republic of Bolivia 3014 Massachusetts Ave. NW, 20008	202-483-4410 to 4412 202-328-3712 (fax)
BOSNIA AND HERZEGOVINA	Embassy of the Republic of Bosnia and Herzegovina 1707 L St. NW, Suite 760, 20036	202-833-3612, 3613, 3615 202-833-2061 (fax)
BOTSWANA	Embassy of the Republic of Botswana 3400 International Dr. NW, Suite 7M, 20008	202-244-4990, 4991 202-244-4164 (fax)
BRAZIL	Brazilian Embassy 3006 Massachusetts Ave. NW, 20008	202-745-2700 202-745-2827 (fax)
BRUNEI	Embassy of the State of Brunei Darussalam Watergate, 2600 Virginia Ave. NW, Suite 300, 3rd Floor, 20037	202-342-0159 202-342-0158 (fax)
BULGARIA	Embassy of the Republic of Bulgaria 1621 22nd St. NW, 20008	202-387-7969 202-234-7973 (fax)
BURKINA FASO	Embassy of Burkina Faso 2340 Massachusetts Ave. NW, 20008	202-332-5577, 6895
BURMA	See Myanmar	
BURUNDI	Embassy of the Republic of Burundi 2233 Wisconsin Ave. NW, Suite 212, 20007	202-342-2574

CAMBODIA	Royal Embassy of Cambodia 4500 16th St. NW, 20011	202-726-7742 202-726-8381 (fax)
CAMEROON	Embassy of the Republic of Cameroon 2349 Massachusetts Ave. NW, 20008	202-265-8790 to 8794
CANADA	Embassy of Canada 501 Pennsylvania Ave. NW, 20001	202-682-1740 202-682-7726 (fax)
CAPE VERDE	Embassy of the Republic of Cape Verde 3415 Massachusetts Ave. NW, 20007	202-965-6820 202-965-1207 (fax)
CENTRAL AFRICAN REPUBLIC	Embassy of Central African Republic 1618 22nd St. NW, 20008	202-483-7800, 7801 202-332-9893 (fax)
CHAD	Embassy of the Republic of Chad 2002 R St. NW, 20009	202-462-4009 202-265-1937 (fax)
CHILE	Embassy of Chile 1732 Massachusetts Ave. NW, 20036	202-785-1746 202-887-5579 (fax)
CHINA	Embassy of the People's Republic of China 2300 Connecticut Ave. NW, 20008	202-328-2500 to 2502
COLOMBIA	Embassy of Colombia 2118 Leroy Pl. NW, 20008	202-387-8338 202-232-8643 (fax)
CONGO, REPUBLIC OF	Embassy of the Republic of Congo 4891 Colorado Ave. NW, 20011	202-726-0825 202-726-1860 (fax)
COSTA RICA	Embassy of Costa Rica 2114 S St. NW, 20008	202-234-2945 202-265-4795 (fax)
COTE D'IVOIRE	Embassy of the Republic of Côte d'Ivoire 2424 Massachusetts Ave. NW, 20008	202-797-0300
CROATIA	Embassy of the Republic of Croatia 2343 Massachusetts Ave. NW, 20008	202-588-5899 202-588-8936 (fax)
CYPRUS	Embassy of the Republic of Cyprus 2211 R St. NW, 20008	202-462-5772
CZECH	Embassy of the Czech Republic 3900 Spring of Freedom St. NW, 20008	202-363-6315, 6316 202-966-8540 (fax)

DENMARK	Royal Danish Embassy 3200 Whitehaven St. NW, 20008	202-234-4300 202-328-1470 (fax)
DJIBOUTI	Embassy of the Republic of Djibouti 1156 15th St. NW, Suite 515, 20005	202-331-0270 202-331-0302 (fax)
DOMINICA	Embassy of the Commonwealth of Dominica 3216 New Mexico Ave. NW, 20016	202-364-6781 202-364-6791 (fax)
DOMINICAN REPUBLIC	Embassy of the Dominican Republic 1715 22nd St. NW, 20008	202-332-6280 202-265-8057 (fax)
ECUADOR	Embassy of Ecuador 2535 15th St. NW, 20009	202-234-7200
EGYPT	Embassy of the Arab Republic of Egypt 3521 International Court NW, 20008	202-895-5400 202-244-4319/5131 (fax)
EL SALVADOR	Embassy of El Salvador 2308 California St. NW, 20008	202-265-9671, 9672
ERITREA	Embassy of the State of Eritrea 910 17th St. NW, Suite 400, 20006	202-429-1991 202-429-9004 (fax)
ESTONIA	Embassy of Estonia 1030 15th St. NW, Suite 1000, 20005	202-789-0320 202-789-0471 (fax)
ETHIOPIA	Embassy of Ethiopia 2134 Kalorama Rd. NW, 20008	202-234-2281, 2282 202-328-7950 (fax)
FIJI	Embassy of the Republic of Fiji 2233 Wisconsin Ave. NW, Suite 240, 20007	202-337-8320 202-337-1996 (fax)
FINLAND	Embassy of Finland 3301 Massachusetts Ave. NW, 20008	202-298-5800 202-298-6030 (fax)
FRANCE	Embassy of France 4101 Reservoir Rd. NW, 20007	202-944-6000
GABON	Embassy of the Gabonese Republic 2034 20th St. NW, Suite 200, 20009	202-797-1000 202-332-0668 (fax)
GAMBIA, THE	Embassy of The Gambia 1155 15th St. NW, Suite 1000, 20005	202-785-1399, 1379, 1425 202-785-1430 (fax)

GEORGIA	Embassy of the Republic of Georgia 1511 K St. NW, Suite 424, 20005	202-393-5959 202-393-6060 (fax)
GERMANY, FEDERAL REPUBLIC OF	Embassy of the Federal Republic of Germany 4645 Reservoir Rd. NW, 20007	202-298-4000 202-298-4249 (fax)
GHANA	Embassy of Ghana 3512 International Dr. NW, 20008	202-686-4520 202-686-4527 (fax)
GREAT BRITAIN	See United Kingdom of Great Britain and Northern Ireland	
GREECE	Embassy of Greece 2221 Massachusetts Ave. NW, 20008	202-939-5800 202-939-5824 (fax)
GRENADA	Embassy of Grenada 1701 New Hampshire Ave. NW, 20009	202-265-2561
GRENADINES	See Saint Vincent and the Grenadines	
GUATEMALA	Embassy of Guatemala 2220 R St. NW, 20008	202-745-4952 to 4954 202-745-1908 (fax)
GUINEA	Embassy of the Republic of Guinea 2112 Leroy Pl. NW, 20008	202-483-9420 202-483-8688 (fax)
GUINEA-BISSAU	Embassy of the Republic of Guinea-Bissau 918 16th St. NW, Mezzanine Suite, 20006	202-872-4222 202-872-4226 (fax)
GUYANA	Embassy of Guyana 2490 Tracy Pl. NW, 20008	202-265-6900, 6901
HAITI	Embassy of the Republic of Haiti 2311 Massachusetts Ave. NW, 20008	202-332-4090 to 4092 202-745-7215 (fax)
HERZEGOVINA	See Bosnia and Herzegovina	
The HOLY SEE	Apostolic Nunciature 3339 Massachusetts Ave. NW, 20008	202-333-7121
HONDURAS	Embassy of Honduras 3007 Tilden St. NW, 20008	202-966-7702, 2604, 5008, 4596 202-966-9751 (fax)
HUNGARY	Embassy of the Republic of Hungary 3910 Shoemaker St. NW, 20008	202-362-6730 202-966-8135 (fax)

ICELAND	Embassy of Iceland 1156 15th St. NW, Suite 1200, 20005	202-265-6653 to 6655 202-265-6656
INDIA	Embassy of India 2107 Massachusetts Ave. NW, 20008	202-939-7000
INDONESIA	Embassy of the Republic of Indonesia 2020 Massachusetts Ave. NW, 20036	202-775-5200 202-775-5365 (fax)
IRELAND	Embassy of Ireland 2234 Massachusetts Ave. NW, 20008	202-462-3939
IRELAND, NORTHERN	See United Kingdom of Great Britain and Northern Ireland	
ISRAEL	Embassy of Israel 3514 International Dr. NW, 20008	202-364-5500 202-364-5610 (fax)
ITALY	Embassy of Italy 1601 Fuller St. NW, 20009	202-328-5500 202-483-2187 (fax)
IVORY COAST	See Côte d'Ivoire	
JAMAICA	Embassy of Jamaica 1520 New Hampshire Ave. NW, 20036	202-452-0660 202-452-0081 (fax)
JAPAN	Embassy of Japan 2520 Massachusetts Ave. NW, 20008	202-939-6700 202-328-2187 (fax)
JORDAN	Embassy of the Hashemite Kingdom of Jordan 3504 International Dr. NW, 20008	202-966-2664 202-966-3110 (fax)
KAZAKSTAN	Embassy of the Republic of Kazakstan Temporary: 3421 Massachusetts Ave. NW, 20008	202-333-4505, 4507 202-333-4509 (fax)
KENYA	Embassy of the Republic of Kenya 2249 R St. NW, 20008	202-387-6101 202-462-3829 (fax)
KOREA	Embassy of Korea 2450 Massachusetts Ave. NW, 20008	202-939-5600
KUWAIT	Embassy of the State of Kuwait 2940 Tilden St. NW, 20008	202-966-0702 202-966-0517 (fax)

KYRGYZSTAN	Embassy of the Kyrgyz Republic Temporary: 1511 K St. NW, Suite 706, 20005	202-347-3732 202-347-3718 (fax)
LAOS	Embassy of the Lao People's Democratic Republic 2222 S St. NW, 20008	202-332-6416, 6417 202-332-4923 (fax)
LATVIA	Embassy of Latvia 4325 17th St. NW, 20011	202-726-8213, 8214 202-726-6785 (fax)
LEBANON	Embassy of Lebanon 2560 28th St. NW, 20008	202-939-6300 202-939-6324 (fax)
LESOTHO	Embassy of the Kingdom of Lesotho 2511 Massachusetts Ave. NW, 20008	202-797-5533 to 5536 202-234-6815 (fax)
LIBERIA	Embassy of the Republic of Liberia 5201 16th St. NW, 20011	202-723-0437
LITHUANIA	Embassy of the Republic of Lithuania 2622 16th St. NW, 20009	202-234-5860, 2639 202-328-0466 (fax)
LUXEMBOURG	Embassy of the Grand Duchy of Luxembourg 2200 Massachusetts Ave. NW, 20008	202-265-4171 202-328-8270 (fax)
MADAGASCAR	Embassy of the Republic of Madagascar 2374 Massachusetts Ave. NW, 20008	202-265-5525, 5526
MALAWI	Embassy of Malawi 2408 Massachusetts Ave. NW, 20008	202-797-1007
MALAYSIA	Embassy of Malaysia 2401 Massachusetts Ave. NW, 20008	202-328-2700 202-483-7661
MALI	Embassy of the Republic of Mali 2130 R St. NW, 20008	202-332-2249 202-939-8950
MALTA	Embassy of Malta 2017 Connecticut Ave. NW, 20008	202-462-3611, 3612 202-387-5470 (fax)
MARSHALL ISLANDS	Embassy of the Republic of the Marshall Islands 2433 Massachusetts Ave. NW, 20008	202-234-5414 202-232-3236 (fax)

MAURITANIA	Embassy of the Islamic Republic of Mauritania 2129 Leroy Pl. NW, 20008	202-232-5700
MAURITIUS	Embassy of Republic of Mauritius 4301 Connecticut Ave. NW, Suite 441, 20008	202-244-1491, 1492 202-966-0983 (fax)
MEXICO	Embassy of Mexico 1911 Pennsylvania Ave. NW, 20006	202-728-1600
MICRONESIA	Embassy of the Federated States of Micronesia 1725 N St. NW, 20036	202-223-4383 202-223-4391 (fax)
MOLDOVA	Embassy of the Republic of Moldova 1511 K St. NW, Suites 329, 333, 20005	202-783-3012 202-783-3342
MONGOLIA	Embassy of Mongolia 2833 M St. NW, 20007	202-333-7117 202-298-9227 (fax)
MOROCCO	Embassy of the Kingdom of Morocco 1601 21st St. NW, 20009	202-462-7979 to 7982 202-265-0161 (fax)
MOZAMBIQUE	Embassy of the Republic of Mozambique 1990 M St. NW, Suite 570, 20036	202-293-7146 202-835-0245 (fax)
MYANMAR	Embassy of the Union of Myanmar 2300 S St. NW, 20008	202-332-9044, 9045
NAMIBIA	Embassy of the Republic of Namibia 1605 New Hampshire Ave. NW, 20009	202-986-0540 202-986-0443 (fax)
NEPAL	Royal Nepalese Embassy 2131 Leroy Pl. NW, 20008	202-667-4550
NETHERLANDS	Royal Netherlands Embassy Temporary: 4200 Wisconsin Ave. NW, 20016	202-244-5300 202-362-3430 (fax)
NEVIS	See Saint Kitts and Nevis	
NEW ZEALAND	Embassy of New Zealand 37 Observatory Circle NW, 20008	202-328-4800

NICARAGUA	Embassy of Nicaragua 1627 New Hampshire Ave. NW, 20009	202-939-6570
NIGER	Embassy of the Republic of Niger 2204 R St. NW, 20008	202-483-4224 to 4227
NIGERIA	Embassy of the Federal Republic of Nigeria 1333 16th St. NW, 20036	202-986-8400
NORWAY	Royal Norwegian Embassy 2720 34th St. NW, 20008	202-333-6000 202-337-0870 (fax)
OMAN	Embassy of the Sultanate of Oman 2535 Belmont Rd. NW, 20008	202-387-1980 to 1982 202-745-4933 (fax)
PAKISTAN	Embassy of Pakistan 2315 Massachusetts Ave. NW, 20008	202-939-6200 202-387-0484 (fax)
PALAU	Embassy of the Republic of Palau 2000 L St. NW, Suite 407, 20036	202-452-6814 202-452-6281 (fax)
PANAMA	Embassy of the Republic of Panama 2862 McGill Terrace NW, 20008	202-483-1407
PAPUA NEW GUINEA	Embassy of Papua New Guinea 1615 New Hampshire Ave. NW, 3rd Fl., 20009	202-745-3680 202-745-3679 (fax)
PARAGUAY	Embassy of Paraguay 2400 Massachusetts Ave. NW, 20008	202-483-6960 to 6962 202-234-4508 (fax)
PERU	Embassy of Peru 1700 Massachusetts Ave. NW, 20036	202-833-9860 to 9869 202-659-8124 (fax)
PHILIPPINES	Embassy of the Philippines 1600 Massachusetts Ave. NW, 20036	202-467-9300 202-328-7614 (fax)
POLAND	Embassy of the Republic of Poland 2640 16th St. NW, 20009	202-234-3800 to 3802 202-328-6271 (fax)
PORTUGAL	Embassy of Portugal 2125 Kalorama Rd. NW, 20008	202-328-8610 202-462-3726 (fax)
QATAR	Embassy of the State of Qatar 4200 Wisconsin Ave. NW, 20016	202-274-1600

ROMANIA	Embassy of Romania 1607 23rd St. NW, 20008	202-332-4846, 4848, 4851, 202-232-4748 (fax)
RUSSIA	Embassy of the Russian Federation 2650 Wisconsin Ave. NW, 20007	202-298-5700 to 5704 202-298-5735 (fax)
RWANDA	Embassy of the Republic of Rwanda 1714 New Hampshire Ave. NW, 20009	202-232-2882 202-232-4544 (fax)
SAINT KITTS AND NEVIS	Embassy of St. Kitts and Nevis 3216 New Mexico Ave. NW, 20016	202-686-2636 202-686-5740 (fax)
SAINT LUCIA	Embassy of Saint Lucia 3216 New Mexico Ave. NW, 20016	202-364-6792 to 6795 202-364-6728 (fax)
SAINT VINCENT AND THE GRENADINES	Embassy of Saint Vincent and the Grenadines 1717 Massachusetts Ave. NW, Suite 102, 20036	202-462-7806, 7846 202-462-7807 (fax)
SAUDI ARABIA	Embassy of Saudi Arabia 601 New Hampshire Ave. NW, 20037	202-342-3800
SENEGAL	Embassy of the Republic of Senegal 2112 Wyoming Ave. NW, 20008	202-234-0540, 0541
SIERRA LEONE	Embassy of Sierra Leone 1701 19th St. NW, 20009	202-939-9261
SINGAPORE	Embassy of the Republic of Singapore 3501 International Place NW, 20008	202-537-3100 202-537-0876 (fax)
SLOVAKIA	Embassy of the Slovak Republic Temporary: 2201 Wisconsin Ave., Suite 250, 20007	202-965-5161 202-965-5166 (fax)
SLOVENIA	Embassy of the Republic of Slovenia 1525 New Hampshire Ave. NW, 20036	202-667-5363 202-667-4563 (fax)
SOUTH AFRICA	Embassy of the Republic of South Africa 3051 Massachusetts Ave. NW, 20008	202-232-4400 202-265-1607
SPAIN	Embassy of Spain 2375 Pennsylvania Ave. NW, 20037	202-452-0100 202-728-2340 202-833-5670 (fax)

SRI LANKA	Embassy of the Democratic Socialist Republic of Sri Lanka 2148 Wyoming Ave. NW, 20008	202-483-4025 to 4028 202-232-7181 (fax)
SUDAN	Embassy of the Republic of the Sudan 2210 Massachusetts Ave. NW, 20008	202-338-8565 to 8570 202-667-2406 (fax)
SURINAME	Embassy of the Republic of Suriname 4301 Connecticut Ave. NW, Suite 108, 20008	202-244-7488, 7490 to 7492 202-244-5878 (fax)
SWAZILAND	Embassy of the Kingdom of Swaziland 3400 International Dr. NW, 20008	202-362-6683, 6685 202-244-8059 (fax)
SWEDEN	Embassy of Sweden 1501 M St. NW, 20005	202-467-2600 202-467-2699 (fax)
SWITZERLAND	Embassy of Switzerland 2900 Cathedral Ave. NW, 20008	202-745-7900 202-387-2564 (fax)
SYRIA	Embassy of the Syrian Arab Republic 2215 Wyoming Ave. NW, 20008	202-232-6313 202-234-9548 (fax)
TANZANIA	Embassy of the United Republic of Tanzania 2139 R St. NW, 20008	202-939-6125 202-797-7408 (fax)
THAILAND	Embassy of Thailand 1024 Wisconsin Ave. NW, 20007	202-944-3600 202-944-3611 (fax)
TOBAGO	See Trinidad and Tobago	
TOGO	Embassy of the Republic of Togo 2208 Massachusetts Ave. NW, 20008	202-234-4212 202-232-3190 (fax)
TRINIDAD AND TOBAGO	Embassy of the Republic of Trinidad and Tobago 1708 Massachusetts Ave. NW, 20036	202-467-6490 202-785-3130 (fax)
TUNISIA	Embassy of Tunisia 1515 Massachusetts Ave. NW, 20005	202-862-1850
TURKEY	Embassy of the Republic of Turkey 1714 Massachusetts Ave. NW, 20036	202-659-8200
TURKMENISTAN	Embassy of Turkmenistan 1511 K St. NW, Suite 412, 20005	202-737-4800 202-737-1152 (fax)

UGANDA	Embassy of the Republic of Uganda 5911 16th St. NW, 20011	202-726-7100 to 7102, 202-726-0416 202-726-1727 (fax)
UKRAINE	Embassy of Ukraine 3350 M St. NW, 20007	202-333-0606 202-333-0817 (fax)
UNITED ARAB EMIRATES	Embassy of the United Arab Emirates 3000 K St. NW, Suite 600, 20007	202-338-6500
UNITED KINGDOM OF GREAT BRITAIN AND NORTHERN IRELAND	British Embassy 3100 Massachusetts Ave. NW, 20008	202-462-1340 202-898-4255 (fax)
URUGUAY	Embassy of Uruguay 1918 F St. NW, 20006	202-331-1313 to 1316
UZBEKISTAN	Embassy of the Republic of Uzbekistan Temporary: 1511 K St. NW, Suite 619 and 623, 20005	202-638-4266, 4267 202-638-4268 (fax)
VENEZUELA	Embassy of the Republic of Venezuela 1099 30th St. NW 20007	202-342-2214
VIETNAM	Embassy of Vietnam 1233 20th St., Suite 501, 20036	202-861-0737 202-861-0917 (fax)
YEMEN	Embassy of the Republic of Yemen 2600 Virginia Ave. NW, Suite 705, 20037	202-965-4760, 4761 202-337-2017 (fax)
YUGOSLAVIA	Embassy of the Former Socialist Federal Republic of Yugoslavia 2410 California St. NW, 20008	202-462-6566
ZAIRE	Embassy of the Republic of Zaire 1800 New Hampshire Ave. NW, 20009	202-234-7690, 7691 202-832-5887 (fax)
ZAMBIA	Embassy of the Republic of Zambia 2419 Massachusetts Ave. NW, 20008	202-265-9717 to 9719 202-332-0826 (fax)
ZIMBABWE	Embassy of the Republic of Zimbabwe 1608 New Hampshire Ave. NW, 20009	202-332-7100 202-483-9326 (fax)